MANAGING SMART

325 High-Performance Tips Every Manager Must Know

MANAGING
SMART

Lynne Milgram, Alan Spector,
and Matt Treger

Cashman Dudley
An imprint of Gulf Publishing Company
Houston, Texas

MANAGING SMART

Cashman Dudley
An imprint of Gulf Publishing Company
P.O. Box 2608 □ Houston, Texas 77252-2608

10 9 8 7 6 5 4 3 2 1

Library of Congress Cataloging-in-Publication Data
Milgram, Lynne.
    Managing smart : 325 high-performance tips every manager must know / Lynne Milgram, Alan Spector, and Matt Treger.
        p.   cm.
    Includes bibliographical references and index.
    ISBN 0-88415-752-0
    1. Management. 2. Success in business. I. Spector, Alan, 1942–   . II. Treger, Matt. III. Title.
HD31.M4374 1999
658—dc21   99-13625
                                                           CIP

Printed in the United States of America.

Printed on acid-free paper (∞).

Contents

SAFETY, 103

RESOURCE MANAGEMENT, 110

GROWTH AND CHANGE MANAGEMENT, 115

MANAGING TEAMS, 150

TIME MANAGEMENT, 154

NEGOTIATIONS, 161

QUALITY MANAGEMENT, 165

LANDMINES, 250

COMMUNICATION METHODS, 264

FAMILY BUSINESSES, 396

Preface

Do you feel prepared to face the challenges that come your way each day? Are you faced with decision-making and managerial responsibilities that are challenging, if not outright intimidating? You are not alone. In an environment of downsizing and streamlining, companies expect more and more from employees. Managers, especially, face an intimidating array of challenges on a daily basis. These challenges can seem overwhelming for even the most seasoned managers, not to mention those newly promoted.

Managing Smart provides step-by-step instructions for mastering more than 300 real-world management tasks. From conflict management to marketing, business strategy to finance, and human resources to leadership, this condensed business curriculum is a quick reference guide that is designed to provide fast answers for solving common workplace situations.

The material in this book provides a general, yet comprehensive, overview of various situations faced by modern managers. While the wide scope of this book makes it difficult to exhaustively cover every topic, we hope to give you a foundation for expanded knowledge and expertise in various managerial concepts and techniques. We hope this collection of information is a valuable addition to an already fruitful and rewarding career.

The tips included here are, of course, intended for purposes of illustration only and may need to be modified for each set of circumstances. While we assume no responsibility for any outcomes that may result from the use of the information presented in this book, we expect these tips to positively contribute to any level of management skills.

We wish to extend a special thanks to Mark Treger, MD, MBA. His expertise, support, and constructive input were extremely valuable in the successful completion of this book.

Lynne Milgram
Alan Spector
Matt Treger

Are You Managerial Material?

Imagine this scenario. You have been with the same organization for five years. From time to time you have been asked to take the lead on projects. You have supervised and oriented new employees. You are beginning to ask yourself whether you are ready for a position in management.

To help decide if you are ready for advancement, think about the following:

- Have you demonstrated job competence? Have you been told that you do your job well? Are problems within the department never attributed to you?
- Do you know how to contribute to and how best to use the resources of your company? Have you taken the initiative of learning about the information network of your company? Do you know what information your company has and how to gain access to it?
- Are you known as a team player? Do you believe in the vision of your company and in its general style of management? Are you part of the corporate culture or do you usually try to buck the system? Do you openly criticize the company or are you known for your loyalty?
- Have you developed a personal support system with your superiors? Are you cordial and courteous to the staff? Has someone been mentoring or grooming you for a position in management?
- Do you have the right skill sets, the right education?
- If you are not an exempt employee, are you willing to become one, and have you discussed the possibility of longer hours and more responsibility with a spouse or other family members who would be affected by such a change?
- Does your current position lack excitement and do you find your motivation for the job diminished?

After you make a candid assessment of your strengths and weaknesses, it is time to start discussing your career development program with your supervisor. Ask him or her to help you set a realistic goal in an appropriate time frame. Discuss the skills you may still need to develop and the opportunities for training that are available to you. If you have been a hardworking and loyal employee, chances are your manager is already thinking about the next steps for you.

2

The Essence of Good Management

According to the *American Heritage Dictionary*, management is (1) the act, manner, or practice of managing; handling, supervision, or control; (2) the person or persons who control or direct a business or other enterprise; (3) skill in managing; executive ability.

As companies downsize, "rightsize," and streamline, some traditional layers of management are being thrown out or restructured. But these changes, even when they cut the managerial ranks, make the role of good management more and not less important.

Quality management offers its company a competitive advantage by providing:

- Entrepreneurial thrust
- Strategic decision making
- Planning and vision
- Low management turnover
- Corporate culture that includes a cohesive management team and positive working conditions
- Job-specific knowledge
- Ethical business practices

All of the above are part of an effective and competitive management focus. Companies that strive to permeate these values throughout the organization will experience real benefits. Ultimately, management holds the key to communicating and implementing the strategies that make an organization successful.

Getting a Handle on Upper Management

Organizations, especially larger companies with significant numbers of employees, typically have several layers of management arranged hierarchically. Even when it functions well, this kind of complex organizational structure often distances employees from upper-level management. What is your relationship with executive management in your company? Are these top managers accessible? Are you able to communicate with them relatively easily? While each organization's culture establishes the nature of such interactions, it is not uncommon to find that a large gap exists between upper management and the rest of the staff.

What exactly do top managers do? Sometimes they seem to be mere rumors of people, never actually seen around the office. Here is a breakdown of some of the most common executive management positions. The responsibilities they entail depend on many factors, including the type of organization (private, public, or government), its size, and the industry.

Board of Directors: Act as consultants to the executives. In a publicly held company they represent stockholders and are ultimately responsible for decisions made by senior management.

Chief Executive Officer (CEO)/President: The two most senior executive positions, with responsibility for the company's overall strategy and vision. Either position, or both, may exist.

Chief Operating Officer (COO): Focuses on the company's internal operations and processes.

Chief Financial Officer (CFO): Oversees the company's finances.

Executive positions may also include a chief technical officer (CTO) or a chief marketing officer (CMO). Managers may hold other titles, such as vice president or director, but their fundamental responsibilities and roles are typically the same.

In recent years, many companies have flattened their organizational structures. Two approaches toward this end are hands-on management styles and environments based on cross-functional teams. Successful managers must understand the dynamics of these teams and develop the skills needed to lead them effectively. Flattened organizational structures are also common in start-up companies. As these companies grow, their organizational structures often become more complex and hierarchical, and change becomes more difficult.

4

The Peter Principle

"In a hierarchy every employee tends to rise to his level of incompetence."

—Laurence J. Peter and Raymond Hull[1]

The "Peter Principle" as theorized by psychologist and educator Dr. Laurence Peter, describes a pitfall of bureaucratic organizations. Employees typically start in low-ranking positions, but when they succeed at their assigned tasks, they receive promotions. This process of climbing up the hierarchical ladder continues until employees reach positions in which they are no longer entirely competent. Since it is generally difficult to demote someone, they remain in these positions, even if they would be more effective and happier at a lower level. As a result, Peter believed, the higher levels of a bureaucracy tend to be filled by such people, who got there because they were good at different, and usually easier, tasks than those they are now expected to perform.

Not everyone agrees with this theory, and it is important to keep in mind that an organization's goal should be to support employee growth and advancement based on performance. Both employees and employers should strive to cooperatively reach their maximum potential.

[1]*The Peter Principle: Why Things Go Wrong* (New York: William Morrow, 1969)

Managing According to Theory X

The way managers view their employees influences managerial practice and style. In the 1960s, Professor Douglas McGregor developed two theories of human nature and human behavior based upon the work of Abraham Maslow (see tip #248). Theory X summarized traditional management thinking, while Theory Y (see tip #6) drew on Maslow's challenges to that thinking.

Managers who adhere to Theory X have a rigid and autocratic style of leadership that is based upon the following assumptions about human nature:

- People are self-interested and prefer leisure to work.
- Because people dislike work, managers need to control, direct, threaten, punish, and coerce them to achieve company objectives.
- Most people prefer being directed and tend to avoid responsibility.
- Most people have little ambition and tend to prefer security and a steady life.

Theory X managers micromanage. They sometimes place undue stress on their employees with rules, regulations, sanctions, threats, and coercive language. Instead of "the stick," sometimes they will dangle "carrots," such as rewards and promises, in exchange for doing the expected job. In either case, they see control as the only means to achieving their ends.

THEORIES

6 Managing According to Theory Y

Managers who practice under the assumptions of McGregor's Theory Y believe that their job is to integrate the needs of the workers with the needs of the company, and to help employees understand that their goals are consistent with those of the organization. This more enlightened approach frowns upon hard-nosed managers who rely on strict control to achieve their ends.

Theory Y makes the following assumptions about people's behavior at work and about organizational life:

- Working is as natural as resting or playing.
- People will become self-directed if they understand and are committed to the objectives of a project or organization.
- People will commit to objectives if they are rewarded for their achievements.
- People can be taught to accept and seek responsibility.
- People are naturally creative and imaginative. They can apply these abilities to organizational problem solving.

Many managers insist that it is more difficult to be a Theory Y than a Theory X manager, because to do so they need to be more sensitive. Theory Y managers must make time:

- To explain
- To understand the needs of the employee
- To foster interpersonal exchange, and to collaborate in problem solving, with members of their staff

The manager remains key to the process. But he or she plays the role of a facilitator and enabler, providing monitoring and feedback instead of strict control. A Theory Y manager believes in empowering employees and enriching their jobs.

Both Theory X and Theory Y try to predict the kind of managerial behavior that will motivate employees to perform to their fullest potential. It is possible that an insightful manager may need to combine some elements from both theories to succeed.

The Hawthorne
Experiments

7

In the late 1920s and early 1930s, Dr. Elton Mayo conducted behavioral studies at the Hawthorne Works Plant of the Western Electric Company in Cicero, Illinois. His research led him to draw numerous conclusions regarding employee performance, productivity, and motivation.

Mayo monitored employee productivity as environmental conditions, such as noise and light levels, varied. Interestingly, it seemed that a change of any sort caused an increase in productivity. When light increased and the sound levels decreased, workers demonstrated greater productivity. When noise became louder and the light dimmer, the workers again boosted their productivity. It appeared that productivity increased as a result of a change.

Mayo also observed greater job satisfaction when employees were able to participate in making decisions. This increase surpassed the effect of offering short-term incentives, indicating that overall employee well-being and performance is not simply a matter of monetary compensation.

General observations drawn from the studies include the following:

- Non-economic factors affect worker behavior and productivity.
- Groups of employees establish norms for productivity.
- There is group pressure to perform at this established level, and those performing both above and below group expectations are socially shunned.
- Workers cannot simply be managed as individuals; the behavior of the group must be taken into consideration.

The Hawthorne experiments have since been studied, questioned, and even refuted by sociologists, behaviorists, psychologists, and others in academia. But regardless of the judgment made about their scientific value, the issues the experiments raised regarding motivation remain interesting. It may well be that money is not the only motivator and that careful attention to work environment and employee well-being will enhance productivity.

THEORIES

8

Herzberg's Job Maintenance and Motivational Factors

Like Douglas McGregor (see tips #5 and #6), Frederick Herzberg, a clinical psychologist and professor of management at Utah University, developed theories of worker motivation based on Maslow's hierarchy of needs. (See tip #248.)

Job maintenance factors are elements that are not necessarily part of the actual job tasks but need to be present at a satisfactory level for work to occur. They are also referred to as *hygiene factors* or, when they are absent or inadequate, *dissatisfiers*. Failure to adequately provide these factors can be detrimental to productivity and may lead to job dissatisfaction. Job maintenance factors include:

- Job security
- Salary and benefits
- Supervision
- Status
- Working conditions
- Company policies and administrative practices
- Interpersonal relationships with other workers

Once the job maintenance factors exist at an appropriate level, *motivators* (or *satisfiers*) can be used to encourage performance. These include:

- Responsibility
- Advancement
- Recognition
- Achievement
- Growth

By supplying the maintenance factors—without which the motivators will generally not be effective—and then focusing on motivators, an organization maximizes worker performance. Herzberg termed this process *job enrichment*.

Applying the 80/20 Rule

Whether you must reduce costs, shorten a project time line, select key employees for promotion, or choose the clients you want your sales staff to visit, start your analysis with the 80/20 rule, also known as the "Pareto Principle." When you look for ways to cut expenses, for example, you may find that 80 percent of your costs come from 20 percent of your expense categories. Likewise, as you examine your customers, you may find that 20 percent of your accounts generate 80 percent of your revenues. Other items you might consider:

- Do 20 percent of your tasks consume 80 percent of your time?
- Do 20 percent of your employees perform 80 percent of your productive work?
- Do 20 percent of your clients account for 80 percent of your sales?
- Do 20 percent of your employees create 80 percent of your discipline problems?
- Do 20 percent of the meetings you attend influence 80 percent of your work?

Write the ratio "80/20" on a piece of paper that you keep near your desk. Before you start a task, use the 80/20 rule to determine the return it will provide on your time investment. Then use it to identify the key items, those which influence 80 percent of your results.

10 Doing Research

The emergence of the Internet has revolutionized the way people do research. Whether you want market data, industry trends, information on competitors, SEC filings, or even reviews of suppliers and distributors, there is an overwhelming amount of information at your fingertips. The following are some of the best sources of business information on the Internet. Most of these services charge a fee for specific information or research requests.

Dun and Bradstreet

Comprehensive information services covering industry trends and analysis, marketing, small business administration, and business-to-business credit data for companies all over the globe.

www.dnb.com

EDGAR Database

EDGAR, the Electronic Data Gathering, Analysis, and Retrieval system, provides corporate filings and annual reports for companies that are required by law to file forms with the U.S. Securities and Exchange Commission (SEC). All information is free.

www.sec.gov

Hoovers Online

This service provides short company profiles. Some information is available at no charge.

www.hoovers.com

Standard and Poor's

This page provides financial and market information about individual companies. Standard and Poor's also maintains several other divisions that specialize in personal finance, bond ratings, financial news, quotes, stock and mutual fund research, recommendations, commentary, and more.

www.compustat.com

LEXIS-NEXIS

The *LEXIS* service provides online research materials for the legal profession, including access to specialized libraries covering all major fields of practice and continuously updated archives of state and federal case law, statutes, and regulations. The *NEXIS* service has become the largest news and business online information service, with financial, demographic, market research, company, country, and industry reports. The service offers more than 13,800 sources of news and business information and adds nearly 120,000 new articles each day from newspapers, magazines, wire services, and trade journals worldwide.

www.lexis-nexis.com

11 Useful Resources—
The American
Management Association

The American Management Association has offered employer and employee management training to the business community for more than 70 years. A manager can use the association's seminars, forums, conferences, and audio, video, and printed material to structure individual training tools for his or her staff.

Membership in the AMA will allow you to network with the association's 70,000 other members and provides access to valuable business information and a means of staying current on management issues. The more than 200 seminars the AMA offers annually can help you to streamline work processes, create self-directed teams, remove barriers to decision making, and increase your ability to respond to change.

Some of the AMA's invaluable annual conferences include:

• The Human Resource Conference. This popular conference offers outstanding, well-known speakers and covers virtually every topic of interest for HR professionals from across the nation and the world.
• Exposition for Executive Secretaries and Administrative Assistants. This conference helps attendees with professional skills and development.
• On-site training. If you have a group of 10 or more you wish to train, the AMA will tailor a seminar to your needs and present it at your site.
• International conferences. These seminars are designed to meet the needs of top corporate executives.

Other topics included in training courses are leadership and management skills, marketing skills, strategic management, inventory management, information systems, financial management, customer satisfaction, and communication skills. Most seminars are offered at both basic and advanced levels. The courses tend to be practical, so that attendees can immediately apply the advice upon returning to work. Seminar leaders are experts in their fields with years of practical experience.

The AMA can be an indispensable resource for managers, offering training, networking, exchange of information, and a foundation for personal and staff development.

Useful Resources— *Harvard Business Review*

In the fall of 1998, the *Harvard Business Review (HBR)* turned 75 years old. While *HBR* has updated its content over time, it remains committed to its founding principles of careful research and analysis of business issues.

Managers and others interested in a career in business should read *HBR* or at the very least be familiar with its contents. The journal, available in print or on the Internet, covers all aspects of business. Subjects discussed in recent issues have included:

- Leadership strategies
- Seller-buyer relationships
- Marketing strategies
- Coaching
- Entrepreneurial issues
- Management challenges

The journal combines such articles with its well-known case studies, providing a mix of the academic and the practical.

The caliber of the articles selected by *HBR* is extraordinary. Since 1959, a panel of business leaders has selected the two or three best articles each year for the McKinsey Foundation awards. The McKinsey Award winners have become classic articles in the world of business literature.

The goal of *HBR* has always been to produce articles that challenge conventional wisdom and make readers think and rethink their views. Managers will find the journal a valuable resource and, more importantly, a source of ideas that challenge the status quo.

13

Belonging to the Chamber of Commerce

Whether your business is a small, community-based operation or a unit of a much larger company, the local Chamber of Commerce can be an excellent resource. The central goal of a Chamber of Commerce is to make the community in which you and your employees live and work a better place. Many of these organizations stay abreast of economic development by conducting studies on housing, retail, industry, and entertainment. In addition, Chambers of Commerce usually maintain a council on small business that actively supports small businesses and provides them with key tools for growth. These features may include seminars, insurance, loan programs, or an information hotline.

Other reasons to belong to the Chamber of Commerce include:

- Making new business contacts. Belonging to the Chamber of Commerce helps you to meet potential customers, clients, and vendors. Many Chambers have after-hours social events, which provide opportunities for networking.
- Increasing company visibility. Investing in a Chamber of Commerce lends credibility, visibility, and marketability to a company.
- Improving your management skills. Managers can take advantage of a Chamber of Commerce's business counseling and seminars for nominal fees.
- Gaining access to low-cost marketing opportunities. Chambers of Commerce often provide opportunities such as trade shows or expositions.
- Helping your community's economy. Most Chambers of Commerce assist companies seeking to relocate or expand their businesses. More companies and jobs in your community mean more potential customers for you.
- Becoming involved in government. Chambers of Commerce speak on behalf of business to elected and appointed officials. Being a member of the Chamber is especially helpful when regulations or legislation may directly affect your business.
- Saving money. Many Chambers of Commerce offer employee assistance programs and other ways of reducing employee benefit costs.

In short, the Chamber in Commerce in your community is a valuable resource that can help your business grow.

SIC Classifications

Comparing your company to others in similar industries is easier and more important than you may realize. The United States Department of Commerce has developed a four-digit code system that classifies all industry within the United States according to its primary activity. The major categories of the Standard Industrial Classification Code (SIC) are:

- Agriculture, Forestry, and Fishing
- Mining
- Construction
- Manufacturing
- Transportation and Public Utilities
- Wholesale Trade
- Retail Trade
- Finance, Insurance, and Real Estate Services
- Public Administration

Let's examine the Services category, which is SIC Code 7. Adding a second digit produces more specific classifications:

• Hotels, Rooming Houses, Camps, and Other Lodging Places	70
• Personal Services	72
• Business Services	73
• Automotive Repair, Services, and Parking	75
• Miscellaneous Repair Services	76
• Motion Pictures	78
• Amusement and Recreation Services	79

Adding two more digits to Business Services, SIC Code 73, generates further subcategories:

• Computer Processing, Data Preparation and Processing Services	7374
• Information Retrieval Services	7375
• Computer Maintenance and Repair	7378

Using the SIC classification system, you can find industry-specific information on sales, debt, profits, and company size. Dun & Bradstreet has also developed a proprietary classification system, which further breaks down each of the above industries by adding up to four additional digits. Another system, the North American Industry Classification System (NAICS), closely follows the SIC and was developed after the North American Free Trade Agreement (NAFTA).

15 Uniform Commercial Code (UCC)

It's not enough to just bill and collect receivables for products and services. It's also important to understand the rules and regulations that govern commercial transactions. The Uniform Commercial Code (UCC), which establishes these rules and regulations, helps protect companies against the loss of income from bad debts.

For example, when someone leases or buys an automobile with a loan, the dealership must have a way to secure its interest in the automobile. By using an agreement established by the UCC, the business can reclaim its interest by repossessing the automobile if the buyer does not make payments or otherwise voids the agreement.

The UCC regulates and clarifies the agreement of both parties. The code sets forth standards of good faith, diligence, reasonableness, and care for commercial agreements. It reduces the risk to creditors of default and establishes a creditor's claim in case of bankruptcy. The UCC makes the United States an attractive place to do business, since it offers protection that is not available in many other countries.

RESOURCES

Management by Objectives (MBO)— Setting *SMART* Goals

Management by objectives (MBO) is a method of managing in which an organization's members jointly establish its goals. The members do not necessarily have to be from the same department or area; they just need to share a common goal or purpose.

The heart of MBO is having the group collectively set *SMART* goals:

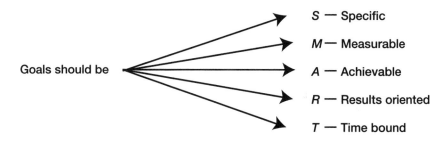

Goals should be

S — Specific

M — Measurable

A — Achievable

R — Results oriented

T — Time bound

Figure 1. SMART *goals.*

MBO provides an organization with improvements in:

- Management performance
- Planning, coordination, control, and flexibility
- Superior-subordinate relationships
- Personal development

The effectiveness of any improvement strategy depends heavily on the commitment management makes, and establishing *SMART* goals is only a small part of the process. Those goals must be actively pursued, and progress must be constantly evaluated, at every layer of the organization.

17

Instituting Management by Objectives (MBO)

Management by objectives (MBO) is a method of managing in which members of an organization jointly establish goals, as well as a structured plan to achieve those goals. Each person's commitment to this improvement process is essential in order for MBO to be effective, and the process typically involves the following steps:

1. One of the first steps in MBO is identifying the members who will be involved and arranging a time to meet as a group. At this stage, basic information about the people involved and the purpose or aim of the department/unit is agreed upon.
2. This stage is an analysis of the people who are involved with or affected by the process being addressed. These are then categorized as customers, owners/managers, suppliers, support services, employees, and external authorities.
3. The next step is to assess the expectations of these stakeholders and evaluate how well they are being met. This helps to set the priority of improvements to be made.
4. A set of objectives is formulated to ensure that the prioritized stakeholder requirements are met. These objectives should follow the guidelines of setting *SMART* goals (see tip #16).
5. Having set the objectives, the actions required are established and main tasks prioritized. This helps make sure that the right things are done in the right order.
6. All the required actions are brought together with progress checks and achievement milestones to form the overall program. This is formally approved by all of the participants, thus sealing the contract for improvement.

Once the action plan is completed, regular reviews take place to monitor progress and to check whether the objectives are being satisfied. At this stage, the action plan can be updated and modified as required, based on the objectives.

The Leadership Grid®

The Managerial Grid, a 1964 book by Robert R. Blake and Jane S. Mouton that has become a managerial classic, describes leadership styles in terms of their orientation toward production and toward people. Blake and Anne Adams McCanse updated the concept in 1991, renaming it the Leadership Grid® in their book *Leadership Dilemmas—Grid® Solutions*, but its central elements remain the same. The Grid defines a manager's approach along the two axes of concern for people and concern for production. The level of concern for each factor is rated on a scale from one to nine.

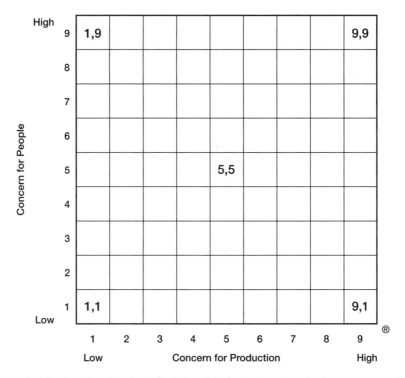

Figure 2. *The Leadership Grid®. (The Grid® designation is the property of Scientific Methods, Inc. and is used here with permission.)*

The management styles represented by the various points on the Grid have received nicknames over the years. For example:

- 1,1: In the lower left-hand corner is the "cream puff" manager who doesn't push for anything.
- 1,9: The upper left-hand corner represents the "do-gooder" manager who is so busy looking out for people that production suffers.
- 5,5: In the center position is the "middle-of-the-road" manager who balances the importance of the people and the work itself just enough to maintain performance at an adequate level.
- 9,1: The lower right-hand corner represents the "hard-nosed" manager who favors production over human concerns.
- 9,9: In the upper right-hand corner is the "professional" manager who is extremely committed to both people and production. This manager builds a team relationship based on trust and respect.

Additionally, two other styles represent a combination of these first five styles. The "paternalistic" manager combines the production "9" of the 9,1 Grid style and the people "9" of the 1,9 Grid style to form a "9+9" combination. This manager uses rewards and punishments to lead employees, as in a parent-child relationship. Lastly, the "opportunistic" manager selects whichever style will serve him or her best in a given situation. This manager is often manipulative and concerned primarily with gaining a personal advantage.

Managers can use the diagnostic tools and the theories that underlie the Grid to identify, study, and change their own leadership styles. Along with finding the optimum balance between concern for production and people, managers also use the Grid for help in understanding, and better responding to, the behavior patterns of their superiors, peers, and staff.

Changing the
Flow of Work

Many traditional organizations are structured with separate and distinct departments. These departments are often functionally oriented, meaning that they each tend to be concerned with only their responsibilities and resources. Departments often compete with one another for resources and recognition, sometimes to the detriment of the company's overall goals.

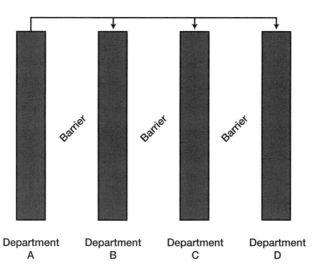

Figure 3. *Functionally oriented departments in a traditional organization.*

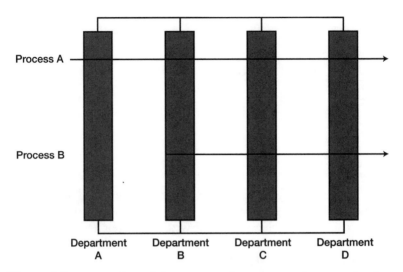

Figure 4. Process-oriented departments in a progressive organization.

Alternatively, consider the way *process-oriented* departments function. The relationships among the departments create a road down which work travels. By focusing on the flow of work across the organization, it is easier to see how each department is a team player in the process and goals of the organization. Building a sense of cohesiveness will bring the departments together as a team that can work cooperatively.

Strategic Use of
Personality Typing

Managers can promote more productive and effective working relationships if they have a basic understanding of themselves and their employees. A knowledge of personality typing, and of tools such as the Myers-Briggs Type Indicator (MBTI), can help the manager measure individual personality traits and use that information to help employees work more successfully. The better the manager understands why people are different and what their individual needs and characteristics are, the more successful any enterprise that relies upon these individuals will become.

Carl Jung first developed personality typing in the 1920s. He based his theory on four functions—Feeling, Thinking, Intuition, and Sensing—and two attitudes, Extraversion and Introversion. Myers and Briggs modified Jung's work in the 1950s, and their model is now widely used to define personality types and differences among individuals. The MBTI identifies eight preferences that indicate key elements of personality and divides them into four scales. In interpreting results, it is important to understand that the MBTI:

- Describes the preferences that an individual answering the MBTI questionnaire indicates.
- Does not describe skills or abilities.
- Assumes that all preferences are equally valuable.
- Is well-documented, with hundreds of scientific studies conducted over a 40-year period.

The four scales are:

- Energizing. The individual will exhibit preference for *Extraversion,* drawing energy from the outside world, people, or things; or for *Introversion,* drawing energy from his or her own internal world of ideas, emotions, or impressions.
- Attending. The preference will be either for *Sensing,* taking in information through the five senses; or for *Intuition,* taking in information through a "sixth" sense.

- Deciding. The individual will show a *Thinking* preference by making decisions in a logical, objective way; or a *Feeling* preference by making decisions in a personal, value-oriented way.
- Living. The individual demonstrates *Judgment* through a preference for living a planned and organized life; or *Perception* through a preference for a more spontaneous and flexible lifestyle.

The four scales and two preferences result in 16 different combinations. These combinations describe particular personality archetypes, each with a four-letter label such as ENFJ, ENFP, ENTJ, or ESFJ.

Examples of these personality styles are:

- ENFJ. These individuals are outstanding leaders who help others become the best they can be. Only 5 percent of the total population demonstrates these preferences.
- ESTJ. These people are responsible and become successful administrators. This personality type is present in 13 percent of the population.
- ENTP. These individuals are inventors, enthusiastic about everything, and sensitive to all possibilities. Only 5 percent of the population falls into this category.
- ISTJ. These people are decisive in practical affairs and considered dependable. Approximately 6 percent of the population demonstrates these personality traits.

By using a knowledge of these styles as they pertain to your employees, you can assess how each worker's traits can best be used for individual and organizational effectiveness. You can better evaluate the worker's leadership style, preferred working environment, potential pitfalls, developmental goals, and potential contributions to the organization. Managers have also found that the MBTI lends insight into their own problem-solving styles and preferred ways of communicating. The questionnaire takes less than 20 minutes to complete, and it is one more tool for furthering strategic planning and organizational effectiveness.

Plan, Do, Check, Act: The Deming or Shewhart Cycle

21

One framework for finding solutions to problems is the Deming Cycle, which was originally introduced by W. Edwards Deming and further conceptualized by Walter A. Shewhart. The cycle consists of four stages, referred to as *Plan, Do, Check,* and *Act* (PDCA). Using the PDCA cycle ensures an orderly approach to problem solving. This framework draws upon scientific method and thus provides rigorous data analysis and verification of results.

Plan Stage

The first step in this process is to identify the primary problem—for example, decreasing sales. The next step is to assign individuals or a team to work on the problem, identify the factors or causes, and develop an action plan to solve the problem.

Do Stage

This involves implementing the action plan on a trial basis.

Check Stage

After it is collected, the data is analyzed and studied to see if it confirms or refutes the assessment of the causes of the problem. Statistical techniques such as statistical process control (SPC) and continuous process improvement (CPI) can be helpful in collecting and analyzing the data.

Act Stage

Once these findings are presented, the action plan is modified as needed.

Keep in mind that this problem-solving technique is a continuous process. Once the cycle ends, it begins over again, and is continually monitored.

MANAGEMENT TOOLS

Approaching a Problem

One of the most powerful skills in management is the ability to solve problems. For many managers, day-to-day activities seem to revolve around "fire-fighting," moving from one unforeseen problem to the next. Developing basic problem-solving skills can help you deal effectively with such challenges, leaving more time for your central responsibilities and for long-range planning.

A systems approach breaks the problem-solving process down into several specific steps. All the activities are interrelated, but it is helpful to consider each one separately.

When faced with a seemingly impossible problem, don't panic or overreact. Take a few deep breaths and then attack the problem systematically, choosing your solution with care. A stepwise approach simplifies a problem and breaks it down into manageable components.

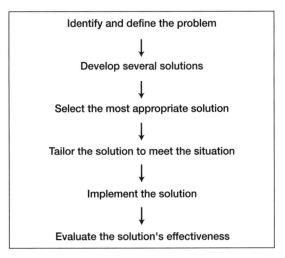

Figure 5. *Systematic problem solving.*

The Gantt Chart

All managers are faced with the challenge of developing work schedules and controlling work in progress. Henry L. Gantt, an industrial engineer, is credited with creating the first production control chart during World War I. Today, many organizations use some version of this chart to plan and visually represent output performance.

The value of the Gantt chart is best understood by example. Your company makes "widgets" (an imaginary product) and you are the manager. Your first order of business is to schedule production orders in the most efficient sequence. You first need to gather all the facts: order #1 will take four hours, order #2 will take eight hours, and order #3 will take two hours. Look at how many machines you have that make widgets, how many hours each can operate before maintenance is needed, and how many hours per day and week they can operate. One approach would be to finish each order first before beginning the next. The flow of work would be orderly but the machines would be underutilized. The Gantt chart demonstrates how you can overlap work, vary the order of production from the order in which the work was accepted, and still keep on schedule through greater efficiency.

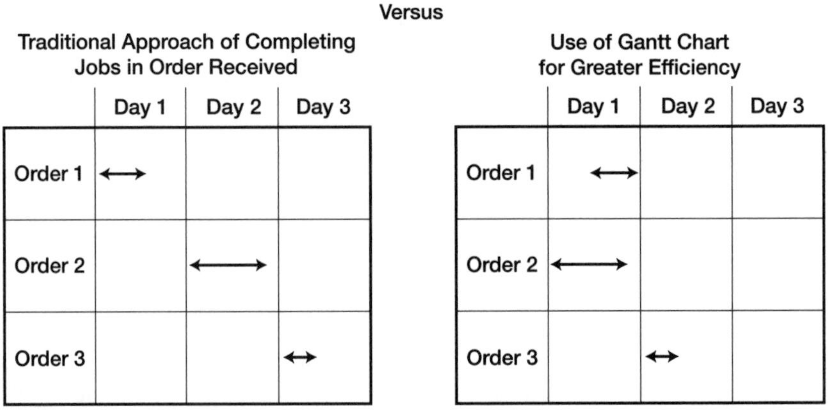

Versus

Traditional Approach of Completing Jobs in Order Received				Use of Gantt Chart for Greater Efficiency		

	Day 1	Day 2	Day 3
Order 1	←→		
Order 2		←——→	
Order 3			↔

	Day 1	Day 2	Day 3
Order 1	←→		
Order 2	←——→		
Order 3		↔	

Note:

• Order 1 requires 4 hours.
• Order 2 requires 8 hours.
• Order 3 requires 2 hours.
• One machine is available to run 12 hours per 12-hour workday.

Figure 6. A traditional approach versus the Gantt Chart approach.

Organizational Charts

An organizational chart is a graphical representation of an organization's hierarchical structure and the flow of responsibility within the organization.

The chart should reflect the chain of command and illustrate the relationships between members of the company. Each employee should have a copy that identifies his or her place in the overall structure and to the immediate supervisor. The chart should be constantly updated.

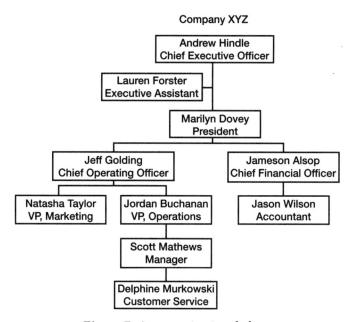

Figure 7. An organizational chart.

25

Writing a Business Plan

The value of developing and writing a solid business plan is frequently unrecognized in the business world. Essentially, a business plan is a report detailing the nuts and bolts of a business concept. It presents a comprehensive picture in which all of the elements related to the business concept must be synthesized and every relevant issue addressed.

Business plans include the following main topics:

- Product description
- Business model
- Management team
- Market analysis
- Competitive analysis
- Resource requirements
- Financial projections
- Critical risks

Entrepreneurs frequently develop business plans so they can seek out investors for a start-up venture. The plan serves as a sales tool that allows a potential investor to evaluate the business opportunity presented. A business plan is also a valuable strategic tool for departments or subdivisions within existing companies.

Think of a business plan as a process, not a fixed product. It is never truly finished, because new information constantly changes it. Many new companies make the mistake of putting their business plans on the shelf once they begin operations. The true value of the plan is that the constant evaluation and revision required to keep it current will help maintain the vision and direction of the company.

Approaching the Strategic Analysis of a Business

In today's marketplace, companies are under constant pressure to maintain both profitability and competitiveness. What is the relative health of your business? Is your business strategy going to sustain future growth and development? To answer these questions, you must analyze three factors: the customer, the company, and the competition.

Customer

It is important to know exactly who the customer is and whether the customer base can be segmented into specific groups. A solid understanding of the customer and the market enables a company to meet customer needs more fully and is essential in determining pricing strategies, marketing efforts, and product development.

Company

A company needs to assess its own relative strengths and weaknesses. By knowing its core competencies, it can more effectively select markets in which to compete. The company should also calculate the cost of doing business and identify the best strategy to attain profitability.

Competitors

There is always a competitor ready to serve a company's customers. Evaluating the competitive forces in the industry allows a company to decide on the best competitive strategy. Understanding competitors and anticipating their reactions is one way to stay a step ahead.

Keep these three Cs in mind—the customer, the company, and the competition. Many business executives tend to focus on one or two of the three Cs, while forgetting to properly address the others—but each one contributes to shaping the nature of the marketplace.

27 Charting a Life Cycle

Would you want to work for an organization that is focusing on the development of a revolutionary new motor unit for record turntables? Or would you rather work for a company that is developing new ways for businesses to take advantage of the Internet? Products, and even entire industries, follow life cycles that break down into a development stage, a growth stage, a maturity stage, and a declining stage. It's important to know where your product, company, or industry is in its life cycle, since each phase brings a different level of sales, profits, and market share potential. Figure 8 illustrates the four life cycle stages.

Development

A distinct market does not yet exist and profits are small. The education process is taking place, and there are some early adopters. Distribution channels are being established.

Growth

Sales grow rapidly, profits increase, competition enters, products are refined, and distribution increases.

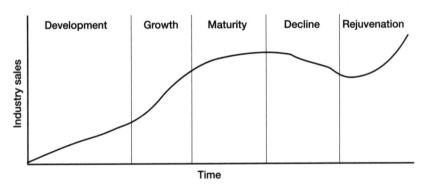

Figure 8. A life cycle chart.

Maturity

Sales slow down and profits level off. There are attempts to boost sales and maintain interest through innovation.

Decline

Sales and profits decrease. Companies are forced to focus on the most profitable areas and cut back spending on other activities in an effort to maintain profits.

Occasionally, a fifth stage may follow the decline phase. The decline phase may turn into a *rejuvenation* phase if, for example, a product undergoes dramatic changes or if new uses for the product are discovered. Sales and profits will once again grow as a result of the repositioning.

These phases are not written in stone. The maturity phase, for example, does not always lead into the decline phase, and may even result in another growth phase based on market factors. A life cycle is a dynamic process; each phase can even have a life cycle of its own.

Forecasting Demand

Ideally, a company wants to produce just enough to meet consumer demand. Producing too much leads to excess inventories, and the selling price may need to be cut to reduce the costs associated with carrying inventory. Making too little means running out of stock and losing potential sales. To avoid these situations, companies anticipate demand and adjust operations accordingly. Forecasting is the art of predicting what future demand will be. Future demand is often difficult to predict, especially if demand fluctuates or if there are many external factors that affect consumer demand.

How can a company estimate future demand? Here are several common approaches:

Surveys of Customers

Asking customers about their purchasing habits and intentions.

Market Tests

Introducing a product into a controlled test market to evaluate consumer response.

Expert Opinions

Using people knowledgeable about a particular field to provide demand estimates. There are also companies that specialize in providing economic forecasts.

Time Series Analyses

Using past sales to predict future sales. The forecast focuses on the elements of time; for example, it will account for changes that occur on a seasonal basis, such as during the holiday buying season.

Statistical Demand Analyses

Using mathematical models to account for economic, environmental, and other external factors that are likely to affect demand patterns.

Each of these methods provides only a piece of the forecasting puzzle. At some point the forecaster must integrate all of the information and make a judgment call based on a mixture of facts and intuition. Like the future, a forecast is ultimately uncertain.

29

Establishing the Objectives of Forecasting

An important part of the forecasting process is establishing the objectives of the forecast. It is possible to have more than one objective for the same forecast. For example, let's say that Wanda's Widget World specializes in the production of widgets and the company is using a forecast to plan operations for the coming year. The forecast has two main purposes: to predict future sales and to estimate the resources that will be required to meet sales estimates.

The dual objectives of the forecast create a precarious task for the forecaster. If sales projections are overly optimistic, material requirements will also be overestimated, and this could result in overproduction and excessive inventory buildup. On the other hand, if sales projections are too low, production may not be sufficient to meet customer demand.

So what should Wanda's Widget World do? Essentially, the forecast must take into account the possible costs associated with each scenario. The optimal solution will likely strike a compromise between the risks of inventory buildup and the risks of running out of stock. Experience and industry-specific knowledge are a forecaster's best guides to finding such a solution.

Understanding
Statistical Terms

Are you familiar with the basic terms used in statistics? Why are these terms important? Most people would be perfectly happy to never answer these questions, but statistics play an important role in even the most common decisions; they are the technical means of collecting and analyzing data to solve problems. They are used in sports, research studies, gambling, and, of course, business. Some of the basic statistical terms you need to understand include:

Population versus Sample

Population refers to all the subjects being studied. For example, all the students at a university, all the employees at your business, or all people living in San Diego County constitute a population. A sample is a subset of a population that can be used to represent the population. But, if the sample is too small, it may not be statistically significant—that is, it may not accurately reflect the population. A sample should provide a confidence level of 95 percent or more; this level is the likelihood that the sample does accurately reflect the population.

Qualitative versus Quantitative Data

Qualitative data involves attributes or requirements that are met or not met.

- *Nominal data* will be compared to other data for similarities or differences. Examples include sex, profession, favorite color, or type of computer of each member of a population.
- *Ordinal data* is data that can be ranked as greater than, equal to, or less than other data. Surveys typically acquire ordinal data when assessing customer preferences or satisfaction levels.

Quantitative data takes the form of actual numerical values. Examples are age, weight, height, income, stock market prices, number of customers, or number of defects.

- *Interval data* involves a scale with equidistant points, such as the distance from 50 to 52 degrees Fahrenheit and from 52 to 54 degrees. The unit of measure is a constant width or interval. Interval data is versatile and powerful, providing useful and accurate statistical information.
- *Ratio data* is data for which a true zero exists. This might be the amount of gas in your automobile or a measurement of time elapsed or of the distance between two points.

For most managers, statistics are a necessary evil. They are important not only for decision making, but also for validating everyday information that may be presented to you. Scientific calculators, as well as popular spreadsheets such as Excel, Lotus, and Quattro Pro, provide the ability to perform statistical analyses, plot data, and create graphs.

Calculating
Productivity

Productivity can be calculated by dividing the units of output by units of input, as expressed by the following equation:

Productivity = Output / Input

Optimal productivity is a ratio of one to one, that is, one unit of output produced for each unit of input. It is unlikely that this target level of efficiency will actually be achieved, however.

The equation for productivity provides a conceptual framework, but it is not immediately useful in a real business setting. Determining what should be measured and how to measure it is often difficult.

Some possible productivity scenarios are:

- Output stays the same while inputs, such as labor requirements, decrease. This is associated with downsizing and "rightsizing."
- Output increases but inputs do not. This is usually a result of achieving greater efficiency within existing operations and processes.
- Output increases while inputs decrease. This is usually only possible when a significant restructuring or reengineering leads to improved operations.
- Output and input increase together. This typically indicates that the company is undergoing expansion.

Productivity is strongly correlated to the competitive ability of an organization. The more productive an organization is, the more effectively it will compete in the marketplace.

MANAGEMENT TOOLS

32

Checking Your Company's Performance Against Others'

From a strategic perspective, a company needs to be assessed within the context of its particular industry. Information is most helpful when compared to industry averages. For example, if you determine that your company is growing at 25 percent per year, that might be good news . . . unless your competitors are growing at 125 percent per year! Likewise, if your company's debt to equity ratio is 50 percent (that is, 50 percent of the company's financing comes from debt) and your competitors' average is 20 percent, it might be worth taking a look at how your competitors are being financed.

Data that deserves analysis and comparison from an industry-wide perspective includes:

- Financial data
- Performance ratios
- Productivity measures
- Labor costs
- Production costs
- Sales projections
- Revenue growth

If your industry is made up of publicly traded companies listed on a stock exchange, these numbers will be easy to obtain. Only by comparing your company to others in the same industry will you be able to fully assess your current and potential weaknesses and strengths.

Encouraging Intrapreneurship

A constant threat to a company's success is the cost of employee turnover. Creative employees need to be recognized and encouraged. Otherwise, these workers will take their innovative ideas elsewhere. One way to keep this type of employee motivated is to offer intrapreneurial opportunities within the company.

Managers should target such restless but valuable employees and make it convenient and rewarding for them to pursue their creativity beyond the normal routine. For example, they may develop their own independent business units, or conceive and develop their own projects and project teams.

A common misconception is that intrapreneurship is a rare characteristic in employees. What managers must understand is that most successful innovations do not arise through a formal planning process. Companies will therefore improve their chances for success if they adopt an effective intrapreneurship program that nurtures creative freedom.

Any company that wants to support individual creativity should:

- Encourage workers to discuss their new ideas.
- Permit employees to pursue those ideas that pass a cost/benefit assessment.
- Accept small failures and setbacks as a necessary part of the big picture.
- Understand that true intrapreneurs need space and freedom and do not fit neatly into traditional company roles.
- Develop less experienced but enthusiastic workers for potential roles as intrapreneurs.

These highly creative employees often intimidate managers, but they need the support, training, and leadership of a management team to accomplish their dreams. The intrapreneur employee is a valuable asset to the company. The innovative organization will develop as many intrapreneurs as it can and profit from their creative thinking and ability.

34 Making Flextime Work

Many businesses find that they are able to offer employees flexible work schedules. Flextime allows employees to balance the demands of work and home and can help ensure a productive and happy staff.

The challenge for the manager is to administer flextime requests consistently and fairly. Here is a procedure to help evaluate requests for flextime and to make flextime work:

- Insist that workers submit a written proposal detailing the reasons why restructuring the job and work schedule will lead to higher quality or productivity.
- Be suspicious of proposals that simply delegate tasks to other employees. Remind potential flextime candidates that they will retain their core responsibilities. Only consider a request to delegate duties if it will mean a development opportunity for the person assuming the duties.
- Schedule a meeting to discuss the proposal. Be cautious, since many proposals are not well thought out and are based on the employee's personal or family needs. While a manager must understand these needs, the flextime arrangement still should be mutually beneficial.
- Don't make the decision at the first meeting. Discuss the implications of the flextime request with your supervisor, human resources department, and other potentially affected employees.
- If the request makes good business sense, but is missing some details, help the employee to make it work.
- Once you agree to a flextime proposal, support it. Do not allow other staff to imply that an employee who is working nontraditional hours or is working at home is therefore not working as hard.
- Meet with flextime employees regularly to reassess their schedules and to evaluate their goals and accomplishments. The success of a flextime plan is the responsibility of both the manager and the employee.

One of a manager's most challenging jobs is attracting and maintaining talented employees. Many competent people will decline opportunities that do not also allow them to meet family needs. Enlightened businesses will offer well-planned, flexible work schedules to attract such employees.

Creating a
Home Office

As today's companies compete for the best people, they have become more open to working arrangements such as flextime and telecommuting. To help assure efficiency when employees work from home, provide a checklist for setting up a home office. Important factors are:

- The right space. To foster discipline, organization, and commitment, there should be a permanent space used exclusively as a home office. Without such a designated space, the employee will tend not to distinguish between home life and work life. This does not have to mean the addition of a room; a corner, hallway, or even a laundry room can become a workplace with creative use of plants or room dividers. The space should, however, provide adequate lighting, telephone jacks, and electrical outlets.
- The right equipment, supplies, and storage space. Shelves for storage can also help to define a workspace. If the storage area is outside the workspace, it should still be conveniently located. Space available should also be a factor in equipment purchasing decisions. For example, a combination printer and fax machine may make more sense than two separate machines.
- The right furniture. Because most work will probably be done at a desk, it is essential that the desk and chair be ergonomically correct. Kitchen chairs or bridge tables do not make appropriate furniture for a home office.
- Phones and phone lines. The office will need at least two designated lines for telephone, fax, and Internet use, a phone with transfer and hold features, and access to the Internet, if possible through the company's server, or through a separate account. Equipment will require service contracts.

An employee setting up a home office will need to discuss with his or her supervisor the equipment that will be necessary and will fall within the budget.

An efficient home office takes thought and time to create. It should be quiet, comfortable, and adequately equipped, designed to provide privacy and to mimic the company's standard working arrangements.

MANAGEMENT TOOLS

36

Managing for the Short and Long Run

In a typical business setting, people are often forced to manage for the short run. Many managers find themselves constantly solving unexpected problems and dealing with crisis. This *reactive* mode makes it difficult to focus on strategy and other broader issues, or to shift into the *proactive* mode from which growth and improvement emerge.

Another problem with managing for the short term is that fewer factors are variable in this time frame. For example, if a company needs to increase production, additional workers can be added within a matter of days, but it takes much longer to add a new production facility.

In the long run, all factors are variable:

- Assets can be sold off.
- Leases can be allowed to expire.
- Contracts can be renegotiated.
- Strategy can be changed.

The reactive mode is also commonly found in large organizations where bonuses and stock prices depend on short-term results. Management's interest in short-term goals frequently conflicts with stockholders' interest in long-term goals.

Business Ethics

Do ethics and morality really exist in the business environment? Do you know what is expected of you in business situations—is it important to distinguish right from wrong, and to act in a way that supports your decision? Is it more important to be honest or to do what your boss asks of you even when you know it is wrong? If you feel pressured to leave your ethics at home, what do you do? Many employees feel that success receives higher priority than ethics.

Certainly, lapses in ethical behavior have occurred in business, just as they have in politics, health care, sports, religion, and philanthropic organizations. So why should you be ethical? The answer is that we should all have moral and ethical concerns as members of our society, and if that's not enough, unethical behavior can easily lead to job loss and/or criminal prosecution.

Although the goal of maximizing profits remains central, in the 1990s many businesses have increased their efforts to control pollution, maintain a healthy work environment without prejudices, increase emphasis on workplace safety, and reduce poverty. Business leaders who stress such goals are described as "enlightened capitalists."

Ethical behavior is just as important for employees as for managers. As organizations downsize, fewer managers are responsible for more employees. It is also more common to use part-time and temporary workers who may have little or no loyalty to the company. The U.S. Chamber of Commerce estimates that as much as $40 billion is lost each year because of workplace theft. It is important to realize that the conduct of a single employee can put an entire business at risk.

Many have jokingly remarked that business ethics is an oxymoron. But if you want to be able to trust your employees, superiors, suppliers, and customers, they must be able to trust you. You must set the example. Making ethical decisions can help your career, just as making the wrong decision can irrevocably damage your prospects.

KEY BUSINESS CONCEPTS

38 Making Ethical Decisions in Business

How do you make a decision that may involve right and wrong and may affect your future career, positively or negatively? In *Managing Business Ethics*, Linda K. Trevino and Katherine Nelson outline an eight-step decision-making process based on a full evaluation of the circumstances:

1. *Gather the facts.* What are the details of the situation confronting you? What caused this situation to occur? All facts may not be available to you, but gather as much information as possible.
2. *Define the ethical issues.* Frame the situation in basic terms of truth, honesty, promise keeping, employee rights, and the rights of the company. Identify as many such ethical issues as possible. It is helpful to present the matter to someone you trust, such as a spouse or good friend. They may see issues that you might have missed.
3. *Who are the affected parties?* Identify everyone who might be affected by the situation, and try to see the situation through each person's eyes. The list might include other employees, management, suppliers, customers, and stockholders in the company. Try testing your potential decision by seeing how each party would react.
4. *What are the consequences?* Look at the consequences that are most likely to occur and at the most negative possible consequences. Which decision would accomplish the most good?
5. *What are your obligations?* Look at your obligations to your boss, employees, and others in terms of right and wrong, truth and integrity. If you think your boss is asking you to do something wrong, you will be better off raising the issue than ending up responsible for unethical behavior.
6. *Will your character and integrity remain intact?* The general rule is that if you would be embarrassed to tell your parents, spouse, or clergyman about your actions, or to see them described in the newspaper, then you need to reconsider.

7. *Have you considered all the alternatives?* Be creative in deciding your course of action. You may have more than two choices; there may be a third that has not occurred to you. If a customer or supplier wants to give you a gift, can you ask instead for a discount for your company?

8. *Are you done?* Last of all, check your gut! Does your proposed decision feel right? If it doesn't feel right, rethink your decision.

Obviously, being ethical is not simply a matter of following a formula. Every situation has its own dynamics that make the ethical concerns unique. But, giving serious thought to the ramifications of a particular decision will always help you make the right choice.

39

Top Down versus Bottom Up

Whether it's a matter of establishing a reputation for customer service or building a corporate culture, policies need support from the uppermost levels of management down through the entry-level positions. The issue is one of setting an example and practicing what you preach. Workers lose morale when they feel that they must adhere to a different set of standards than management. Achieving change means everything must be supported from the top down.

Trying to work without the support of the upper management can be very discouraging and frustrating. It is highly unlikely that any such bottom-up effort will be successful for any length of time. It is extremely effective, however, to have an open line of communication from the bottom up. Input and suggestions from the staff are key to a company's success. All employees must be able to contribute and make a difference, and they can't do this if no one is listening. Employee suggestion boxes are a step in the right direction, but they are only effective if the suggestions are given sufficient attention on a regular basis.

There are other ways for upper management to show dedication and support. One manager went the extra mile to establish the type of communication he wanted within the company. He not only told his employees that his "door was always open," but he actually had the door to his office removed. What better way to demonstrate sincerity and commitment?

Sticking to the rules and treating all employees the same is also important. Playing favorites will send the wrong message and only end in frustration.

Consistent and reliable management is essential. When top management walks the walk and talks the talk, there will be far-reaching effects throughout the organization. Transformations do not happen overnight, however, especially major changes in a large corporation. Changing a corporate culture is a significant undertaking that typically takes five to seven years.

Supply and Demand

40

The theory of supply and demand is one of the most fundamental concepts in economics. In Figure 9, a typical supply and demand graph, the horizontal axis represents quantity and the vertical axis represents price.

The graph shows that as supply increases, demand decreases, and vice versa. The point at which the two lines intersect is the equilibrium point. Draw a line from this point to the two axes to determine price and available quantity. To see how supply and demand affect price, let's imagine that torrential rains in Colombia have devastated the coffee crop. If coffee is in short supply, what happens to the price? It's easy to guess that coffee prices will increase, but let's use the graph for verification.

When the supply of coffee decreases, the supply curve will shift over to the left, that is, quantity available will decrease. This change is represented by the dotted line. There is now a new equilibrium (the point where the supply and demand curve intersect), and a line drawn to the price axis indicates a price above the previous one.

In general terms, as the supply of an item decreases, the price will go up. Conversely, if an item is in great abundance, the price is likely to drop. But other factors also contribute to supply and demand, such as the competitive environment, consumer preferences, availability of substitute products, and general market trends.

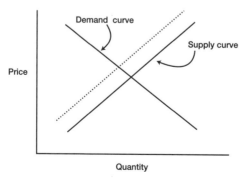

Figure 9. A supply and demand graph.

41

Taking Advantage of Economies of Scale

It's probably no surprise to hear that buying products in bulk is often cheaper than purchasing smaller amounts. The same phenomenon underlies the concept of *economies of scale*, which applies to purchasing, manufacturing, maintenance, and even marketing. Examples of economies of scale include:

- Lower construction costs for tract homes and planned communities
- Greater efficiency of production lines
- Savings when purchasing a "family size" product
- Discounts offered on larger orders or purchases

Economies of scale often provide a distinct competitive advantage for companies. As companies grow, they are able to capitalize on increased volume. For example, suppliers will frequently offer deeper discounts as order sizes increase. Production volume may also justify the purchase of specialized equipment, or vertical integration on the side of suppliers or distributors. The results are lower production costs and the ability to offer a product at a more competitive price.

Economies of scale do not happen automatically; they must be actively recognized and pursued by management. Like bulk purchasing, economies of scale can provide savings, but only for the smart shoppers.

Law of Diminishing Returns

At some point, increased effort put into a task or operation will not result in an equal increase in output. Let's look at a production line as an example. Suppose five workers are able to produce 100 items each hour, or 20 items per person. Six workers are able to produce 132 each hour, or 22 items per person. The additional worker has increased overall productivity from 20 to 22 units per person per hour. But in this case, it turns out that adding one more worker to the line, for a total of seven, results in 147 units produced each hour, or 21 units per person.

Table 1
An Example of Diminishing Returns

Number of Employees	Total Units Produced per Hour	Units Produced per Person
5	100	20
6	132	22
7	147	21

Seven workers produce fewer units per capita than six workers did, indicating the point of diminishing returns for this production line. The reason returns begin to diminish may lie in the structure of the task, the equipment, or increased difficulty of the task when more workers are sharing one production line. Whatever the cause, identifying such points of diminishing returns can help increase the efficiency of your business.

43

Understanding the Competitive Nature of Your Environment

Competitive pressures differ from industry to industry, but in every organization management decisions should take into account not only internal issues but also the competitive landscape.

A useful framework for evaluating competitive pressure is the "Five Forces of Competition" model developed by Michael Porter of the Harvard Business School. This model incorporates five factors that characterize the competitive nature of an industry:

Economic Power of Customers

Is it easy for the customer to switch to a different product?
How important is your product to the customer?
Does the customer have many competitors to choose from?
Can your product be created or made by a potential customer?

Economic Power of Suppliers

Do you have several suppliers to choose from?
Do they offer comparable quality?
How important are the inputs obtained from suppliers?
Is it easy to switch suppliers?

Competition from Substitutes

Are there alternative products that will fulfill the same customer needs?
What price will customers pay before they decide to switch to a substitute?

Rivalry Among Competing Firms

What are the number and size of your competitors?
Is demand for your product growing or is the market saturated?
What is the basis of competition?
How are competitors differentiated?

Threat of Potential Entrants

Are there barriers to entry that prevent new companies from entering the market?

How would existing firms react to a new entry?

No single force is necessarily more important than any other. Customers, suppliers, and competitors each pose critical challenges. Each force, as well as interaction between the forces, will characterize the competitive nature of an industry.

44

Competitive Advantage

No company can exist in a bubble; a competitor is always lurking somewhere in the marketplace, waiting to steal market share, customers, and profits. Success in today's business environment requires a company to establish and maintain competitive advantages. Organizations can increase their competitiveness by excelling in any of a number of areas:

Information Systems

Managing information—obtaining, organizing, distributing and evaluating it is something organizations must do well in order to respond quickly, both to internal circumstances and changes in the marketplace.

Technology

Companies can gain a distinct competitive advantage by using technological advancements to automate and simplify processes and to make them more efficient.

Location

A company's location may offer strategic advantages, such as better access to raw materials, transportation, distribution channels, markets, and other infrastructure elements. Workforce requirements also have a strong influence on location. Many companies move their manufacturing operations to countries that provide cheap labor.

Research and Design

There is strong pressure to constantly outperform the competition by developing new and improved products.

Marketing

Marketing is one of the most commonly overlooked aspects of competitiveness, but it is nonetheless crucial. What good is a product or service if no one knows about it? Developing a cohesive and effective marketing strategy is key to establishing and maintaining a competitive presence.

Pricing

Pricing products lower than the competition is a difficult competitive advantage to maintain in the long run. Short-term price reductions are used by large companies to drive out competition which cannot afford reduced or negative profits.

A competitive advantage must be closely linked to the forces that shape the marketplace and the industry. Each company must determine how it can best compete and develop a competitive strategy suited to its strengths and resources.

45

Sustainable Competitive Advantage (SCA)

An asset or skill that gives a company a competitive advantage (see tip #44) in the marketplace is more valuable if it is difficult for others to imitate or copy. Such a sustainable competitive advantage allows the company to reap the benefits from the differentiating factor until other substitutes are made available. An SCA can be related to marketing, production, or even a developed customer base or logo, and it can be achieved by many different strategy formulations. Several examples include:

- A strategy of differentiation involves offering a product that is substantially different from the competition. This differentiation is sufficiently unique as to be difficult to emulate. Obtaining patents and other legal protections are common ways to preserve potentially competitive advantages.
- A low-cost strategy offers customers a lower price for a product or service, such as a Casio watch or health care from an HMO.
- When business units within a larger organization combine sales and marketing or expenses such as office space, billing personnel, plant equipment, and human resources personnel, they are able to reduce their costs.
- A focusing strategy involves concentrating on a specialized product or service, or on a small buyer group. Examples include clothing stores for tall men or plus-size women, or an auto muffler service or oil-change service.
- A preemptive strategy focuses on being the first supplier with a new product or service. Microsoft and Intel are examples of this preemptive strategy.

Developing and maintaining a sustainable competitive advantage is crucial to a business's long-term health. There are many strategies for developing and maintaining this necessary advantage over your competitors. Any sustainable competitive advantage must be constantly monitored and updated to remain effective. Which type of SCA strategy does your organization employ? Survival may depend on it!

Barriers to Entry

In a competitive environment, establishing and maintaining a competitive advantage can often mean the difference between success and failure. Numerous factors influence a company's performance in a given industry, among them the competitive nature of the environment, consumer demand, and the particular risks of doing business in that industry. What if an industry has not been defined yet? For example, what if Company XYZ is going to sell a product that is new to the world? There is not yet any competition to speak of, but this will likely change if the product generates profitable returns.

How long will Company XYZ be able to enjoy exclusive sales of its product? One way to assess this is to evaluate the *barriers to entry* that exist. Barriers to entry are factors that help determine the difficulty another company would have in establishing itself as a competitor. Let's take a quick look at some common barriers to entry:

Capital Requirements

How much money is needed to enter a market and establish a competitive presence? The more expensive it is to compete effectively, the smaller the number of entrants there will likely be.

Learning Curve

How much time does it take to understand a market and to learn the tricks of the trade? Experience in an industry helps a company make efficient and timely decisions that provide a significant competitive advantage.

Distribution Channels

This is one of the most frequently overlooked factors, but it is critically important. Competitor 123 may make a product that is identical, or even superior, to Company XYZ's, but unless this company has a distribution channel to get the product to the consumer, it will never compete effectively.

Economies of Scale

Generally speaking, as companies increase production volume, the costs associated with each unit produced tend to decrease. Larger companies are able to enjoy the advantages of economies of scale and can frequently offer products at a lower price.

Barriers to entry are unique to each industry. For example, creating a new airline requires large amounts of capital and will mean facing intense competition and significant regulatory requirements. Starting a new web-based music store, on the other hand, requires far less capital and presents a completely different competitive environment. In each case, a company must decide which industry or market it is best suited to compete in effectively.

Controlling an Industry

The following terms describe the competitive forces and the distribution of market control that characterize an industry:

Monopoly

A single player controls the market and is able to keep others from entering. The monopoly is able to enjoy large profits since no competition exists. Counterweights are government intervention, intended to keep prices reasonable, and anti-trust legislation, intended to give other companies a fair chance at competing in the marketplace.

Oligopoly

Several large companies are the dominant players in an industry. Roughly speaking, an oligopoly exists if four or five sellers together control more than 60 percent of the market. The soft drink, fast food, and long-distance phone service industries are all examples of oligopolies.

Monopolistic Competition

Many companies are competing for market share and there is little difference between the product offerings. It is relatively easy to enter this market as a new competitor. An intersection with gas stations on each corner is a good example of monopolistic competition.

Perfect Competition

A large number of sellers are competing, and the actions of any one competitor have virtually no impact on the market. For example, if an Idaho farmer decides to grow more potatoes, there will be little effect on the market price.

Understanding how your company fits into the market environment will help you position yourself to compete most effectively.

48 Supply Chain

A supply chain is the sequence of steps involved as a product evolves from raw materials and travels into the hands of the customer. A typical product will be the result of efforts from many different and independent companies. Figure 10 gives an example of a supply chain.

To be competitive, a company must review and assess each segment of the chain. Successful companies typically have a well-integrated supply chain; that is, there is smooth and efficient transition from one segment to the next. In developing a supply chain, it is important to consider potential strategic alliances with partners who will fit into and contribute to the supply chain.

Building and maintaining productive relationships with both suppliers and distributors is key to preserving or improving the performance of the supply chain. Many companies vertically integrate, which means they take over the activities of their suppliers or distributors (see tip #92). For example, a manufacturer may decide it would be more cost effective to process raw materials in-house.

While each component of the supply chain needs to be evaluated, it is the chain's overall effectiveness that influences an organization's ability to compete. Developing and maintaining a highly efficient supply chain is one of the critical elements of success.

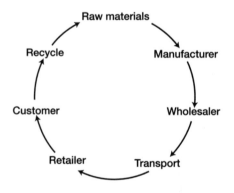

Figure 10. A supply chain.

Value-Added Chain

The concept of a value-added chain is relatively straightforward. As a product travels from suppliers of materials to the manufacturer and on to customers, its value increases at each point. The companies involved add value by producing a finished product from raw materials, adding function to a product, making a product more attractive to consumers, or moving a product closer to consumers. Figure 11 represents a simplified value-added chain.

There are many other potential links in a value-added chain. One example would be a reseller. In the computer software and hardware industries, companies often seek resellers to help sell and support products. Much like franchisees, resellers are given exclusive territories to protect profits and limit competition. In return, they add value to, and increase profits from, the product.

Each partnership should be constantly evaluated to make sure that it is in fact adding value. For example, having three suppliers for the same products may not be cost-effective. While the concept of a value-added chain is straightforward, it takes attention and commitment to ensure its continued success.

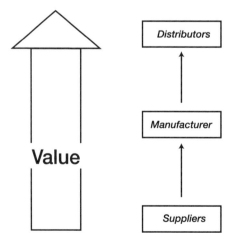

Figure 11. A value-added chain.

50 Mission Statement

A mission statement is a brief, concise expression of a company's fundamental purpose and goals. Here is an example of a mission statement for Company XYZ:

To provide innovative and superior products while offering the highest quality in customer service and care. Aggressive research and design combined with strategic marketing and a complete commitment to quality will establish our products as the industry leader.

The creation of a mission statement is only the first step; the next step is to circulate the statement throughout the organization. Many companies make the mistake of formulating a mission statement and then putting it on the shelf to collect dust. A mission statement will be a wasted gesture unless it is incorporated into everyday business operations. The mission statement must be reviewed and updated frequently, with input from the entire corporation. Everyone must be aware of the mission of the company and must buy into the mission statement.

Do you know what your company's mission statement is? If one does not exist, your company would benefit from taking this step to identify its primary goals and express the values that are its highest priority.

Sharing a Vision

One of the sure signs of a good leader is his or her ability to share a vision. After all, it's no good to have a great idea, or a clear vision of the direction a company should take, if you are unable to communicate it effectively. A good chief executive officer is the source of the vision for a company, and this vision needs to be spread throughout the organization.

Doing so requires passionate delivery in addition to excellent communication skills. Selling a vision is four parts salesmanship and six parts passion, which is why your own strong belief in and commitment to a vision will help you spread it. Some of history's most powerful figures have been charismatic leaders who believed deeply in their own visions and excelled at sharing them.

Typically, visionary leaders are associated with change and with doing things that have not been done before. They are willing to experiment and take risks, to consider new ideas, and to listen to others. The leaders of the future are willing to turn the organization upside down, that is, to regard the customer and the customer contact people as the top rather than the bottom of the organizational pyramid.

Effective leaders must have the vision to see things that others do not see. They must regularly reexamine their view of the world, constantly ingest a great deal of information in order to stay current, think broadly, and modify their actions accordingly.

52

Understanding the Cost of Goods Sold

It is important to know the cost of goods sold (COGS) in order to calculate your profits. The COGS is your capital investment in your business. Sales minus the COGS will give you your gross income.

Sales – COGS = Gross Income

Gross Income – Operating Expenses = Profits

COGS is a non-taxable item since it is the cost of continuing your business. If you have inventory, compute the COGS by taking the cost of initial inventory, adding the cost of purchases, supplies, and labor, and subtracting the cost of the final inventory. Inventory is defined as all merchandise held for resale to customers in the usual course of business.

Inventory costs include all costs necessary to acquire and bring the merchandise to the site of the sale. Therefore, inventory costs include:

- Freight, returns, allowances, discounts, and storage
- Insurance premiums on the merchandise
- Employee expenses for handling merchandise
- Property tax on merchandise
- Losses from deterioration or obsolescence of merchandise
- Earnings from alternative investments of the capital expended on inventory

There are four generally accepted methods of pricing inventory (see tip #291). Table 2 is an example of a COGS calculation using the periodic inventory method. Negative numbers are indicated by parentheses.

Table 2
Calculation of Cost of Goods Sold

Sales		$ 200,000
Cost of Goods Sold:		
Beginning Inventory	($120,000)	
Purchases	($40,000)	
Cost of labor and supplies	($20,000)	
Less: Ending Inventory	$50,000	
Total Cost of Goods Sold		($ 130,000)
Gross Profit		$70,000

Company Performance from a Financial Perspective

How does a business define and measure good performance? Sales and profits provide one measurement of past and present performance.

Return on assets (ROA) is the sum of profits, divided by assets. The equation breaks down further into

$$ROA = Profits/Assets = (Profits / Sales) \times (Sales / Assets)$$

What target should be set for a strategic plan? The "hurdle rate" is the rate of return on assets (ROA) on an investment that needs to be cleared for the project to be viable. A company's ROA must meet or exceed the cost of capital. The figure used for cost of capital is usually the interest rate on government bonds, which are considered to be the most secure investment. This is the minimum amount that an investment in the business should earn; otherwise, the money could better be invested elsewhere, and at lower risk. Investors expect a higher rate of return for a higher risk.

Economic Value Added (EVA) is another way of evaluating corporate performance. The EVA method deducts the cost of capital from the net operating profit. A positive value indicates that the company has contributed to shareholder value.

American companies use increased stockholder value as a measure of performance. Shareholder value analysis takes the present values of future cash flows (see tip #320) and residual value and subtracts the market value of any debt. The result indicates the company's future versus its past financial performance.

From a global perspective, it is interesting to note that American companies typically place more importance on the return to the investor, or ROI, while Japanese companies place prime importance on market share increases. It's also important to keep in mind that while the measures discussed here are useful, there are other important indicators of strategic performance.

KEY BUSINESS CONCEPTS

54 Measuring Performance— Beyond Money

Measuring a company's performance only in financial terms will paint an incomplete picture. Other measurements must be added to the financial calculations to determine the long-term viability and health of a business. A business that is successful today will not be successful in the future if the company's strategic plan does not address the following:

- Customer satisfaction and brand loyalty
- Product service and quality
- Brand/firm associations
- Relative cost
- New product activity
- Manager/employee capability and performance
- Strategic options

It's hard to identify any one category as the most useful indicator. What is more likely is that complex interactions between these various categories will help determine the existing and potential profitability of a given organization.

Many successful companies have not paid enough attention to these issues and have learned the hard way that paying attention to them is necessary for continued success.

Corporate Culture

When you are at work, is there a relaxed, upbeat atmosphere? Does the boss stop and ask employees how their families are doing? Is everyone in a suit and tie? How would people react if you showed up at work with your one-year-old daughter? Chances are that each company has its own set of standards and accepted behaviors. These attitudes and values that are prevalent throughout an organization are termed *corporate culture*. Factors that influence the culture range from the organizational structure to the attitudes and actions of management to the dress code. A company actively cultivates a particular kind of corporate culture to help establish its identity. For example, Microsoft has set a very loose dress code with flexible working hours. Both formal and informal frameworks define corporate cultures.

The formal framework refers to the

- Structure of the organization
- Chain of command
- Rules and regulations

The informal framework can include

- Open-door policies
- Accessibility of management
- Dress codes
- Special event and rituals
- Standard manners of speech and behavior

These informal characteristics vary from company to company and also according to the culture of the host country. As business enters the global marketplace, culture becomes an even more complex issue. Japanese companies, for example, have a distinctly different way of doing business, and American companies must respect and understand these differences. The same also holds true for Japanese companies coming to the United States and Mexico. Each company must ask itself how well its corporate identity fits into the culture of its business environment.

The merger of two organizations often creates interesting dynamics as two cultures attempt to integrate. This effort is frequently unsuccessful and the culture clash may sink profitability and eventually end in a breakup. Changing a corporate culture, whether or not this change is part of a merger, takes years and requires support from top management as well as from all other levels. There are managerial specialists who focus specifically on helping companies through this process.

Types of Corporate Culture

There are four major styles of corporate culture: academy, baseball team, club, and fortress. The internal values of each kind of company often reflect external circumstances. Let's take a closer look at the characteristics of each one:

Academy

These companies focus on long-term employment and internal career advancement. Many of the Fortune 500 companies adhere to this more traditional type of culture. Employees usually receive high-quality, extensive training and are then expected to repay the organization through committed and long-term employment.

Baseball Team

These companies focus on short-term employment and usually have limited resources to put toward employee development. They look purely for talent and are willing to pay a premium for it. Employees are considered to be free agents with little or no obligation or loyalty to remain with the company.

Club

These organizations stress the importance of the group. Priority is placed on doing what is good for the group rather than just for the individual. Management typically interacts directly with employees and maintains open channels of communication. A CEO who desires few special privileges is likely to encourage this type of culture.

Fortress

These companies are in a state of flux. They are often in serious trouble and in danger of going out of business. They are unable to offer long-term employment security and even the best employees may lose their jobs. Management tension reflects, or creates, the prevailing uncertainty.

Which type of organization do you work for?

57

Planning a Public Relations Crisis Response

Most companies do not deal with crises on a daily basis, but managers must be prepared to handle a crisis or a serious incident when it arises. Having a crisis response plan prepared in advance, and honing your response skills in case of an emergency, may prove invaluable. The manager's role during a serious incident is no small task, and many companies will seek help from public relations consultants during times of crisis. The goal of crisis response is to retain public confidence in your company and protect the welfare of your workforce, while satisfying the public's right to know by supplying timely, honest, and accurate accounts.

The definition of a crisis is an issue so severe that it threatens the integrity or existence of an organization or institution. Examples are the Monica Lewinsky scandal or the Valujet, TWA, and Swissair crashes. How and when a company responds to such issues will determine whether or not the public continues to have confidence in the company.

Surviving a crisis depends upon a thorough and well-thought-out plan and a commitment to continuous communication with the public throughout the crisis. Suggestions for a successful crisis response plan include:

- Make a plan and provide staff to support it. Commit to training those involved and give them the opportunity to rehearse their roles. Key elements of the plan are a statement of corporate policy, division of responsibilities, contingency plans, resources, and points of contact.
- Use technology. During a crisis, establish a web page with frequent updates concerning the incident. The site will be used by media and public news seekers and can be a referral source for your callers.
- Keep your phone lines free. Following the Valujet crash in 1996, the company received as many as 100 voice-mail messages an hour. Anticipate the need for information and send fax releases that may decrease the incoming calls. Use cellular phones and make sure that every crisis team member has an up-to-date telephone directory.
- Establish an e-mail network for the crisis team. Make sure a key person monitors the network for messages and update messages frequently.

- Have laptops available to monitor e-mails from the field. Have digital capabilities to send images, such as photographs of a disaster site, if necessary.
- Prepare for high-visibility visitors, and have the necessary staff available for their visits. Treat all visitors professionally.
- Get the good news out. Seek out opportunities to tell the good stories.
- Keep notes and learn from your mistakes. Change plans based on evaluation, feedback, and experience.
- When the crisis ends, tell everyone.

Your success during a crisis will depend heavily on what you do or don't do. You will be judged by the rapport that you have established with the community and the media both prior to and after the crisis. Establishing a plan that relies upon honest and timely responses will help you survive catastrophe and may even boost your public image.

What Is an Information System?

An information system (IS) consists of an organized combination of people, computer hardware, software, communications networks, and data resources that collect, transform, and spread information throughout an organization. Modern industry relies on computer-based information systems and on information technology (IT).

Users of IT are:

- *End users*—the people who use the information or information system. Most employees are end users. Managers are also end users, and a good working knowledge of your IS will increase your chances of success.
- *Information system specialists*—the individuals who work with the information system and the technology behind it. The systems analysts, operators, and professional computer programmers set up the IS, update it, and keep it functioning.

Aside from the usual word processing and e-mail functions, you should be familiar with a spreadsheet program to help provide effectively analyzed information, a database management program to provide reports on organizational performance, and any specialized software needed for your own work activities (see tip #60). Your employer will usually provide training programs, either in-house or off-site. Take advantage of these opportunities to upgrade your computer skills; they will be invaluable in any future position.

IT serves three vital roles in a business:

- Support of business operations. This includes inventory control, sales of goods or services, purchase of equipment, expenses, and financial management.
- Support of managerial decisions. By analyzing sales, overhead, competition, and performance of groups and departments, management will have the information necessary for decisions regarding production, purchasing, hiring and firing, promotions, and growth.
- Support of your business's competitive advantage. Information analysis can also help a company make decisions that will give it an advantage over the competition. Examples include price reductions, addition of services, and new merchandise or product production.

Computer Basics

A computer is more than just a sophisticated calculator—it is a system of interrelated components that input, process, output, control, and store information. The earliest computers were large, extremely expensive mainframes. With time, the price and size of computers has decreased dramatically and now personal computers, or PCs, can perform all the functions of their larger predecessors.

The most important component of the computer on your desk is the *central processing unit,* or CPU. The CPU controls the interpretation and execution of instructions. Technological advances have increased the processing speeds of computers exponentially. Operating speeds used to be measured in milliseconds (thousandths of a second) and are now being measured in microseconds (millionths of a second) and nanoseconds (billionths of a second). Computers are able to process several million instructions per second, or MIPS. Processing speed is also measured in millions of cycles per second, or megahertz (MHz).

How does a computer work? Essentially, a computer processes data by tracking the presence or absence of magnetic or electronic signals in the circuitry or media (such as floppy disks or CD-ROMS) it uses. These signals are a form of *binary representation,* meaning that there are only two possible states or conditions. Let's take a look at the most fundamental unit of data, the *bit.* The bit, an abbreviation for the words "binary digit," can have a value of either zero or one. A *byte* is a group of bits that the computer treats as one unit. A byte usually consists of eight bits and is used to represent one character of data. For example, in the American Standard Code for Information Interchange (ASCII) format, the letter M is represented by the following byte: 01001101. Each letter and number has its own unique sequence that the computer uses for processing.

Sophisticated programming languages have been developed since the earliest programming languages were introduced, such as Fortran, Java, Visual Basic, Delphi, and COBOL.

60

Computer Software

While computer *hardware* consists of the computer itself and other physical devices, such as modems, printers, and video screens, computer *software* refers to information processing systems. These are generally categorized into two major types of programs:

- System software
- Application software

System software supports and manages the information processing tasks. It includes the operating system (such as Windows or DOS), system utilities, security monitors, and software development packages. *Application software* includes general-purpose programs, such as word processors, database managers, graphic design packages, and application-specific programs that may be designed for manufacturing, capital budgeting, engineering, or any number of other specialized areas.

A computer system consists of several interacting components:

- *Input of information into the system.* The input data is known as raw data.
- *Processing of the information to produce the desired data.* The processed information is only as good as the raw data; if the raw data is inaccurate or incomplete, the final data will be of poor quality or will be useless.
- *Output of information.* The production and delivery of the data in the desired form to the user.

Which software programs should you learn and use in your work? There are several general types of computer software programs that will enable you to perform your job better. You should become proficient in a word processing program (Microsoft Word or WordPerfect), a spreadsheet program (Microsoft Excel or Lotus), and a program for presentations (Harvard Graphics or Microsoft Powerpoint). You should take advantage of all the relevant computer software training programs that your company makes available to you. Learning these programs will save you time and allow you to do a better job. These skills will also be necessary for promotions and future job opportunities.

Operations Support Systems

Information systems play a role in both the operations and management of a company. The role of information systems has been expanding as systems have evolved and become more sophisticated. The systems that support operations management consist of:

Transaction Processing Systems

These systems record and process data from business transactions. The data may include inventory, customer lists, sales, and costs. In batch processing, transactions accumulate over time and are processed periodically; in real-time processing, the processing takes place at the time of the transaction.

Process Control Systems

Process control systems (PCS) are support systems that make routine decisions automatically. The computer can be instructed to make decisions when a certain threshold is reached. Examples include reordering items once the amount on hand drops below a given level. The system can monitor data such as number of orders, and adjust the numbers of units to be produced and the amount of raw materials needed accordingly.

Office Automation Systems

Office automation systems (OAS) collect, store, and process information. These systems include word processing and e-mail programs. With desktop publishing packages, which include word processing, graphics, and page composition capacity, you can produce materials such as newsletters, manuals, brochures, and books. Image processing allows the input, processing, and retrieval of text, handwriting, graphics, and pictures. Electronic data management (EDM) provides an interface among image processing, word processing, e-mail, and voice mail, so that information can be forwarded to other end users. Computer graphics present data in graph or chart form. Computer-aided design (CAD), used by engineers and architects, employs computer graphics in the design of mechanical, electronic, and physical objects.

INFORMATION SYSTEMS

62 Management Support Systems

Management support systems (MSS) provide a systems framework that organizes information systems applications. Integrating all systems allows management and integration of the information and makes it available to all managers. The operational support systems (see tip #61) supply the information.

Management support systems include:

Management Information Systems

Management information systems (MIS) are the most common management support systems and provide information to support decision making. Information comes from internal sales, inventory, and cost databases, which are continually updated by the transaction processing system. This system will generate displays and reports automatically on a predetermined schedule or on demand. You can also obtain information from external sources, in order to measure your company against the competition, or to keep current on the economy and on industry and government changes that affect your company.

Decision Support Systems

Decision support systems (DSS) use decision models to process information supplied by the transaction processing and management information systems. Managers can generate the information they need and use the models as an aid in decision making. A spreadsheet, for example, can generate different information for different scenarios, such as different sales levels or costs. These "what if" changes can help the manager to make a decision regarding operational or strategic changes or to explore alternative strategies.

Executive Information Systems

Executive information systems (EIS) provide middle and upper management with selected information necessary to make strategic decisions. Key factors used to make strategic decisions are programmed into the EIS. These information systems are user friendly and frequently present data in graphic form.

A working knowledge of these management support systems helps management obtain the information necessary for executive decisions and can make a real difference in the continued viability of the company.

Using Artificial Intelligence

Computers that can see, feel, and act like people? While it may sound like science fiction, artificial intelligence (AI) simulates such processes of the human brain as reasoning, learning, and problem solving. More and more, computers are developing the ability to "think," although there is still a long way to go before they reach the complexity of a human brain.

Artificial intelligence has led to the development of *expert systems*. An expert system uses a large collection of information on a specific topic in order to serve as an expert, or consultant, to users. It consists of a knowledge base and a software module that provides answers to a user's questions. Expert systems have proven useful in financial planning, diagnosing illnesses, and recommending repairs in a manufacturing plant.

Most computer operations are linear in nature, that is, they follow a sequential, straight path. Artificial intelligence, on the other hand, uses something called *neural networks* in processing information. Neural networks function more like the brain and are able to integrate several types of information at once. The difference is best demonstrated with an example:

Let's say you are walking downtown and you are about to cross a busy intersection. Linear processing would view crossing the street as a simple matter of going from point A to point B, and would factor no other information into the operation. Now let's consider how neural networks would handle the situation. Before crossing the street, the computer would consider other factors that may be relevant to the operation, much the way a human would. Is there a crosswalk available? Is there a bus approaching at 35 miles per hour?

Another powerful feature of expert systems is the ability to learn from experience. In crossing the street, for example, the computer could learn that it should first check for oncoming buses. The system can then take this knowledge and use it in future decision-making processes.

64

Computer Viruses

How do you and your company safeguard the information stored in your computer? An estimated 100 new computer viruses are developed each day. As a result, virus detection and destruction has become big business, and virus detection software needs constant upgrades to detect and destroy the new invaders. As a general rule, be cautious about downloading any data or program, whether from a CD-ROM, floppy disk, e-mail message, or the Internet, when you are uncertain about the source. It is simpler in the long run to avoid downloading a virus than to detect and destroy a virus that may destroy your hard drive.

The most common types of computer viruses are:

Appending Virus

These are among the more virulent viruses. They may rest for months without detection and then may be activated by a trigger such as a certain date or word. They can erase the File Allocation Table (FAT), which tells the computer where the files are on the hard drive. When the FAT is deleted, the hard drive is dead and the data and programs cannot be retrieved.

Overwriting Virus

These viruses are activated when a program is executed. They attach themselves to the program and overwrite it, usually destroying it.

There are several good computer virus software programs available, such as McAfee Viruscan and Norton Symantic. These virus detection programs can be updated monthly to keep pace with new viruses.

Computer Safety

Do you know how easy it is to obtain sensitive or proprietary information from your computer? Have you taken any precautions to make sure that your data is safe? Even the most sophisticated computers at U.S. government sites have been penetrated and compromised, but there are many steps you can take to protect your data.

The first step you can take is to set up a password that must be entered to access your computer programs or data. It should not be your name, date of birth, or other information about yourself that would be easy to obtain. You should always sign off when you leave your desk. Remember, too, that if your modem is activated and connected to a telephone line or a network, your data can be obtained remotely.

Routinely back up your computer files to floppy disks, or other media such as tape drives. You can set your computer to back up files periodically.

Never download files from the Internet or those attached to an e-mail unless you are sure of the source. You could unknowingly download a latent virus, which might show up at a later date. Never give out personal information such as your birthday, social security number, credit card numbers, or passwords on the Internet unless you are sure that the site is secure.

Routinely use antiviral software (see tip #64) to check your software for latent viruses, and update your antiviral software regularly.

Computer security is a growing industry, and many companies provide services to help protect data. Since almost all your company's important information—including sales, inventory, profits, losses, interoffice memos, minutes of important meetings, and plans—is likely stored on computers, security is extremely important to the company's health and growth.

66 What Every Manager Needs to Know About Marketing

Marketing is critical for every business, and every manager can benefit from being familiar with fundamental marketing concepts. A company will utilize a marketing mix, or a variety of marketing tools, to achieve its goals. The "Four *P*s" of marketing provide a framework for characterizing the marketing mix.

Price

- What type of pricing strategy is most appropriate? Should the product be perceived as "low-cost" or "premium"?
- How are competitors pricing their offerings?
- What is the market willing to pay?

Promotion

- What is the best way to create awareness of your product?
- How can you encourage people to try your product?
- Which media are best suited for your advertising efforts?

Product

- What features do consumers desire?
- What are your product's quality and design attributes?

Placement or Distribution

- What distribution channels are available?
- How much are competitors able to control distribution channels?
- Will retailers put your product on the shelf?

Each of the *P*s should be considered in the context of the others to make sure the marketing mix is strategically consistent.

The *SWOT* Analysis

One of the most useful ways to characterize an organization's overall strategic situation is the *SWOT* analysis. It provides a simple framework by using four general classifications:

S : Strengths
W: Weaknesses
O: Opportunities
T : Threats

The first two classifications apply to the organization's *internal* strengths and weaknesses:

Strengths

What does the organization do well?

What are some competitive advantages?

Can the organization establish patents and protect ideas?

Weaknesses

What does the organization lack?

What problems exist within the organization?

The last two classifications refer to the *external* opportunities and threats faced by the organization. They help to determine the nature of the environment and to assess the company's market potential.

Opportunities

Is there a significant unmet need?

Does a large market exist?

Can the organization get the advantage of being the first to meet this need?

Threats

How many competitors exist?

Are there barriers to entry into the market?

Are there regulations in place?

A *SWOT* analysis is most typically used in a marketing context. By assessing internal strengths and weaknesses and external opportunities and threats, it is possible to determine how well a product or service is poised to compete in the marketplace. The analysis is also useful in planning how to best position an offering or product (see tip #70).

Wanting and Needing

A want and a need are not the same thing. This may seem a simple observation, but the difference between the two provides an extremely useful perspective for dealing with products, customers, and even employees.

Needs

Anything necessary to sustain life is considered a need. Food, water, air, and shelter are the most basic needs. Failure to satisfy a need results in a sense of deprivation and could be life-threatening.

Wants

Wants may specifically satisfy needs but also reflect more specific preferences. For example, a person may need food, but specifically want a pizza.

What one person considers a need, another may not. This is often due to socioeconomic and cultural influences. In America, for example, a car is commonly considered a need. In Japan, it may be viewed strictly as a luxury item while a bicycle is considered an absolute essential.

The distinction between wants and needs is most often used in a marketing context to determine the type of customer demand for a product or service. It is applicable in almost every context, however. A company is considering removing a coffee machine that has been freely available to employees. While management may view coffee as an unnecessary benefit that is not directly related to productivity, there are likely to be several employees who feel differently, and so the results may not be worth the savings.

When making decisions, your business must consider how its view of wants and needs may differ from the view of employees or customers.

69

Who's Driving Your Efforts?

The basic function of most organizations is to provide a product or service to a customer. While this sounds straightforward, many large companies have made poor strategic decisions because they have not understood the basic nature of their efforts. A question as simple as "Why are we in business?" provides a surprisingly effective framework to help make the right strategic decisions.

It is useful to classify an organization's efforts as either *product driven* or *market driven*. The distinction is most often used in a marketing context, but one of the most important realizations a manager can have is the pivotal role marketing plays at every level of an organization.

Product Driven

A product-driven company focuses its efforts on pushing a product into the marketplace. Often the product is a discovery from the research and development or engineering departments, and the creators desperately want to find a commercial application for their innovation. But the company must ask itself whether or not there is actually a market for the product. In other cases, the technology behind a product may be driving the company. Often this product aims to satisfy a need or want that the customer does not recognize. This was largely the case with fax machines in the late 1980s. Adoption was slow since consumers were unsure of the advantages associated with faxing documents.

Market Driven

A company may instead focus its efforts on being market driven. The goal is to identify a want or need that is currently unmet in the marketplace and to provide a solution. More and more companies use this approach in order to remain competitive.

Even though people often consider marketing to be nothing more than advertising and public relations, it is essential that every department be focused on serving the needs of the market. If these needs are not communicated effectively throughout an organization, longer-term profits will be jeopardized and competitors will have the opportunity to gain market share.

Positioning

As mentioned earlier, of the components instrumental to success, marketing continues to be one of the most commonly overlooked. Executive management tends to be heavily preoccupied with operations and finances, and most organizations lack an executive officer dedicated to marketing. While some companies are recognizing the importance of marketing efforts, there is still a long way to go.

Why is marketing so critical? The principles of marketing help establish not only what products are likely to succeed in the marketplace, but also how they will compete most effectively. How will a product or service be unique? How will it be differentiated from the rest of the competition? To position a product, you must make strategic decisions about how best to compete in the marketplace.

For example, let's say you want to make a better mousetrap. Will your mousetrap be a high-quality device that is more expensive than other mousetraps, or will it be a low-cost alternative to current offerings? How you choose to position your mousetrap will determine not only your target customers but also the marketing methods you will use to reach them.

The basis of a product's positioning is usually price, quality, or service. A product positioning map illustrates how a product or service fits into the competitive landscape. Figure 12, on the following page, shows the positioning for your new mousetrap. Let's say that your mousetrap is made out of strong and lightweight titanium steel for maximum effectiveness and durability. Most of the competitors make cheap wooden mousetraps that cost far less.

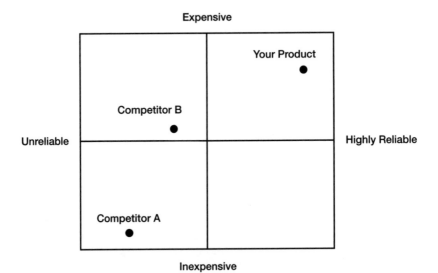

Figure 12. Product Positioning Diagram.

A Checklist for Salespeople

Salespeople provide information about products and services and strive to form relationships with potential buyers. Historically, selling has been more telling than asking. But today's successful salespeople will need to develop the skill of asking questions if they want to stay competitive in their field.

In the course of their communication with potential buyers, salespeople will need answers to some general questions:

- Who is the decision maker in the organization? Are you speaking to the decision maker and are there other people who need to be involved before the sale can close?
- What are your customer's specific objectives? Ask him or her, "If I could grant you two or three wishes, what would they be?"
- Ask your potential buyers if they are looking for the service or product today. If a buyer is not ready for your service or product, find out why. The reason for delay may make it worth your while to continue to build the relationship or, on the other hand, may make it futile for you to continue to try to make the sale. For example, the buyer may already be involved in a long-term satisfying relationship with another vendor.
- Ask potential clients what worked and what didn't with previous vendors. The answer to this question will help you formulate your selling campaign.
- Ask them why they buy from their current vendor. Do not accept better service or better pricing as an answer. Probe for specifics and assure them that all vendors can provide the same price or quality of service. Stress instead the uniqueness of your product and what you will specifically do for the account.
- Ask to name the new trends that they see ahead in their industry. This answer will help you classify buyers as trendsetters or followers, and as being content or discontent with their current marketing position. If they insist that they are not ready for new developments, you can lend your expertise with examples of how you can help them acquire a cutting edge in the market.

• Ask a buyer to tell you where, on a scale of one to ten, you stand as a potential seller. This preliminary reading will help determine what work you need to do to close the sale.

Keeping a checklist of questions to ask your potential buyers will assist you in evaluating the future seller-buyer relationship. A skilled salesperson will let the customer talk. Once the necessary information is gleaned, the salesperson can then respond with a worthwhile and convincing presentation.

Successful Selling

The goal of every sales organization is to become a leader in its industry. Although companies strive for competitive advantage by developing unique characteristics, top-performing sales companies appear to share many similarities. For success in selling, businesses should be:

- Committed to building long-lasting, mutually beneficial relationships with their customers
- Efficient in their operations and constantly striving to improve efficiency
- Investing heavily in research and development to exceed customer expectations
- Consistently offering top-quality products and services to their customers and allowing the customer the flexibility of purchasing only specific features
- Ranked as an industry leader and highly regarded by customers and competitors

Essential to the success of a sales organization is customer satisfaction. Research has discovered that to ensure a healthy buyer-seller relationship, a company needs to:

- Convey an image of expertise. Buyers need to be satisfied with both the company and the salespeople that service them. They expect the organization to be a stable business entity recognized for leadership and will insist that salespeople be knowledgeable about the competition, well versed in the business, and personable.
- Be dedicated to the customer. The customer will judge the organization and the salesperson on how well problems are solved, how products and services are priced, and how much dedication is given to becoming a real business partner.
- Offer guidance and be sensitive to changes. Customers expect that the company will adapt to changes in the marketplace and adjust pricing accordingly. The buyer will also expect the company to be able to coordinate all aspects of the product or service and provide a total package based on current needs.

- Confirm capabilities. Customers expect references and on-site inspections. Likewise, they expect full disclosure of weaknesses, and recommendations of competitors that may perform aspects of the needed services more efficiently than you can.

Today's buyers are savvy and demanding. They expect to receive dazzling customer service and high-quality products. As a manager you need to evaluate your company's strengths and weaknesses and devise an action plan to achieve the image of a top-performing sales organization. The characteristics discussed here can guide you toward achieving that status in the eyes of your customers.

Defining Sales Territories

The importance of pairing a sales territory with an individual salesperson is that the salesperson can better relate his or her effort to performance. Ownership in a territory builds pride and morale. Establishing sales territories will allow a manager to develop a more efficient team and to better assess performance.

One way to assign territories is to use the following steps to define workload:

- Divide your current customers into sales volume categories.
- Calculate the frequency with which each type of account should be called upon and the approximate time each call will take.
- Determine the workload involved in covering the entire market.
- Determine how many salespeople are currently available to service your customers.
- Calculate each salesperson's time by the number of jobs and the anticipated time required for each assignment.
- Calculate the number of salespeople needed for your market.

To conclude your analysis, you will also need to design the territories. Steps for territory design include:

- Establishing a basic control unit
- Approximating the market potential in each unit
- Combining units into groups or territories and performing workload analysis for each unit
- Rearranging groups based on workload analysis and unique characteristics of sales accounts
- Assigning salespeople to the newly defined sales territories

Sales territories with salespeople assigned to specific accounts provide customers with a personal touch. Establishing relationships is key to successful business operations, and sales territories help your staff build relationships with customers.

14

The Changing Sales Call

Sales managers and salespeople have long blamed each other when sales expectations are not met. Managers frequently complain, for example, that salespeople are not selling hard enough, while salespeople reply that the company is not advertising appropriately. Even though this type of disagreement is not new, there do seem to be new factors to consider in the selling equation.

Downsizing and cutbacks have affected the service industry. It is estimated that 17 million jobs in sales will be eliminated in the next few years. Further, there is a changing attitude toward sales calls. In the past, salespeople had ready access to their customers. Nowadays, even long-time customers are often reluctant to see sales representatives. With the evolving business environment, salespeople will have to rethink ways to succeed in business-to-business sales. Some new strategies are:

- Knowledge in your field. Today you are expected to be an expert. You will not even get through the customer's door to make your presentation without a reputation for expertise. In the past it was what you sold that was important to the customer. Now what you know is as important. Most successful salespeople will be well versed on one or a few products rather than on a wide range of items.

- Understand your customers and their business. This means taking the time to educate yourself. Do not underestimate your customer or assume that you can get by with glib remarks.

- Communicate your competence. You may not be invited to make a sales call but that doesn't mean you're barred from getting your message to the customer. Take the opportunity to participate in panel discussions, and give educational in-service presentations to the customer's staff. Remember you are reinforcing your expertise. The sales cycle, the period between first contact and signing the customer, is increasing. You as the salesperson need to stay in front of your potential prospects. Likewise, your sales manager must understand that finalizing the sale can take much longer than in the past.

The salesperson's goal is attained when the buyer decides that he or she wants a partnership with the salesperson. Reaching this point requires patience and communicating the sales message in a variety of ways. The sales call is no longer the primary instrument for selling the product. Salespeople need to be expert not only in their own product or service, but in their customers' business. The skilled salesperson of the future will be able to motivate the buyer to do business by delivering an indispensable total package.

75 Designing Effective Compensation Programs for Salespeople

In response to changes in the marketplace, salespeople are changing the way they sell. Managers and supervisors need to respond to the new selling strategies by rethinking the structure of compensation packages.

Traditionally, sales compensation packages have consisted of:

- Base salary
- Automobile, if needed for the job, and related expenses
- Expense budget
- Commission (a percentage of revenue or fee per unit sold)
- Bonus (a percentage of salary or fixed amount paid when specific performance criteria are met)
- Non-monetary compensation, such as trips and prizes

These basic elements of the sales compensation package were adequate in former years. But today the sales cycle has increased and it is necessary to raise the base salary to compensate. Another important market change is the shift towards partnerships and long-term relationships. In response to these alliances, there should be compensation for retaining business and extending the length of current contracts. Incentives for new business should not be on a commission basis when the market has consolidated into fewer buyers and when the goal is to establish long-term alliances with new customers as well.

Effective compensation programs should reinforce the company's sales objectives:

- Increase market share
- Meet specific market targets
- Retain business and increase the lengths of current contracts.

Note that sales and marketing strategies and incentive plans must be customized to reflect regional and other differences among markets. This approach will help maximize selling results and sales representative satisfaction.

Providing Dazzling Customer Service

Today, most companies' mission statements will contain some phrase about delivering quality service to the customer. Some organizations will use the term "service excellence," while others will speak of "total customer satisfaction." Customer service has been a buzzword for the nineties and will continue to be one of the most important factors in determining business success. What exactly does it mean to provide dazzling customer service?

The first step to being recognized as a leader in customer service is to understand who the customer is. It is easy to recognize your external customers, that is, your vendors, suppliers, contractors, and clients. While companies concentrate their efforts on their external customers, most organizations do not stress the importance of dazzling your internal customers as well as your external ones. A company that cannot communicate effectively on the inside will find itself unable to do so on the outside. A manager should not tolerate a display of rudeness by one employee to another. This type of behavior is counterproductive and will likely cause a snowball effect.

Once the organization realizes who the customer is, the next step is to evaluate where you are in delivering customer service. How does the customer rate you? What are your strengths and weaknesses? To assess your delivery of customer service, do a customer satisfaction survey. Remember to survey both internal and external customers. Ask questions that will tell you how well you are communicating, listening, and negotiating, and how well you solve problems. Have the customer define what good customer service is and explain why they would or would not continue to do business with you. Another important group to survey is the customers who leave you. Make certain that you ask enough questions to allow you to understand the loss of business.

Dazzling customer service depends upon skill in listening and communicating. A manager must ensure that his or her front-line staff is well trained in the art of communication. Because conflicts will always arise, a second important skill is empowerment. Managers need to give their staffs guidelines that are useful in resolving conflicts rapidly. Many businesses will authorize a dollar amount that employees can use to resolve problems. Other organizations will give employees as much leeway and creativity as it takes to resolve a conflict. Management must evaluate the benefits and costs of good customer service and determine how that equates with staff empowerment. Keep in mind that most customers understand conflict; what causes the customer to depart is delay in resolution of the conflict.

If your goal is to provide dazzling customer service, you will need to take a realistic look at where you are today, set your goals, and devise an action plan to achieve them. The result will be well worth the effort.

Ensuring a Successful Trade Show

77

In devising your strategy to increase your customer base, you should consider participating in a trade show. Trade shows offer a profitable means of reaching hundreds or even thousands of potential new customers, at relatively less cost than more conventional ways of doing business.

The number of trade shows in the U.S. and abroad is increasing, with thousands held each year. These trade shows present opportunities for sellers and buyers to meet face to face. They offer a chance to comparison shop, to present a positive image of your company, and to introduce new products and services. References that list where and when trade shows will take place include: *Tradeshow Week Magazine, Tradeshow Week Data Book,* and *Gayles Encyclopedia of Associations.*

To ensure that your trade show will be successful:

- Clearly define your goals. Who are your customers and what shows do they go to?
- Be prepared to interact with the buyers. You cannot just sit at your booth waiting for customers. When people enter your booth, be attentive. You need a minimum of two staffers at the booth.
- Prepare a 60-second presentation that describes your product and/or service and the benefit you will bring to the customer. Offer proof and statistics to validate your claims. Have testimonials, articles, interviews, and pictures.
- Read your audience. Can this person afford to buy your product? Are you talking with the company's decision maker?
- Keep a database of your potential customers. Get their business cards and write down personal information about them on their cards. Follow up after the show.
- Consider ways to increase traffic to your display. You may use a consultant to help you develop product demonstrations, contests, comical skits, game shows, dramatizations, and other attention-grabbing devices.

At a trade show, the customer comes to you. Trade shows are fast becoming an easy, less costly, and more profitable way to reach a large number of potential customers. Managers who intend to use trade shows to grow their businesses need to plan creative and entertaining presentations and to be willing to sell themselves and their businesses to large crowds.

MARKETING AND SALES

97

78

Granting Credit

People often decide where they will go for products and services based on where they can use their credit cards. The same is true in transactions between companies. Available credit terms may be the most important factor in selecting a supplier. Similarly, customers may weigh a credit option when deciding whether or not to do business with you. While offering credit may make you attractive to customers, it does present certain risks. One of the key ways to minimize this risk is to grant credit to the right customers and organizations. The bottom line is to assess who is likely to pay and who is not.

How can you determine whether or not someone deserves credit? There are several ways to check credit histories that will help you evaluate the risk of granting credit.

- The simplest method is to check customers' payment history with your firm. Have they paid their bills on time in the past? This will indicate their likelihood of making future payments.
- There are companies that sell credit information reports detailing payment histories and other relevant information. These companies often publish reference books that contain credit ratings.
- Analyzing an organization's financial statements also provides valuable information for assessing creditworthiness.
- Banks can provide information on the payment histories of other firms.

Obtaining the information is often the easy part, but the tough part is deciding whether or not to actually grant credit. The "five Cs of credit" help guide firms in making this crucial decision:

Capacity: Will operating cash flows allow the customer to meet credit obligations?

Capital: Does the customer have sufficient financial resources?

Character: Is the customer willing to meet credit obligations?

Collateral: In case of default, does the customer have an asset that can be seized?

Conditions: What are the general economic conditions?

Offering credit may serve as an attractive business tool, but there is always a degree of uncertainty involved. You will have your own bills to pay, regardless of whether your customers are paying theirs. Proper evaluation of credit information will enable you to best assess which customers are worth the risk.

79

Offering Trade Credit

Trade credits are often an attractive option for companies. Essentially, a trade credit is a discount on a payment received before it is actually due. For example, suppose a supplier typically gives you 30 days to pay a bill and has just sent you a bill for $100. That supplier could offer you a trade credit of 2 percent if you pay your bill in fewer than 30 days. That means you would save $2.

A trade credit may be represented as follows:

2/10 net 30

This simply means that you will get a 2 percent discount if you pay your bill within 10 days, as opposed to the 30 days normally allowed. So if your bill is $100, you will only need to pay $98 if you pay within 10 days.

Of course, there is a cost associated with offering trade credit. In this example, the company is willing to receive $98 as opposed to $100. Why then would it offer a trade credit? Well, there can be a significant difference between being *owed* $100 and actually *having* $98.

Companies want to collect their accounts receivables as soon as possible, and trade credits offer an incentive for customers to pay sooner. For the company offering the trade credit, it can be more beneficial to have $98 within 10 days than to wait for $100 at the end of 30 days. In the extra 20 days the money can be invested or used for various financing requirements. *When* you get money is as much a consideration as *how much* money you will get. If you have to wait for your money, it will be worth less when you receive it.

Enforcing the Robinson-Patman Act

In 1914, Section 2 of the Clayton Act prohibited certain forms of price discrimination. It was amended in 1936 by the Robinson-Patman Act to protect businesses against certain types of price discrimination. The act was born from the belief that large firms could pressure retailers for price concessions not available to smaller firms. This act afforded protection and the potential for substantial awards to firms that often become victims of price, advertising, and service discrimination.

Let's imagine that you are the victim of unfair price discrimination. How should you decide whether to pursue legal action? What are the costs and what are the potential gains?

Expenses might include:

- Attorney's fees. Although many attorneys will be retained on a contingent-fee basis, there are still fixed expenses, payable in advance for the first few months of litigation. This sum will be in the range of $10,000–$20,000.
- Filing fee, $100
- Fees for service of summons and complaints, $25 per defendant
- Copying costs, $2,500
- Deposition transcripts, $3,500
- Telephone, postage, fax, $1,000
- Travel, $1,500
- Research online, $1,500
- Witness fee, $300
- Expert witness fee, $5,500
- Data processing, $1,000
- Reserve, $1,000

The total costs of starting the action are approximately $30,000 to $40,000. To decide whether or not to proceed with the suit, you must now look at the potential gain.

Winning Under the Robinson-Patman Act

The remedies for unlawful price or service discrimination under the Robinson-Patman act are substantial. In fact, businesses that believe they have been the victims of such unfair business practices should exercise their right to file a price or service discrimination lawsuit.

The law states that the plaintiff can recover:

- Damages for the four-year period prior to the filing of the action and for a period of two to three years or more beyond the trial date
- An automatic tripling of the actual damages
- An award for legal fees based upon actual attorney hours, which can exceed the award for damages
- The right to prohibit the defendant from any further violations of the Robinson-Patman Act
- The right to obtain a judgment which orders the defendant to divest itself of acquisitions. This divesting could end the defendant's monopoly, or attempt to gain a monopoly, in the industry.

The plaintiff can also be awarded interest on damages for unnecessary delay on the part of the defendant; is entitled to recover costs including filing fees, witness fees, travel fees, and deposition fees; and may also be awarded damages for proven claims of interference with business relations, breach of contract, state antitrust claims, and other such claims.

It is obvious from the remedies available to the disfavored retailer that Congress is encouraging small businesses to file these lawsuits. But in each case it is important to compare the initial out-of-pocket expenses with the potential awards before deciding whether to proceed with a suit or not.

Protecting the
Workplace

Workplace violence is increasing. Recent statistics have reported 160,000 assaults on employees and more than 1,000 murders committed annually at the workplace. While in the past a threat toward a coworker may have been brushed off, now these potentially dangerous remarks must be taken seriously.

Employers cannot realistically eliminate all threats of workplace violence, but they must recognize it and respond to it immediately and effectively when it occurs. Managers must also be responsible for reducing the threat of violence in their offices. The law is clear as to the employer's responsibility. Under the Occupational Safety and Health Act (OSHA), employers are charged with providing a workplace "free from recognized hazards that are causing or are likely to cause death or serious physical harm."

To help provide a safe environment, the manager needs a zero tolerance policy for:

- Committing physical assaults, including shoving or hitting
- Harassing or threatening communication
- Stalking or unauthorized surveillance
- Threatening or intimidating an employee or employee's family
- Bringing firearms or weapons to the office
- Coercing employees

Managers should realize that workplace violence has become a priority issue. The forward-thinking manager will prepare, recognize, and protect his or her employees against this potential hazard.

SAFETY

83

Warning Signs for Workplace Violence

Workplace violence does not come without warning signs. A supervisor must recognize these signs and minimize the risk of workplace violence through careful hiring of employees. This means conducting thorough background investigations and checking work history and references before hiring an applicant.

Under the laws of negligent hiring or negligent retention, the legal system expects the employer to provide a safe working environment and to maintain competent, nonviolent workers. But even with the most diligent of background checks, some employees will be hired that are potential or real security risks. Look for the following:

- Employees who are chronically absent on Mondays
  may have a drug or alcohol problem
- Employees displaying concentration problems
- Employees who abruptly change their appearance or dress
- Employees who continually make excuses or attempt to
  blame others
- Employees preoccupied with discussions of violence
- Employees who identify violence as a solution to problems
- Employees who threaten or intimidate coworkers

It is also the manager's job to defuse violent situations and to report employees to counseling when appropriate. Training programs to help people learn conflict resolution skills should be made available. Employers should encourage workers to report threats or suspicious conduct to their supervisors and must pay attention to all warning signs of potential workplace violence, in order to ensure safety for their employees and to minimize legal exposure.

Establishing a Safe Internal Work Environment

Safety and security in the workplace are everybody's concern. Do not wait for a crisis or criminal act before establishing both routine and emergency safety and security regulations. Most of these will be matters of common sense, but they must be implemented and enforced.

Safety Tips:

- Be sure you have procedures established for emergencies, accidents, burglaries, or unruly customers or employees.
- If there is an emergency, know how to report it.
- Know where an emergency kit is located.
- Know where fire extinguishers are kept and how to use them.
- Know locations of fire alarms or other alarm systems.
- Establish evacuation plans for major catastrophes and decide who should be notified when problems occur after hours.
- If you occupy an office in a large building, you and your employees need to know the building's emergency procedures and be familiar with all its exits and entrances.

To Avoid Accidents in the Office:

- Keep individual work areas clean.
- Clean up spills immediately.
- Keep aisles clear of electrical cords, computer cables, and any other hazards that could cause a fall.
- Keep file drawers closed when not in use.
- Try to avoid opening more than one file drawer at a time.
- Do not use chairs, desks, or other office furniture as a stepladder.
- Have employees report all equipment that is not functioning well, especially any electrical item that may be causing shocks.
- Keep sharp objects like thumbtacks, razor blades, or letter openers in safe places.
- Try to keep the equipment in good ergonomic positions to avoid back strain, eye strain, or hand strain.

85 Establishing a Secure Internal Work Environment

Safeguarding your business, your office, your equipment and your employees and their property is a very important part of your day-to-day operations. Security is everyone's concern, and one of the most powerful prevention tools is awareness.

One of the first things that should be done is to make sure the office or workspace is set up so that there is good natural surveillance. Access to the office should be limited and strictly controlled. Guests, clients, or customers should be escorted to their destination or announced to the person expecting them. After the business is finished, the guest should be escorted out. Do not hesitate to ask unfamiliar people to identify themselves. Do not be afraid to ask "Can I help you?" If you run an office where there may be problems, does your receptionist have a panic button or alarm for emergencies? Can he or she control the lock on the front door?

Washrooms located outside the office can pose a problem, especially if the public can access them. They should be kept locked at all times with a key available from the receptionist. Individuals can hide in the washroom shortly before closing, then enter the office after everyone leaves for the day. All washrooms should be checked before locking up for the night.

Keys, alarm codes, and computer codes should be issued only to those who genuinely need them. Keep strict records on their issuance. Make sure all keys are marked "Do Not Duplicate." Alarm codes can tell you who entered the building or office after hours. If a disgruntled employee leaves, you may consider changing all locks, alarm codes, and computer codes.

Employees working after hours should report to someone outside of the office. They should let that person know when they are leaving and if necessary that they arrived home safely. Arrange an escort or security guard to take employees leaving after hours to the parking garage.

Instruct employees not to enter an elevator containing someone they feel is suspicious.

Be sure employees lock up valuables when they leave for lunch, a meeting, or the weekend. Along with their own property, this includes items such as stamps, petty cash, and checks.

Avoiding Employee Accidents

Companies must guard against employee accidents, which represent a significant expense. The annual bill for work-related accidents is estimated to be $50 billion and increasing. The human cost is even higher. You cannot put a price on the pain and suffering that accompany a disabling injury. The good news is that since people are responsible for accidents, many can be avoided with careful planning.

Accidents occur when people are careless or inattentive, when equipment fails, and when supervision has been poor. It is management's responsibility to properly educate staff concerning the dangers of the work, ensure that equipment is maintained and inspected, and invest time and energy into protective equipment and other safety and health measures.

The "80/20 rule" (see tip #9) applies to accidents in the workplace. While the great majority of employees never have accidents, there are a few accident-prone workers that encompass the bulk of the accident claims. Studies have shown that most of these employees will become accident free when placed in proper job assignments with sufficient training.

The manager is also responsible for assuring that:

- Safety rules and procedures are enforced.
- Proper housekeeping and sanitation are carried out.
- Protective devices are adequate.
- Rules about safety clothing are enforced.
- Ventilation is adequate.
- Appropriate tools, materials, and supplies are used.

Do not feel pressured to cut corners or to place workers in hazardous situations even when project demands are aggressive. A responsible manager should consider it his or her job to reduce the number of employee accidents significantly, and beyond that, to prevent them.

SAFETY

87

Planning for a Business Disaster

Major disasters such as fires, earthquakes, and even terrorist attacks are possible threats to businesses. Statistics following major disasters have revealed that:

- As many as 60 percent of businesses do not reopen after a major disaster.
- Without contingency planning, many companies lose a considerable portion of their customer base.
- Those organizations that do recover have an emergency operations plan in place, have trained their staff for disaster response on the job and at home, and have formulated both recovery and resumption plans.

Companies that lack a plan to handle natural or man-made disasters will risk not being able to resume normal business operations if an emergency occurs. Managers must be able either to develop such plans or to enlist outside consulting firms to assist them in emergency planning.

The components of an emergency operations plan are:

- Executive summary. This identifies the types of emergencies the plan will address and the policies of the organization regarding them. It will also list the responsibilities of key personnel and the location of the emergency operations center.
- Emergency management. This section outlines potential safety issues, emergency management structure, emergency response procedures, and plans for communications, recovery, and business resumption. Included are instructions on insurance issues.
- Resource list. This is a list of customers, agreements, and contracts and of resources for supplies, equipment, and services. It also identifies emergency telephone lists and facility maps.

All personnel must be trained in the role they will play during a business emergency. Each worker should be able to answer the following basic questions: "Where do I go? What do I do? And how do I do it?" Management must hold drills to test the effectiveness of the plan. These should involve high-level training, and, going beyond simple fire drills, can consist of single function drills, paper drills, functional real-time exercises, or full-scale simulations of actual disaster events.

Managers should perform a cost/benefit analysis of the risk that natural or man-made disasters pose to their businesses. With this analysis they will be better armed to determine how vulnerable their organizations are and what degree of emergency plan and training is needed for workers.

Buying Versus Leasing

Adding new pieces of equipment to an operation can mean substantial outlays of capital, and today's rapidly changing technology forces businesses to consider whether leasing or purchasing an item would be more advantageous. This question applies to photocopying machines, fax machines, telephone systems, large pieces of industrial equipment, new warehouses, or offices. To analyze whether to lease or buy, review the projected cash flow statement for both alternatives. If the only consideration is one of cost, then the option with the lower net present value (NPV) (see tip #320) would be the best scenario. The following information or estimations also need review:

- Cost of capital (what will the item cost?)
- Purchase or financing terms
- Useful lifetime of asset for depreciation
- Salvage value (can it be sold when its useful life is over?)
- Total income tax rate
- Leasing conditions
- Any additional costs associated with leasing or buying

Factors besides cost may play a part in your decision. For example, is the item actually available for lease? Luckily, almost *anything* can be leased today. The main advantage of leasing is that you can acquire the asset with less capital outlay (see Table 3). The company may be able to lease the item without a down payment, as opposed to either buying it outright or financing it with a 20 to 25 percent down payment.

In a lease, however, there is no equity in the equipment and there is no depreciation to write off as an expense. Additionally, lease payments cannot be canceled during the term of the contract even if the asset becomes obsolete. Purchased equipment has a salvage value since it is actually owned by the company. The main advantage of leasing is that it requires less cash up front than a purchase does. Seriously consider leasing assets that will be heavily used, like photocopiers. Also consider leasing items that will probably be kept for less than five years and that will lose value over time—like computers and automobiles.

Table 3
Leasing Compared to Purchasing

Leasing	Purchasing
Decreased initial cash outlay	Down payments usually required
Easier credit terms	Stricter credit restrictions for bank loans
No financial restrictions for new purchases	May need lender's permission for future equipment purchases
Easier to update or substitute equipment	May not be able to update equipment
Short-term lease allows evaluation of item	Item would be purchased and then sold if not needed
Maintenance provided	Pay for maintenance or have service contract
Leasing payments fully deductible	Depreciation can be written off as expense

89

Implementing a Lease

If you have the authority to sign a lease, the following quick review of basic concepts may be very helpful. Remember that a lease is a contract and that contract law prevails. A lease permits property owned by one person (lessor) to be used by another person (lessee) for a given amount of time in exchange for fixed compensation.

A *true lease* gives the lessee the right to use the property but no equity in it, while a *financial lease* is most often used to finance the purchase of the item. The financial lease usually parallels the lifetime or usefulness of the asset, cannot be terminated, and requires the lessee to maintain the property. Normally the lessee can buy the asset at the end of the lease for a nominal fee. Under a *sale* or *lease back* lease, someone buys the property and immediately leases it back to the previous owner. This gives the lessee both cash back and use of the asset.

In negotiating a lease, always consider the following:

- Length of lease (if you may need an extension, be sure renewal is possible)
- Payment plan (know when payments are due, and what the penalty for a late payment will be)
- Insurance terms (decide who pays for insurance, who is responsible if the item is lost, stolen, or destroyed, and who pays to replace the equipment)
- Maintenance (determine if it is included with the lease and if it is adequate to keep the item functioning without added expense)
- Upgrades (find out if you can upgrade the property or equipment while it is being leased)
- Right of first refusal to purchase equipment after the lease expires
- Amendments to the lease (find out if early cancellation is possible and what happens if it becomes illegal to use this equipment or if your company goes out of business)
- End of lease costs (discuss who will be responsible for removing the equipment)

Before signing any lease, be sure you shop around and compare different leasing companies. Know their reputations, and do not be afraid to ask for a modification or change in the standard lease agreement. If a lease agreement is complicated, get legal advice.

Purchasing Equipment

If you are in a position to directly purchase a piece of equipment, make sure you get the most for your money. The most important guideline is to shop around rather than take the first deal. In order to make useful comparisons, know what you want, what features are necessary, and how much you are willing to spend. Be sure to negotiate. You have nothing to lose in seeing if you can get a better price, more features, or better terms.

Also, consider purchasing used equipment. A competitor that is going out of business or remodeling may be willing to part with something you need at a substantially reduced price. Office furnishings are a good example. Look in trade journals for equipment you need. Products like computers, irregulars or factory seconds sometimes come with a new product warranty. Other used equipment may still have an original warranty that can be transferred.

Remember that tax savings will partially offset the expense of the purchase. The IRS allows deductions for items such as equipment costs and other business-related expenses. Companies should consult with a qualified accountant to determine the tax benefits that may be available to them.

Next, your business has to decide whether to pay cash or finance the new purchase. If you decide to finance it, be sure to compare the different financing arrangements available through banks, financing companies, the manufacturer, or the vendor. Carefully review the requirements of the loan. What collateral will be needed? Do you have to use other assets to secure the loan and, if so, what restrictions may be placed on them? Find out if the loan comes with any other restrictions, such as a required minimum cash balance.

Finally, see if you actually need to purchase a service contract with the new piece of equipment. If the equipment is extremely reliable, you may spend more on a service contract than you would to fix or replace the item. If it is less reliable, a service contract may mean significant savings. Remember that even service contracts can be negotiated.

91

Outsourcing

Outsourcing means using an outside provider for a task or function that would otherwise be performed within the company. Outsourced functions are usually not part of a company's core competencies. The advantage of outsourcing such tasks is that it allows the company to focus more closely on those core competencies.

The manager needs to evaluate what resources are necessary to perform the job in-house. If the resources do not already exist, then one solution may be to outsource. The decision would depend on the costs, the time frame for the project, and the availability of a company that will do high-quality work. One advantage of outsourcing is that it replaces fixed costs with variable ones, which may be beneficial in some instances (see tip #280). The questions to ask in deciding to outsource a task are:

- Do you have the necessary resources internally?
- Are there specialized skill requirements for the task?
- Is the need for these specialized skills only short-term?
- Is there a time frame that will be difficult to meet due to lack of resources?
- Do you have adequate managerial staff to supervise the outside provider?
- Is the managerial staff sufficiently trained to handle this oversight?
- Do these tasks distract from core competencies?
- Does your company want to reduce risks associated with the task?
- Would in-house resources soon be obsolete and would additional funds be needed to keep them current?

Outsourcing will fail if managers do not do their homework. They must commit to explaining the project fully, to maintaining close communication with the outsourcing company, and to ensuring frequent oversight. While the terms of the contract are also crucial, the key to successful outsourcing is close managerial supervision.

Integrating Every Which Way

Integration means broadening the operational and production capabilities of an organization. It is a strategic move that will usually provide significant cost benefits. There are two primary categories of integration, *vertical integration* and *horizontal integration*.

Vertical Integration

To visualize vertical integration, consider the sequence of events that occurs in the production of a given product (see Figure 13). Company X receives raw materials from Supplier Y and then sells a product to Customer Z. This process can be depicted as a vertical series of steps, like a staircase.

Now, say that you are Company X and, instead of purchasing your raw materials from Supplier Y, you decide that you want to produce them yourself. This is termed *backward vertical integration* since you are climbing down the stairs and incorporating a preceding step into your operational activities.

Further, suppose that Company X sells a product to Customer Z. Company X can use *forward vertical integration* to take over the function of the customer. The company is moving up the staircase and incorporating the next step into its operational processes. It may seem strange for a company to become its own customer, but there is a difference between a *customer* and an *end-user* (the final customer). For example, if a company sells raw materials to a processor, the processor is a customer. The company, however, may decide to process that raw material in an effort to expand its products and services. A lumber company, for instance, may mill its own wood.

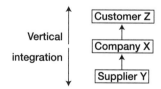

Figure 13. Vertical integration.

Horizontal Integration

A company uses *horizontal integration* when it integrates within the same level of the distribution channel. This is analogous to stepping off the staircase and exploring the possibilities on a given floor. For example, Company X sells life insurance to Customer Y. By horizontally integrating, Company X could offer several other services, such as disability insurance or financial services, to Customer Y through the established distribution channel.

Integration may provide more than just greater cost efficiency. Vertical integration gives the company more control over quality and production costs. Horizontal integration enables a company to take full advantage of existing distribution channels and to increase its offerings. Understanding these fundamental concepts of integration will help you assess if it provides a strategically viable option for your company.

Downsizing

Have you heard rumors at your company about downsizing, rightsizing, optimizing, mergers, acquisitions, reductions in force, or terminations? It's not unusual in today's business environment to see some or all of these changes. Even successful companies like Kodak, Levi-Strauss, and Citicorp have downsized for the sake of continued profitability. Job security seems to be a thing of the past. Now more than ever you must rely on your education, experience, and skills to survive in the business world. What's the best way to protect yourself from falling prey to one of these threats?

Maximize Your Job Security

How long have you been with the company? Do you have seniority or will you be the first one to go? Have you had excellent reviews or have you had warnings and bad performance evaluations? The best way to protect your job security is by doing your job well. Look for ways to improve your department's performance and reduce costs. Always have your reports and assignments ready *before* they are due. You can also look for continuing education both within and outside the company to upgrade your job skills. This will make you more desirable to your company, as well as more attractive to other companies. Many companies provide skill upgrading and new skill training as a substitute for job security. Take advantage of such offers. You never know when you might need new or improved skills.

Try to network with others in your field. Keep track of job openings and salaries that relate to your job description. There may be better offers available at other companies. If this is so, approach your superior and ask him or her to match the salary; be prepared to leave for the better job if necessary. Remember that you may have to change companies to receive a promotion or an increase in pay. You should be working to advance your career. Look for the additional training or job change that will help you accomplish this.

If You Are Given Notice

Ask to speak to your superior and/or your human resources specialist to find out why you are being terminated. If you think you are being discriminated against, speak to legal counsel. Find out what resources will be available to you in the form of additional training, job placement services, severance pay, counseling, and continued health care (see tip #266). If you are a federal employee, resources are available on the Internet (Federal Employees Survival Guide) at www.safetynet.doleta.gov.

Try to negotiate a severance package and seek help from your union or a knowledgeable friend. Always take time to consider the company's offer. Never sign anything without reading carefully and don't sign any release of liability without legal counsel.

Immediately check with job placement services and with other members of your network. You may also have to consider temporary work to pay your bills until another full-time job becomes available.

Managing Downsizing

You just got word from your superior that the company will be downsizing. There will be terminations in your department. You will need to react quickly to control fear and helplessness and to provide support and counseling to both terminated and remaining employees. Layoffs will mean increased stress, decreased morale, and increased workloads for the employees who are left.

There are several steps you should take to manage this situation:

- Discuss with your manager the details of the downsizing. Decide when the staff will be informed; the information will leak out sooner than you think. Decide which employees will be terminated and how the work will be done with a reduced work force. Discuss alternatives to termination, such as job sharing or part-time employment. These alternatives will need to be coordinated with your company's human resources department.
- Arrange a meeting with all employees to discuss the downsizing and the reasons for it. Do this before rumors begin.
- Have job counseling resources available at the time of the meeting. If your superior has approved this, stress that these resources will remain available to the terminated employees for three months.
- Meet individually with each employee being terminated. Make sure they understand why the company has had to take this step. Discuss the services your company is making available, such as job placement, job training, counseling, continued health care, and, if available, part-time employment. Your company may decide to use an outplacement firm to help terminated employees find new jobs.
- Keep remaining employees well informed about the changes and make counseling available to them. Fear that they will be terminated as well may affect job performance, and they will also face heavier workloads because of the decreased workforce.

It will take some time for morale in your department to improve and for you and your employees to adjust to the changes. Keep in mind that counseling may be necessary for you as well as for your employees.

95 Knowing the Basics of Business Process Reengineering

For some organizations, the concepts of gradual change and continuous improvement have become less useful in the face of globally competitive marketplaces and rapidly advancing technology. Companies need to move quickly, and business process reengineering (BPR) is an approach to make change happen fast. BPR is a management technique used to redesign processes, organizations, and cultures. It entails large-scale evaluation and modification and is intended to provide rapid and dramatic improvements.

In its most extreme form, BPR disregards the characteristics of a current process or situation and, in essence, starts from scratch. While more traditional reengineering would focus on making incremental changes to a process, BPR dictates a complete overhaul.

The general steps in BPR are as follows:

- Identify the objectives and define the scope of the engineering project.
- Gather relevant information to be used in designing the new process; this may come from employees, customers, competitors, or other knowledgeable sources.
- Create and implement an action plan.

Is BPR necessary for your organization? Even if your organization is running smoothly and people are performing satisfactorily, that doesn't mean there is no room for improvement. For example, say that employees are doing an excellent job at their assigned tasks, but perhaps the tasks themselves are not necessary.

BPR is a tool that induces managers to examine the flow of work and identify improvement opportunities, and, due to the potential magnitude and impact of changes resulting from BPR, it requires commitment from all levels within an organization.

Preparing for Change

Today's employees must be flexible and prepared for continuous changes in their workplace. Managers must not only counsel their workers on the importance of preparing for change, but they must also understand that change is necessary for growth. Some ways in which you can prepare for change while planning your career are to:

- Discuss your thoughts about change with a trustworthy friend. Pick someone who is honest with you and may not necessarily agree with you on all accounts. It will be useful to hear another perspective. An open discussion about change is an important step in recognizing your true feelings on the matter.
- Make a private commitment to a personal discipline and adhere to it daily. This effort helps to build self-confidence, an essential step for change.
- Educate yourself about your company and your industry. Be familiar with industry trends, which are good indicators of future changes. Proactive responses to change are possible when you understand the big picture.
- Define a mission statement for yourself in regard to your work. What are your responsibilities to your customers, company, and team? A clear understanding of purpose and goals is helpful for evaluating your responses to change.
- Evaluate your finances and strive to remove all debt. Debt tends to keep you tied to your current employment and prevent you from feeling free to pursue new avenues.
- Commit to and complete one personal growth project annually. Changes at work may not always be under your control, but such projects will give you a sense of moving forward in your personal life.

Change is a continuous and inevitable process. Accepting this will allow you to grow in your professional and private life. Today's business world offers no long-term guarantees of employment. You must think of your current job in terms of a one-year contract. Review the terms and conditions of that "contract" on a regular basis to make sure you are satisfied. If your job is not developing your talents and your interests, you must be willing to make a change. Thinking about change and preparing for it will help you move on when the time is right to do so.

97

Overcoming Resistance to Reengineering

When a company decides to reengineer, the task of actually making it happen often falls on the shoulders of middle management. Reengineering means dramatic change, and it is often met with intense resentment. A manager will succeed in change management if he or she follows a carefully defined process.

The first decision is how long the process of reengineering will take. It can take as little as few months to accomplish results, or as long as several years. To better understand how long the process could be, answer the following questions:

- How convinced are senior managers of the urgency of the situation? Are they ready to commit staff and resources to the process?
- How complex and large will the change be?
- What is the company's track record for similar attempts to reengineer? What were the outcomes of those attempts?

Often managers will develop action plans, with key staff responsible for different phases of the plan. The following is one example of such a plan:

- Discuss with your staff the reasons why change is inevitable. Explain the sense of urgency and enlist staff to help implement the solution. Focus on where the organization needs to go to ensure success.
- Define the organization's current processes, goals, and measurable performance. Explain why current performance falls short of goals and customer expectations.
- Create a new process based on input from staff and customers. Redesigning with employee support improves the potential for successful outcomes.
- Develop a strategy and detailed plan to implement the new vision. Test the process as it develops and, upon completion, commit to continuously improving the new design.

While all change meets some degree of resentment, by following certain general principles a manager can help guard against resistance. Change will be better accepted if the manager maintains excellent communication, enlists the support and participation of staff, and practices effective leadership by inspiring shared visions.

Doing Business in Other Countries

The global business environment is bringing the world closer together. While international business may provide attractive and profitable opportunities, many issues must be considered before jumping into the international arena.

Below are just a few of the potential sources of problems:

- Language barriers
- Cultural differences
- Government regulations
- Legal issues
- Economic stability
- Quality control
- Management issues
- Operational logistics

The Price Waterhouse *Doing Business* series of publications provides information on doing business in 80 countries across the world. The series also contains tax law summaries for 120 countries. For more information on the *Doing Business* series and other resources available from Price Waterhouse, refer to www.trade.com/infosrc/pw, or the new PricewaterhouseCoopers website at www.pwcglobal.com.

Cultural and Language Pitfalls in the Global Marketplace

Not even the largest companies always surmount the challenges of international business. While it is difficult for any company to fully understand the culture and language of a foreign marketplace, Americans have a reputation for ignoring and misunderstanding cultural and language differences. Some of the more humorous examples come from marketing attempts:

- Translated into Spanish, the Coors slogan, "Turn it loose" read as "Suffer from diarrhea."
- Gerber began selling baby food in Africa with the same packaging used in the U.S. that displayed a Caucasian baby's face. To their dismay, they soon learned that in Africa, product labels usually bear a picture of the package's content to overcome language barriers.
- Chevy introduced the Nova automobile in Mexico without changing its name. In Spanish, "no va" means "does not go," and so, not surprisingly, sales were not as brisk as anticipated.

Further, companies need to be aware that a widespread custom in one country may be inappropriate in another.

- The Japanese frequently close their eyes when listening intently. Americans often assume they are rudely falling asleep. Meanwhile, the Japanese view American businessmen as far too casual, lacking in proper respect. Additionally, the ten- to twenty-second pauses that are common in Japanese conversation can make Americans who are unaccustomed to them very nervous.
- In many cultures, it is inappropriate to point, and it's considered extremely rude to point at a person. Be aware of this when giving a presentation. It's never a good idea to offend your audience!

Employee-Management Relationships in the Global Environment

As more and more companies expand globally to remain competitive, more executives find themselves moved around the world. Taking an assignment abroad may improve your chances for future promotions. But what should you do in a management position in a foreign country?

In Mexico, it is traditional for managers to take a personal interest in their employees' families, acting as father figures. They frequently help find housing and arrange health care, and they often participate in family events such as weddings, funerals, and celebrations. The managers also know that many workers in the northern cities work to earn money, then leave to return to their families in poorer areas in Mexico. Japanese and Korean corporations have encountered problems when they tried to run plants in Mexico the way they would run plants in their own countries.

In Japan, employees have traditionally been hired for life. They expected to be taken care of in return for their loyalty, although recent economic developments have begun to change these patterns. It is also traditional in Japan for business decisions to be discussed with workers at all levels until a final decision is made with the input of all employees. Gifts, including their wrapping, also play an important part in employee relationships.

We must understand other cultures in order to respect them. If you are chosen to spend time in a foreign country, try to learn as much as possible about that country and its religions, culture, and language. Many large companies offer courses or hire consulting firms to provide this information to their employees. This is good business and shows a degree of respect for the host country.

101

Strategic Planning

Strategy is the great Work of the organization. In situations of life or death, it is the Tao of survival or extinction. Its study cannot be neglected.

—*Sun Tzu, from R. L. Wing,*
The Art of Strategy: A New
Translation of Sun Tzu's
Classic, *The Art of War*

Strategic management has evolved from budgetary planning and control in the 1950s, to corporate planning and corporate strategy in the 1960s and 1970s, to analysis of industry and competition in the 1980s, and finally to the search for a competitive advantage in the 1990s.

There are certain critical elements common to all strategies:

- Long-term, simple, and consistent goals are necessary. If there is confusion regarding these goals, the strategy will be ineffective in the long run.
- Implementation of the goals must be effective. Objectives must be clear, the organization must understand itself and its environment, and it must demonstrate commitment and consistency.

Henry Mintzberg, in *The Rise and Fall of Strategic Planning*,[2] identifies three "fallacies of strategic planning":

- *The Fallacy of Prediction*
  You must recognize that the external environment, including the behavior of your competitors, is unpredictable.
- *The Fallacy of Detachment*
  Strategy must be integrated with the management process and must be continually updated. The data used for strategic planning must come from the managers in your company.
- *The Fallacy of Formalization*
  The flexibility necessary for success comes from informality, which leads to the promotion of organizational learning.

In essence, strategic planning means planning how to win. An overall strategy gives an organization direction and helps guide individual decisions.

---

[2]Henry Mintzberg, *The Rise and Fall of Strategic Planning* (New York: Free Press, 1994).

Goal Setting

It is the manager's job to set goals. It is a common mistake, however, to confuse plans with goals. Plans are the means to achieve your goals. Before you can begin planning, you must set targets or goals.

While higher executives tackle longer-term strategic goals, most managers are responsible for short-range targets. Once the manager has these targets in sight, he or she must develop policies and plans to reach them. Establishing specific procedures and schedules will allow the goals to be put into operation.

The following are guidelines for setting goals effectively:

- Pick reasonable department goals that align with the goals of the company. It is important that these goals help the employees to understand how they add value to the mission of the company.
- Evaluate the department's strengths and weaknesses. The goals should be to make use of the talents and skills of the department, while also addressing its deficiencies.
- Review goals that have been met and decide on appropriate new targets in the light of past achievements and customer feedback.
- Don't set goals in a vacuum. A manager needs support from the employees who are responsible for meeting targets. Workers are more motivated to reach goals when they have had a role in setting them.
- Set priorities among the goals and make certain that the employees understand what this hierarchy of goals is. Employees cannot meet the most important objectives if they are unsure which of the department's objectives these are.
- Consider the needs of other departments when setting goals and watch out for roadblocks. Take into account the likelihood that other business units will be drawing upon the same resources you need to achieve your goals. Realistic planning, prioritizing, and knowledge about other department's activities will help you reach your most important targets.

Managers will be measured by the goals they set and achieve, so it is important that they set goals carefully and realistically. New managers in particular will have greater success when they take a step-wise approach to goal setting.

STRATEGY AND DECISION MAKING

103

Decision Making

Of all the hats that a manager must wear, probably one of the most important is that of the decision maker. To be a more effective decision maker, it is helpful to understand the range of decision-making styles. Dr. Michael J. Driver of the University of Southern California has done the most significant work on decision style theory.

A decision style is the way we learn and process information and apply that knowledge to making decisions. Our decision style is based upon past experiences. The key drivers of decision making are the complexity of the information and the number of solutions to the problems that are generated.

The four basic styles outlined by Dr. Driver are *decisive, integrative, hierarchic* and *flexible*. They vary in the amount of data used to make a decision and in the range of options considered. For example, a manager who uses the decisive style will typically depend upon minimal data to arrive at a single solution, while a manager with an integrative style will typically draw on as much data as possible to generate several reasonable alternatives. The manager who uses the hierarchic style will use large amounts of data to come to one optimal conclusion. The flexible decision maker relies on minimal data but will generate a variety of options or will continually shift focus as he or she reinterprets the data.

While most managers tend to favor one of these four styles, they may use another style as a backup when speed is necessary. The decisive and flexible styles are the most common fallback choices. Managers will also often display mixed styles. They may use one style, perhaps the decisive style, for simple problems but change to another, such as the integrative style, for more complex situations.

Focusing on Decision-Making Styles

104

Managers should strive to understand employees' decision-making styles and keep these styles in mind when assigning tasks. Each of the four major decision-making styles—*decisive, hierarchic, flexible,* and *integrative*—has characteristics that are advantageous in some situations and burdensome in others.

The employee using the *decisive* style is fast, loyal, reliable, consistent, obedient, and orderly. But this style can also come off as rigid, inflexible, and simplistic. Decisive employees are often uncomfortable with change and have negative feelings about themselves. Managers can help develop such individuals by supplying positive reinforcement and feedback. Supervisors should shy away from giving these employees creative projects. Decisive people will be more effective if others help them analyze complex data.

The worker who uses the *hierarchic* approach is logical, thorough, controlled, complete, and rigorous. But he or she can also be argumentative, tyrannical, perfectionist, and suppressive. Hierarchic individuals are perfectionists who cannot delegate and rarely give credit to others. They should not be appointed to front-line management positions. Such employees may improve, however, through experience with team projects.

The *flexible* style involves adaptability, speed, spontaneity, and intuitiveness. But the tendency toward a multiple focus type can sometimes mean a shallow, fickle, poorly focused, or ill-planned approach. The employee who uses this style of decision making often appears spineless and is often not taken seriously by coworkers. Supervisors should avoid giving these employees jobs that require concentrated efforts.

Those with an *integrative* decision-making style can be creative, open, informed, empathetic, and cooperative. But in this case the multiple focus approach can appear indecisive, passive, untimely, confused, wishy-washy, or over-intellectual as well. Integrative people focus on the process instead of results. They do not pay attention to detail and tend to delegate too much. Because of their indecisiveness, they should not be placed in positions of control. Managers should take advantage of their creativity and assign them to teams with a more decisive support staff.

A thorough understanding of the major decision-making styles helps managers pair employees with the right assignments. This insight is another useful tool in managing effectively and improving organizational performance.

STRATEGY AND DECISION MAKING

105

Using Decision Styles to Accomplish Goals

The four major decision styles each offer advantages and disadvantages. There is no one style that will best fit with all situations. For example, a person most comfortable with the decisive style of decision making (one who uses a minimal amount of information to reach a satisfactory decision) would be well suited for a job requiring speed and consistent behavior. Likewise, a manager would be wise to choose a person with a flexible decision style (one who relies on minimal information but adjusts the decision based on new or reinterpretation of the material) if the employee is expected to rely upon ingenuity or adaptability to do the job.

Analyzing the decision style of an employee and the characteristics of a task requires a careful approach. The first step is to evaluate the demands of the job:

- What kind of data is needed? How complicated and substantial is it?
- What is the time frame for completion?
- How many ways can the job be approached?

Next, evaluate the applicant's decision style:

- Decisive
- Hierarchic
- Flexible
- Integrative

Then choose the job that best fits an individual's decision-making style. But rather than rely simply upon a job description, make an in-depth analysis of the job requirements. Similarly, do not assess an employee's decision-making style based on one-time observation. You need to appraise the employee's work in as many situations as possible before concluding what decision style he or she generally uses. Careful and accurate assessment of both job requirements and individual decision styles are necessary to best match employees to jobs and accomplish company goals.

Understanding
Due Diligence

The ever-changing world of mergers and acquisitions means you may soon be called upon to help gather information about your company or to review information about another company. After a formal letter of intent to buy a business has been signed, delivered, and accepted, there is a designated time period in which the buyer will have the opportunity to carry on a "due diligence" examination of the company being bought.

If you are on the *buying* side, consider the following aspects of the company you are planning to purchase:

- Financial records, contracts, leases, and loans
- Sales reports and inventories
- Assets and liabilities
- Maintenance records
- Current and past due receivables
- Payroll and payroll benefits
- Customer lists
- New products
- Marketing plans
- Any pending litigation or tax audits
- Cost of insurance and any insurance problems
- Audited financial statements

In addition to reviewing all the documents, the buyer should tour the facilities, talk to the employees and perform its own financial analysis. Know who the customers are, who the suppliers are, who the major competitors are, and what the market is like.

If you are on the *selling* side, you also need to do your homework. Some of the questions you need to ask are the following:

- Can the buyer come up with the money for the sale?
- Does the new entity have the proper management experience to maintain the business?
- What kind of reputation does the new company have?

- What plans does the new company have for the old company?
- Will they keep existing employees and, if so, for how long?
- Have you withheld any information that may come back to haunt you after the deal closes?

With luck, after each side has completed its due diligence, there will be a successful change of ownership that will satisfy all parties.

Recognizing Ways to Cut Costs

In today's highly competitive environment, there are increased pressures to minimize costs without sacrificing quality. As a manager, you will have to recognize cost-cutting opportunities and exercise sound judgment about what can and cannot be cut. Before you make any changes, however, you need to understand the goals of your organization, the nature of the company's projects, and the various personnel that make the efforts successful. Carefully study your operations and collect information from your employees, customers, and suppliers before you make any decisions.

To help recognize cost-cutting opportunities, determine what your budget is, make a list of all your costs, and then prioritize your expenses. Can you apply the "80/20 rule" (see tip #9) to your prioritized expenses? For example, do 80 percent of your expenses accomplish 20 percent of your activities? If so, could a portion of the expenses be outsourced to other departments or vendors?

Here are some additional areas that may offer opportunities to reduce costs:

Rent

- If you need more space, evaluate the costs of moving; consider renting extra space, or sharing space with another department.
- If you have too much space, consider leasing it out.

Insurance

- Review all insurance policies yearly. This includes medical, casualty, auto, disability, personal injury, and business interruption insurance. Check to see that you are getting the best rates, and assess whether you still need the same amount of coverage.

Utilities

- Does your building use automatic timers on heating, air conditioning, and other utilities?

Supplies

- Establish long-term relationships with reliable, quality suppliers. Often they can match competitors' lower prices. Keep up regular communication with your suppliers, give them information regarding your needs and problems, and request their participation in solutions.
- Combine purchases with other departments if there is not a central buying office.
- Always ask for volume discounts.
- Consider alliances, jobbers, and consortiums to purchase supplies in volume.
- Maintain a minimum amount of inventory and, if possible, use the just-in-time approach (see tip #141).

Pay bills on time to avoid additional charges and see if there is a discount offered for early payments. Make sure you consider all the ramifications of any changes before they are instituted. Discuss anticipated changes with those who will be affected; they may give you additional insight. Giving them an opportunity for input also means they will accept the changes more readily.

Getting Creative About Cost Cutting

In cost cutting, try to think of some of your *fixed costs* as *variable costs* (see tip #280) and evaluate overhead expenses for ways to trim. Some areas of overhead to consider are:

Office Perks

The cost of coffee, water coolers, sodas, and snacks can add up very quickly. But in deciding which perks you might eliminate or reduce, consider the benefits to your employees as well as the costs.

Telephone

Reassess your phone system. Should you own or rent? Do you have too many lines, or not enough? Your telephone company can help you by determining how busy your lines are, the length of time callers are put on hold, or how often they get a busy signal. Do you need cellular phones, toll-free numbers, limited access to in-house long-distance service, Yellow Pages advertising, or voice mail?

Auto Expenses

Are company automobiles necessary or can employees use their own cars and be reimbursed? If they are necessary, is it better to lease or buy?

Subscriptions

Check the relevance and value of journals and technical magazines.

Services

If you hire outside services like cleaning, gardening, or maintenance, review these contracts and see what can be renegotiated. Do you have lawyers, accountants, or payroll services on retainer? Would it be cheaper to pay for these services as you go, or bring them in-house?

STRATEGY AND DECISION MAKING

Checkbook

Periodically review the checkbook and see where the money is going.

When it comes to cutting costs, it's important not to get carried away. Always consider the benefits that the company and its employees derive from a given expense. Extreme cost cutting may act to lower morale, and that will create the greatest expenses of all. If you go too far, you may reduce your costs but lose valuable employees who cannot be replaced.

Your Market Value

Do you know what you are worth in today's job market? In order to decide whether to ask for a raise or look for another job, you need to know your value to the business. Wages began to climb in 1997 with unemployment at a record low. Meanwhile, increased worker productivity, control of health costs through managed care, and leaner employee benefits have all increased the profitability of many companies. Some employees can negotiate an increase in wages at their current companies without much trouble. This is especially true for "behind the scenes, stay late, get the work done" employees, who are often the most seriously underpaid.

But leaving your current job or even getting laid off may be the best thing that can happen to you in today's job market. There is a great deal of competition for workers in many fields with perks offered by many companies to entice new employees. Excite, an online search-engine company, pays for a masseuse to relieve stressed workers and gives stock options to new employees.[3]

Below are a few helpful sites for determining your market value:

"What Am I Worth?"

Drake, Beam, Morin, Inc. provides information on job searches, salaries, and negotiation at this website, as well as updated hyperlinks to other sites with salary information.

www.dbm.com

"Careers, Not Just Jobs"

This service of the *Wall Street Journal* lists current salary tables taken from the *National Business Employment Weekly*.

www.careers.wsj.com

---

[3]"You Deserve a Raise Today," *U.S. News & World Report*, May 4, 1998.

The Bureau of Labor Statistics website lists government reports and surveys on wages and unemployment in different regions, updated monthly.

www.bls.gov

CareerBuilder, Inc., provides information on job searches and the cost of living in U.S. cities and foreign countries.

www.careerbuilder.com

Yahoo also provides a list of professional organizations on the Internet at www.yahoo.com/business_and_economy/organizations/trade_associations.

Obtaining all this information regarding your job and career may help you obtain a raise, find a better job, or change careers. If you find that your company is not compensating you appropriately, it may not be too soon to look for a position with another company.

Types of Resumes

People often neglect to give their resumes the attention they deserve. But an updated resume is important even if you have a job. It represents a concise summary of your experience and qualifications. Applications for grants, contracts for projects, and business plans will often require a resume. Update yours frequently. Working on it a little bit at a time makes it easier to keep it accurate and ready for use. Types of resumes include:

Traditional Resume

You can use this type of resume if your work history does not contain gaps, your new job is related to previous experience, and you have held professional jobs.

Functional Resume

If there are gaps in your work history, or your work experience might seem unrelated to the job you are applying for, a functional resume is more useful. List your previous employment, then discuss what you found satisfying, what responsibilities you held, and how you handled problems.

You can also discuss course work, volunteer work, or military experience. A variant of the functional resume is the skills emphasis resume. This should highlight your job objective and present the relevant skills you possess. Skills that can be emphasized include ability or experience in leadership, retail and sales, writing, computers, finance, or management.

111

Building a Resume

A resume is the first step in your own marketing program. You must be able to communicate your qualifications to others, or you will never be asked for an interview.

The resume needs to be concise and should keep the reader's attention. All information must be factual and accurate. Don't overburden it with extraneous information that will bore the reader or it will end up in the wastebasket. Aesthetics are extremely important, since a resume is considered to be a reflection of your attention to detail as well as your skills. It must be typed, tidy, and well written.

Remember, you will only get 20 or 30 seconds of the employer's time before he or she goes on to the next resume. Ask yourself what your potential employer is looking for. The most pertinent information to include is your:

- Name, address, and telephone number
- Career/job objectives
- Educational background
- Work experience, both full-time and part-time
- Military service
- Special qualifications or achievements such as awards or publications
- Community activities
- Personal interests, skills, and hobbies
- State that references are available, but don't list them on the resume itself. Do make a list of references that you can present at an interview.

A successful resume will attract the reviewer's attention and make him or her want to know more. This first impression you make is extremely important, and without a concise, well-structured resume, you will not be considered for the job regardless of your qualifications. It is a good idea to give your resume to several people for review and feedback before giving it to a potential employer.

Job Search
Networking

Twenty years ago, networking to gain access to employment opportunities was a little known concept. This has changed, however, as widespread elimination of jobs has become a fact of life. Employees changing jobs within a company still fill the vast majority of open positions. But networking is quickly rising as a means of gaining employment, and most experts feel it will continue to grow in importance.

The process of networking has also become more acceptable. Professionals were once reluctant to talk to candidates for job openings that didn't yet exist. However, since many professionals have themselves been victims of layoffs, they have become believers in the value of networking. They realize that the purpose of networking is not to call strangers and ask for a job, but to gain knowledge and collect information.

Networking creates exposure to potential employment opportunities by increasing your contact with professionals who know of these opportunities and now know of you. The more people you contact, the more you increase your chances of accessing previously unknown career opportunities.

Networking is time-consuming and requires commitment and organization. You need certain tools to network successfully. An example is a voice mail system, perhaps one that automatically pages you for messages. You do not want the person who is returning your call to get a busy signal or no answer at all. When you do get messages, call back immediately. Your promptness in returning calls will reflect your general follow-up skills. You should also have a filing system for the people you have contacted and the information you have received. This can be as simple as an index card system or instead be a sophisticated computer database system.

It is essential to have an up-to-date, well-written resume. If you are out of practice, ask an outsourcing agency for advice on writing a clear, concise resume. You may need multiple resumes that stress different aspects of your work or educational experience if you are applying for different positions.

It is estimated that up to 80 percent of available jobs are never publicly advertised. Networking is a powerful tool to penetrate this "hidden job market." Your friends and contacts, and even strangers, can help give you potential job leads. When you master the skill of networking, it is like having hundreds of people working to find you a job.

Fundamentals of Effective Networking

It has become a common scenario—you find yourself without a job and you want to use networking to help you job hunt. You take out your Rolodex and business card file. Now what?

First, don't limit your network. Make a list of professional colleagues, vendors, former coworkers, and anyone else you have met during your professional career, as well as friends and social contacts. Everyone is a potential source of information and of further contacts.

Next, develop a clear and concise message to use. You will need at least two versions, one for the people you know personally and one for those you do not know. Write these messages down and practice them. You will also rehearse what you will say when leaving voice mail messages. Use powerful phrases when speaking to new contacts, such as "I am John Smith" instead of "My name is John Smith." Don't be afraid to state that you are networking in search of new job opportunities. Since your time will be limited, develop a short dialogue about your past experience and the opportunities that interest you.

Your first call to a new contact should include the following elements:

- Introduction
- Source of contact
- Reason for call
- Brief overview of your background
- Statement of your job interests

If the recipient has received your call positively, then you may learn of opportunities within his or her company or you may be referred to yet another contact. Make sure you end the call with a sincere thank-you and record the information for future reference. Follow up immediately with any new contacts you may have received. If you had a personal visit, make sure you send a thank-you letter. Keep in touch with all your contacts periodically, at least once a month, to inform them of your progress and to make sure they keep you in mind.

Finally, expand your network. Continue to work on adding new people to your contact list. Use social gatherings, meetings, professional associations, and conferences to this end. You can even use company brochures and directories, newspaper articles, and phone books to look for potential leads. Networking has become an acceptable means of searching for a job. With practice and confidence you can make almost anyone into a contact who can help you with employment opportunities.

114 Dressing for Success

Dressing properly and appropriately is extremely important. It can be the difference between making the right impression and making the wrong one. The type of occasion, the time, and the location all help determine what will be appropriate. A convention, for example, usually means casual dress. If the meeting is in Hawaii, shorts and a tee shirt may be acceptable. If you are a speaker or presenter, however, a suit is still the way to go. When planning a job interview, think about how you want to present yourself to the interviewer, since your attire does make a positive or negative statement about you.

"Business casual" dress can mean anything from loosening your tie to wearing jeans and polo shirts. It is best to check your company's definition of the term before dressing down on casual days. Generally speaking, shorts or very short skirts are not appropriate for a work environment. Some work situations have relaxed dress codes with casual clothing permitted or expected all week long, while others require a suit every day.

Grooming is also important. If you are unshaven, or your hair is unkempt, you will not make a good impression on others. Cleanliness includes clean hands with trimmed, clean fingernails. Make up should not be heavy or overdone.

Remember that the first impression you make at a job interview or with a superior or customer is difficult to change. Your dress, appearance, and demeanor can set the stage for positive future interaction or can trigger the end of a relationship.

Establishing Dress Code Guidelines

All companies have some kind of dress code. While some businesses may allow a more casual look, others will insist upon true business attire. It is important for the manager to be familiar with and supportive of the company's dress code and to set an example by dressing appropriately.

An employee's appearance is an integral part of the way he or she meets internal and external customer expectations. Dress should reflect the wearer's professionalism and that of the organization. Attire should never be disrespectful or distracting to other employees or customers.

The following are some suggestions for establishing dress guidelines:

- Clothing should not be provocative or revealing. Examples might be tight-fitting, see-through, or low-cut garments, tank tops, or cropped shirts. Skirts and dresses must be sufficiently long.
- Clothing should not present a threat to safety, as open-toed sandals, thongs, or flip-flops could.
- Inappropriate garments usually include shorts, sweatpants, sweatshirts, warm-up suits, and other gym-like clothing. Most offices do not consider jeans appropriate even on casual days.
- Torn, frayed, or cut-off type clothing is not acceptable.
- Clothing with slogans or images that are derogatory, insulting, or disrespectful is not acceptable.
- Underwear and shoes must be worn at all times.

The manager must make sure employees know that dress code violations can lead to disciplinary actions.

116

Dual-Career Couples

Dual-career couples face a variety of challenges. If you are offered a position in another city, how will your spouse be able to find a job there comparable to his or her current one? Or will it be necessary for him or her to take a lower-paying or less satisfying job, or to remain behind altogether? If you begin a family, how will you handle child care? Will one or both of you decide to sacrifice position or pay, or reduce work hours, to spend time with your children?

Many companies provide special assistance programs to help the spouse of a relocating employee find work and adjust to the new community. Many communities also offer resources for dual-career couples including aid with relocation problems, jobs and child care information centers, and other useful contacts and forms of assistance.

According to the U.S. Bureau of Labor Statistics, 48 percent of all workers come from dual-earner couples. Only 9.4 percent come from so-called "traditional families," with a male breadwinner and female homemaker. By the year 2000, estimates are that two-earner couples will head 51 percent of all families, up from 41 percent in 1980.

Dual-earning couples are often less free to travel, relocate, or work extended hours, especially when they have children. Such workplace demands can create conflicts with family responsibilities for either spouse. Each couple must find its own way of balancing family life with continued personal and professional growth for both partners.

Employee Relocation

Workers can find themselves relocating for many reasons. They may be taking a new job at a new company or transferring within a company. The company itself may be moving, merging, or being bought. Corporations spend enormous amounts of money each year recruiting new employees and transferring existing ones. As a manager, you need to know the problems that both management and the employee will face in a relocation. It is a matter you may, over the course of your career, experience from both sides.

Several different departments may take roles in the recruitment and relocation process, such as weighing the costs of recruitment or deciding how much money to allocate an employee or a new hire move.

Until recently, new hire relocation packages usually offered minimal reimbursement, providing payment for moving expenses, a small amount of money for incidentals, and sometimes an advance trip to find new housing. Now there is greater variation among companies in the kinds of packages offered. Some corporations have set dollar limits on the amount they will spend on any relocation. Others classify new hires according to years of experience and kind of job. A more comprehensive relocation package may go to someone in upper-level management or a hard-to-fill position. The latter is especially true in cases where there is fierce competition among employers for employees with certain types of skills.

Some important questions to ask in determining the type of package to offer a new hire are:

- Is the employee married or a parent?
- Does the employee support other family or take care of someone?
- Does the employee rent or own his or her home?
- What is the difference in cost of living between the two areas?

Corporations must constantly review their relocation policies and ask the following questions:

- Did we get the employees we needed in the past year's recruitment?
- How many refusals were due to the relocation package offered?

- Are we competitive?
- Are the new employees satisfied?
- What else can we do to make relocation attractive?

A well-designed relocation policy can increase a new hire's satisfaction with the company, thereby boosting retention and saving the company money, since the recruitment and relocation process have to be paid for less often.

The Entrepreneurial Perspective

The term *entrepreneur* is a current buzzword. Even large companies are benefiting from maintaining an entrepreneurial perspective. Nevertheless, there is still widespread misunderstanding of the basic concepts of entrepreneurship. An entrepreneur is commonly considered to be a risk taker seeking large financial rewards. The principles of entrepreneurship, however, extend far beyond this simplification.

An entrepreneur constantly pursues opportunity and then figures out a way to take advantage of it. He or she does not immediately consider financial constraints or other resource limitations, instead first researching and evaluating an opportunity to determine whether potential rewards are high enough to make the necessary investment worthwhile. In short, entrepreneurs take calculated risks.

Not everyone is cut out to be an entrepreneur. Many people prefer to maintain a comfort level, a stable environment that reflects the status quo. Innovations arise when people think "outside of the box," that is, look at things from a new perspective and with a new set of rules. But the degree of uncertainty associated with doing this is enough to discourage many people from venturing forward.

How can the entrepreneurial perspective benefit an organization? An entrepreneurial company is able to respond more quickly to changes in the marketplace. Larger organizations with more traditional management tend to move more slowly and are therefore at a comparative disadvantage.

PERSONAL AND CAREER DEVELOPMENT

119

Understanding Group Processes

Teams are an important aspect of nearly every modern business. They encourage communication, cooperation, and a shared sense of purpose. But not all teams function effectively, and ensuring they do so can require a significant amount of effort. The first step toward working effectively as part of a team is understanding group dynamics.

When teams form, they characteristically go through four phases: *forming, storming, norming,* and *performing*.[4]

Forming: This is the initial phase, in which team members get acquainted and, while being generally polite, begin to assess their roles in the context of the group.

Storming: Members actively establish their positions within the team, and personality conflicts become readily apparent. Typically, some people will be jockeying for a leadership role, while others will act as mediators to help reduce friction within the group.

Norming: Eventually, people settle into roles within the group. They may do so reluctantly, but pressure from the rest of the group will generally encourage them to accept the majority rule. Once the norming phase has run its course, the group is in a position to operate effectively.

Performing: This phase begins once the team members are familiar with one another and have established a structure that works for them. There may also be a "de-forming" phase as the team reaches the end of its project or task.

These stages will not necessarily be quite so distinct from one another, and the time frame for each stage will vary by project. Nonetheless, understanding these phases will help keep the team process moving forward. Remember also that a team effort takes input and effort from each member of the team.

---

[4]Tuckman, Bruce W. "Development Sequence in Small Groups." *Psychological Bulletin,* Vol. 63, 6:334–99, 1965.

Differentiating Formal and Informal Groups

Workplace groups can either be *formal* or *informal* groups. Formal groups are created by the organization with a strategic purpose, while informal groups are a byproduct of the working environment and are not directly controlled by the company.

Formal Groups

An organization may set up a formal group to complete a project, act as a steering committee for a particular effort, or to address a specified problem. Such *task groups* are usually temporary in nature. *Functional groups,* another type of formal group, are a permanent part of the organizational structure and typically form departments or divisions.

Informal Groups

Informal groups are formed by employees without direction from the company. Workers who share common interests, beliefs, or attitudes will often cluster into informal groups. Employees may simply enjoy the activities of the group, or they may participate for social or work-related reasons.

The cohesiveness and effectiveness of both informal and formal groups is largely determined by the compatibility of group members. While an informal group is based on shared interests or beliefs, a formal group will not necessarily reflect any shared personal attributes. Building a cohesive group requires people who can readily communicate with each other and interact in a productive manner.

MANAGING TEAMS

121

Avoiding the "Road to Abilene"

Have you ever been part of a group that made a decision, only to realize afterward that no one really agreed with the decision that was made? Or have you ever acquiesced to a group decision because you didn't want to make waves? When these components are combined, it is possible that a group of bright people will knowingly make a bad decision.

Dr. Jerry B. Harvey, a professor of management science at George Washington University, characterized the phenomenon as the "Abilene Paradox." Years ago, on a hot summer day in Texas, Harvey's family decided to drive to the town of Abilene to try a new diner. The drive was long, the car had no air conditioning, and the food turned out to be lousy. No one said anything negative until the return home. Then, one after another, they all complained that it had been a miserable time, and each person claimed that he or she had agreed to the trip only out of the belief that everyone else wanted to go. If none of them had really wanted to go to Abilene, why did they all agree to do so?

How does a simple drive to a diner apply to business? Consider the decision-making process that was involved. In truth, no one had really wanted to go in the first place. Publicly, they are politely agreed while keeping their true feelings to themselves. Collectively, they decided to follow a course of action that everyone knew was wrong because they failed to communicate with one another.

Harvey used this story to identify a potential danger of decision making in organizations. The main culprit in this dynamic is each individual's decision to maintain public silence despite what he or she knows to be true. To Harvey, whenever a group is about to do the wrong thing while knowing it's the wrong thing, it is "on the road to Abilene."

Groupthink

While an effective group can be very productive, there are also pitfalls that can arise from a group environment. People often reach a unanimous agreement even when the facts point to another, perhaps more appropriate, conclusion. Irving L. Janis used the term "groupthink" to describe this process in his book *Groupthink: Psychological Studies of Policy Decisions and Fiascoes*. The following factors may indicate the potential for groupthink:

- There is team pressure on each member to agree with everyone else.
- The group feels separated from the consequences of its actions.
- General closed-mindedness prevails.
- The group ignores suggestions that its thinking is irrational.
- Members censor thoughts that go against group ideas.

The end result of groupthink is a group that does not think straight. Judgment and decision-making abilities become clouded and the members grow unable to effectively consider alternative courses of action. A group can fixate on a particular solution that is not the most appropriate or rational. There is speculation that the phenomenon of groupthink may have contributed to the decisions made prior to the *Challenger* disaster.

How can you prevent group pressures from giving rise to irrational reasoning and poor decision making? Here are several general guidelines:

- If you are a group leader, remain impartial.
- Encourage disagreement among group members.
- Turn to a third party for an objective assessment of a decision.
- Have another meeting so people can rethink a particular decision.

Being aware of the groupthink phenomenon can help to prevent its potentially disastrous impact on a group's decision-making abilities.

123 Time as a Resource

It is important to see time as a resource to be managed. Keep a detailed record for several days of how your spend your time, then analyze it. Are you wasting time with tasks that others could do better? Are there tasks you should delegate to your employees to free up time for your management duties? Do you spend a great deal of time visiting with coworkers or on routine tasks? Establishing priorities for all your tasks is crucial to gaining better control of your time.

List your activities first by category, then by priority. High-priority items are those that help you reach your objectives and advance your career. They may include assignments from your senior management and additional education. Medium-priority items are tasks that need to be done on an everyday basis, such as returning phone calls and writing reports. Low-priority items can be done when you have the time. Examples might be playing racquetball with a friend or cleaning your desk.

As you keep the several-day schedule of your activities, record your time in 15-minute blocks. At the end, break down the time spent into activity categories, such as talking on the telephone, handling mail, sending and receiving e-mail, and attending meetings. Think about your time in terms of the following "time wasters" described by R. Alec MacKenzie, a management consultant and author of the American Management Association book *The Time Trap*.

Telephone Calls

Frequent interruptions are disruptive. You need to decide whether it is more efficient to handle all your own calls, use voice-mail, or have a secretary route the calls and give you only those that are necessary.

Visitors Without Appointments

If the visit does not concern an immediate problem, and you are involved in important tasks, you might suggest meeting later in the day or sometime in the next several days.

Meetings

Most business people say 50 percent of the time they spend in meetings is wasted.

Crisis Situations

Try to anticipate problems and solve them before they occur. If you spend all your time putting out fires, you will not be able to gain control over your job.

Lack of Objectives, Priorities, and Deadlines

Set your own priorities. Make sure you give your employees deadlines and keep track of their projects. Expect regular reports and help them keep on track with suggestions and encouragement. Attempting too much at once, and underestimating the time it will take to do it all, is another example of failure to set priorities.

Personal Disorganization

A cluttered desk and a general lack of organization will prevent you from accomplishing your objectives.

Delegation

Involvement in routine tasks that should be assigned to others will mean insufficient time to accomplish your own work. Staying at work until 10 p.m. every night is not the solution. You need to learn to delegate.

Leadership

Failure to set clear lines of responsibility and authority among your employees will affect morale, and you will not have an efficient work team. Indecision and procrastination, as well as unclear or nonexistent instruction and communication, are other examples of poor leadership. To be a good manager, you must reverse any of these tendencies. You must also set standards for your employees and use progress reports that enable you and your superiors to keep track of developments. Finally, you need to know when to say no.

Information Systems

When you send inadequate, inaccurate, or delayed information to others, or accept such information from them, you hamper the company in accomplishing its goals.

Fatigue

Working long hours and driving yourself hard doesn't always help you do your best work. You need to be rested to think well. Remember that the quality of your work is more important than the amount of time worked. Find ways to relax and enjoy yourself.

124

Getting the Most Out of Your Day

Every manager needs to juggle a busy schedule that includes meetings, phone calls, progress reports, presentations, routine activities, and unforeseen events that often pop up at the worst possible time. On top of all this, personal commitments may often conflict with planned work.

There are a multitude of schedulers and daily planners available in book form, for your computer, and even for palm-sized minicomputers. All of them can help you schedule more effectively; the key is finding the system that works for you. Set your goals and then put a priority on those tasks that will move you toward those goals.

- If you have an assistant, make sure he or she understands your priorities. Determine which one of you will keep your schedule.
- Determine which activities are important and which ones can be dropped or delegated. Don't waste time on the little things.
- To help prioritize, take advantage of the "Pareto Principle" or the 80/20 rule (see tip #9). Choose the 20 percent of your activities that will generate 80 percent of your results. Then pare down or delegate the remaining 80 percent of your activities.
- Set aside blocks of time for different categories of activities.
- Leave time for the unexpected. Both problems and opportunities can present themselves when you least expect them.
- As mentioned earlier, keeping track of your activities in 15-minute time blocks for a few days will help you find out how much time you spend or waste on activities.

One hour wasted per day by an employee earning $20,000 per year costs the company approximately $2,500, or 12.5 percent of the employee's salary. Adhering to these principles of time management can help you, as well as the company, to make deadlines easier to meet and to maximize the amount and value of the work you can accomplish each day.

Power Napping

Many employers consider sleeping on the job to be grounds for termination. But research has found that it is quite common to experience low energy levels around mid-afternoon, especially for those workers who are already sleep-deprived. To combat the urge to close their eyes, workers will hit the coffee or snack machines. What studies have demonstrated is that napping for 15 or 20 minutes will refresh and renew alertness better than anything else. Hence, some companies are beginning to look at napping as an important part of a productive workday.

An estimated 80 percent of all college students take naps during the day. Unfortunately there are many working people who think they can function well even without enough sleep but in fact spend much of their time feeling groggy. Napping after work, however, can sometimes only worsen matters by making it difficult to fall asleep at bedtime and thus perpetuating the cycle of sleep deprivation.

The midday nap is an institution in many cultures. Some companies now follow their lead by providing nap rooms and encouraging employees to take 15 to 20 minute naps if they begin to fade in the afternoons. Other organizations will allow napping in the lunchroom or at the employee's desk during break times.

Managers are also educating their staffs about sleeping better. Some helpful hints are:

- Go to bed at the same time every night, even on weekends.
- Get up at the same time every morning, if possible without an alarm.
- Avoid alcohol at least two hours before bedtime.
- Be sure your bedroom is quiet, comfortable, and dark.
- Reduce caffeine after 2 p.m.
- If you can't fall asleep because of worries about work or personal matters, write them down and address them the next day.
- Remember that "sleep debt" is like a bank account. You should put back what you take out.

Children have always napped in preschool and kindergarten. Perhaps adults should adopt the habit of napping as well. Of course, it will be up to innovative supervisors to realize that allowing napping on the job may result in greater productivity.

126

Taming the Paper Chase

If you are like the average worker, you spend hours each week just searching through the mess on your desk. To avoid this, develop some sort of organizational system. It does not have to be the traditional "in box" and "out box"—it just needs to be a system that works for you.

- Organize your materials into broad categories such as "Correspondence," "Current Projects," and "To Do." Consider using the same categories to organize the files on your computer.
- Keep your important files within easy reach; otherwise you will tend not to use them, or you may waste time repeatedly getting them.
- Do not set mail aside because it will soon be buried. Go through it to identify and handle items immediately.
- Make a concerted effort to clean your desk at the end of each day.
- Handle each piece of paper only once. Take action as each item comes to you. Don't revisit the same paperwork over and over again.

Following some of these guidelines can help keep the amount of time you spend wading through paperwork to a minimum. Remember that your organizational system will likely need to evolve as your job requirements change.

The Benefits of Telecommuting

127

Telecommuting arrangements allow employees to work from locations other than the office. This can mean working at home, but it also refers to working from hotels, airports, client offices, and even cars, trains, or airplanes. You may think that telecommuting would require high-tech equipment such as computers, modems, fax machines, and voice mail. But many employees can accomplish their responsibilities with a phone and a notepad.

Telecommuting may be an ongoing arrangement—for example, an employee may work from home two days a week—or it may only be used occasionally for special projects or circumstances. In either case, both full-time and part-time employees, managers and non-managers, can benefit from telecommuting. It can reduce travel time for exempt employees who spend most of their time in the field. After a major disaster that affects the workplace, allowing employees to work from home will help the company resume functioning as quickly as possible. Other tasks that can be handled by telecommuters include:

- Preparing documents, doing financial analysis and reporting, and writing training programs, proposals, newsletters, handbooks, and brochures
- Preparing performance reviews
- Doing data entry
- Making sales calls by phone to potential customers
- Handling customer service calls that are taken 24 hours a day on a toll-free number

There are numerous benefits of telecommuting for both the employee and the manager. The employee is more productive because there are fewer interruptions and distractions. He or she is more committed and loyal because the manager has been flexible. The manager saves the company overhead expense by using office space more efficiently. The labor pool increases, now including people who otherwise could not work for your company. The employer is in compliance with laws such as the Americans with Disabilities Act and the Family and Medical Leave Act by helping those employees who

TIME MANAGEMENT

cannot work in the office but can be productive from home. The flexibility an employer demonstrates by allowing telecommuting will enhance employee commitment, loyalty, and retention, and an organization with little or no turnover is more likely to be successful.

Learning to Negotiate

Do you avoid negotiating because it is stressful, intimidating, or unpleasant? Do you shy away from potential disagreements with customers, higher-level personnel, peers, or friends? Are you afraid of creating a hostile environment? Don't be! Whether you realized it or not, you have had practice negotiating your whole life. Every time you compromised with your parents over toys, allowances, curfews, or household chores, you were negotiating. Further, the art of negotiating is a priceless tool. Knowing how to negotiate can improve your personal position and that of the company you represent. The following are several ways to help ensure successful negotiations.

Negotiation Preparation

- Determine what you, and the company you represent, want out of the negotiations.
- Determine what the opposition wants out of the negotiation and why they want it.
- Determine beforehand what points can and cannot be conceded and what circumstances will make you willing to walk away without any agreement.
- Do your homework. Know your facts and supporting evidence. Know your opponent.

Negotiating Techniques

- Strive for a win-win agreement. The most successful negotiation makes everyone feel they have won.
- Keep in mind that nearly everything is negotiable.
- Understand what others are saying—both their words and their underlying meanings.
- Select the time and place for the negotiations.
- Set the guidelines and control the negotiations.
- Be fair.
- Be creative.
- Attack the problem, not the negotiator. Do not become emotional.

- Understand what the best alternative to a negotiated agreement would be from both your and your opponent's perspective.

Becoming a successful negotiator can help build self-confidence, reduce conflict, and ultimately lead to improved productivity. As with other skills, practice makes perfect, so use each negotiation experience as a learning tool.

Polishing Negotiation Techniques

What is the secret to becoming a skilled negotiator? Practice, practice, and more practice. Each day gives numerous opportunities to practice the art of negotiation. Start practicing with simple situations like garage sales, a family conflict, a minor work problem, or resolution of a problem with a room-mate. You can then quickly apply the skills to situations that have more impact on your everyday and business life. These might include buying a car, asking for a raise, convincing customers to buy from your company, or getting the budget for your department increased.

In order to be a better negotiator, you need to know what you really want to accomplish, and why you want to accomplish it. Next, determine who has the power to negotiate with you, and, finally, decide whether to call it quits if you cannot get what you want. This requires doing your research thoroughly, because in some cases you may even decide it would be in your interest to give up your job and go elsewhere if you cannot get the agreement you want.

Before going to the bargaining table:

- Know what the best deal possible would be.
- Know what the least acceptable deal would be.
- Know what deal you will most likely achieve at the conclusion of the negotiations.

And, speaking of bargaining tables, consider the arrangement that would best facilitate negotiations. This might be sitting at a round table, sitting opposite the person with whom you are negotiating, or sitting side by side and attacking the problem together.

It's also a good idea to keep in mind the difference between *interests* and *positions*. Interests are the reasons why you want what you want and why your opposition wants what it wants. Positions are the means each side will use to achieve these goals. Also remember to separate the people from the problem and not to let personalities interfere. Never attack a person, only attack the issues. Your goal should be to reach a conclusion through collaboration between the negotiating parties.

NEGOTIATIONS

130

Picking a Negotiation Strategy

It is common to negotiate with the same parties over and over again. You must therefore consider very carefully how your actions and demeanor will affect these working relationships. Even if you see people at the bargaining table only once, your reputation will still be at stake. Always be honest and fair in your dealings with others. After the agreement, both sides must feel good about honoring the new commitment. An excellent negotiator is one who can carry the day and still find that the opposition would not hesitate to negotiate with him or her again.

The importance of learning to listen cannot be emphasized enough. Treat others with respect. When someone else states a position, restate it to be sure you understand. If someone else becomes angry, stay clam. Shouting at each other is confrontation, not negotiation.

Decide on whether you are going to use a collaborative (cooperative, or win-win) or competitive (win-lose) negotiating strategy. In a win-win situation, both sides feel good about the decision. This produces a much better chance for a successful conclusion, since both parties' needs are satisfied. In a win-lose situation, one side feels good and the other does not. In most negotiations, the key is to try to turn even a win-lose situation into a win-win solution.

Listed below are some helpful hints to try to change win-lose to win-win:

- Create new alternatives
- Separate interests from people
- Look for common goals
- Listen, listen, listen
- Accentuate the positives and reduce tensions

Beware of the intangibles that may play an important role in the outcome of the negotiations, such as:

- Time constraints
- Location and setting of negotiations
- Personalities of the negotiators
- The value your opponent places on a particular point in the negotiation, such as salary versus a good school system for his or her children

Following these tips should help you negotiate more effectively and allow all parties to leave the bargaining table with a sense of accomplishment.

The Importance of Quality

As markets have become more global, businesses find they need to compete on both national and international levels. This increased competition has resulted in a wider range of choices for consumers and has shifted power from the suppliers to the customers. Quality has become a critical competitive issue in this environment.

A quality product is one that meets or exceeds the customer's requirements or expectations. This may sound as though quality is a matter of personal interpretation, but there are fundamental characteristics that quality products and services share. Quality can be a factor of:

- Performance
- Materials
- Aesthetics
- Durability
- Functionality
- Value
- Service

Traditionally, consumers have expected products and services to be either high-quality, convenient, or cheap. They now want them to be all three. This means that to have any hope of remaining competitive, you must understand what your customers want and expect in each of these categories, so that you can best meet and exceed their expectations. Consumer research is a specialized field that provides this information.

TQM Basics

Through total quality management (TQM), organizations set up structures that foster the design, production, and delivery of quality products or services. The focus of TQM is on both external and internal customer and supplier relationships.

External TQM

An organization must anticipate the requirements of its customers and meet them by providing continuous improvements in quality. It must also require continuous quality improvements from its suppliers. A successful TQM program will fully incorporate suppliers and will establish clear joint goals through open communication. Never underestimate the importance of suppliers. It's impossible to produce quality outputs from inferior inputs.

Internal TQM

Internally, each employee must examine his or her role as both a supplier and a customer within the chain of activities. For example, on an assembly line, a worker acts as a "customer" of the previous workstation and a "supplier" for the next workstation. Under the TQM model, each worker needs to be aware of the quality issues involved in his or her task and how they relate to the quality issues for activities upstream and downstream. Cooperation and teamwork are essential principles of TQM.

And Whose Job Is It, Anyway?

Most importantly, TQM must be supported from top management on down. All too often, companies make a lot of fuss about using the principles of TQM, only to put the program on the back burner due to a lack of commitment and follow-through from upper management.

The activities of an organization are coordinated to reach a particular goal, and the pursuit of quality must be similarly coordinated. Quality is everyone's job, and employees must work together for a TQM program to attain its potential.

Transitioning to TQM 133

Incorporating TQM principles into a business is a slow process that usually takes five to seven years. No progress can be made without the involvement of management and of all employees. The fundamental goal of TQM is to continuously improve quality while reducing costs. The result will be a business that is better able to maintain a competitive advantage in today's global environment.

Moving toward a TQM philosophy is a major undertaking. Consider the following steps to aid in such a transition:

- Train employees at all levels. Training should cover the importance of quality, problem-solving tools and skills, teamwork skills, and customer-focused quality improvement processes.
- Use information systems to measure quality, track improvements in quality, and identify customer problems.
- Management support and involvement is essential. Without it, no progress will be possible. Managers must show by example to generate real commitment from employees.
- Rewards are extremely important. These can be tangible, such as raises, bonuses, and promotions; or intangible, such as verbal praise.
- Keep communication flowing. Large group meetings, workshops, newsletters, videotapes, and small group meetings all help facilitate the exchange of ideas and thoughts.
- Special roles and titles, such as facilitator or quality officer, can prove useful.
- The formation of steering committees, implementation teams, and other groups helps to develop a sense of involvement.
- Processes like setting quality goals and performing quality reviews will also give a sense of direction to the employees.

Even successful companies must commit themselves to continuous improvement of quality in order to survive. Giant corporations that have experienced rough times, such as Chrysler and Apple Computer, have regained some of their previous stature by getting back to the core principles of TQM.

134 Quality Management— The Kaizen Method

The word *Kaizen* originated from a Buddhist term meaning "renew the heart and make it good." Today the Kaizen process is a method of quality management, with the goal of company success through continuous improvement.

Like other quality improvement programs, Kaizen depends upon top management's clear commitment to the process. Senior management must commit to developing a strategy for continuous improvement. This method is not a quick fix nor does it have an ending point.

The Kaizen process targets the following areas:

- *Shop floor.* The process concentrates on improving existing manufacturing processes to meet specific customer-driven needs.
- *Support areas.* The administrative offices that support the shop floor will also be improved.
- *Product development.* Improving the process of product preparation and development ensures that measures to optimize quality are in place from the outset.

Some of the approaches commonly used in Kaizen quality management are:

- *Just-in-time,* which reduces work-in-process inventory by operating on principles of minimal inventory and quick delivery
- *First-time quality,* which applies methods such as mistake-proofing (designing parts, processes, or procedures so that mistakes cannot happen), to reduce causes of re-work, defects, and scrapped products
- *Total productive management,* which reduces downtime and maintenance costs by improving housekeeping and preventive maintenance
- *Administrative improvement,* which focuses on processes used in customer relations, accounting, and marketing

There are many consultants available to help a company implement the Kaizen process or any other continuous quality improvement program.

Quality Circles

Dr. Kaoru Ishikawa of the University of Tokyo developed quality circles in the 1960s. Quality circles integrate much of the philosophy of quality management pioneer W. Edwards Deming and contribute to a total quality management program (see tip #132).

Quality circles are typically teams of 8 to 10 employees who work in the same department or area. A supervisor will usually serve as a group facilitator, helping the group discuss a variety of work-related issues. The group reaches decisions by consensus, following an established procedure for identifying, analyzing, and solving quality-related issues.

Quality circle members are volunteers, and groups are encouraged to have meetings and make decisions on their own. Interestingly, these quality circles have been much more popular in Japan than in the United States, despite the movement toward team-based work environments in the U.S. Some people suggest that this is due to the Japanese ability to work well in groups. While American adoption of the quality circle process has been increasing, many managers still seem reluctant to share responsibilities with their employees as the process requires.

Some companies using quality circles have reported benefits that go beyond improvements in quality. Among the benefits mentioned are better communication between management and employees, higher employee morale and a deeper sense of involvement in the company, and improved problem-solving skills.

According to the International Association of Quality Circles, the most successful programs are long-term, well-established ones in large, non-manufacturing companies. The estimated average net savings contributed by each circle member is approximately $1,000.

136

What Is Benchmarking?

A *benchmark* is a level of quality established by one company that other companies use as a goal. The American Productivity & Quality Center defines benchmarking as "the process of identifying, understanding, and adapting outstanding practices and processes from organizations anywhere in the world to help your organization improve its performance." Their definition intentionally uses the word "outstanding" and not "best," since what is best for your organization depends on your particular situation and needs.

Paul Allaire, president of the Xerox Corporation, stated, "The prime purpose of benchmarking is to understand those practices which will provide a competitive advantage in the market place; target setting is secondary."

There are four main types of benchmarking. *Internal* benchmarking compares one unit in an organization to another. *Competitive* benchmarking analyzes strategies, processes, and practices used by competitors and other companies in the same industry. *Process* benchmarking assesses best practice processes and functions, regardless of industry. *Strategic* benchmarking analyzes emerging trends to help shape and implement strategy.

As mentioned already, benchmarking does not always need to take place within the same industry. For example, a good example of process benchmarking is the airline industry benchmarking off a race car pit crew. Both rely on efficient, synchronized service to reduce turnaround times and ensure reliable performance. Another example is a cosmetics company that benchmarked from an ammunition manufacturer. Having trouble seeing the connection between makeup and bullets? Consider the similarities between a lipstick tube and a bullet shell.

Benchmarking—
Past, Present, and
Future

Each year, The Benchmarking Exchange (TBE) reports on the most actively benchmarked business processes from the preceding year. The purpose of the annual ranking is to show the business processes that are receiving the most attention and to provide insight into what to expect in the coming year.

In 1997, human resources and information systems were the most commonly targeted areas for benchmarking. It is interesting to note that assessments of other companies' benchmarking efforts came in third. For more information on the resources available through TBE, visit its website at http://www.benchnet.com/.

Table 4
The Benchmarking Exchange's 1997 List
of Most Actively Benchmarked Business Processes

Business Process	1997 Ranking
Human Resources	1
Information Systems	2
Benchmarking	3
Purchasing/Accounting	4
Customer Service	5

QUALITY MANAGEMENT

138

Approaches to Benchmarking

It takes a certain degree of humility to admit that someone else is better at something than you are. This realization, however, sits at the heart of the benchmarking effort. You must be wise enough to recognize superior practices in other organizations in order to learn how to match or surpass them.

Once you decide to benchmark, here are two frameworks to aid in the process.

The 10-Step Benchmarking Process

1. Identify the benchmarking subject.
2. Identify the companies whose methods you will study.
3. Determine the data collection method and collect data.
4. Determine the current competitive gap.
5. Project your future performance.
6. Communicate your findings and gain acceptance for them.
7. Establish functional goals.
8. Develop action plans.
9. Implement plans and monitor progress.
10. Once the benchmark has been reached, set a new benchmark.

The American Productivity and Quality Center Benchmarking Model (www.apqc.org) breaks the benchmarking process into four main stages:

1. Plan.
2. Collect data.
3. Analyze data.
4. Adapt and improve.

If you want assistance with your benchmarking effort, you will find that an entire industry dealing specifically with benchmarking issues has developed.

Perspectives on Benchmarking

Do you and your company's executives know how your business is doing? How do you rate compared to your competitors? Answering these questions through the benchmarking process has become easier, with huge amounts of data about other companies available both on software and on the Internet. This knowledge can help you improve customer satisfaction, identify changes in the industry, and change the direction of your business to gain a competitive advantage.

There are two major categories of information that can be used for benchmarking:

1. *Financial information*

   It is extremely useful to compare your company's financial situation to industry norms, looking at sales, profits, debt, inventory levels, inventory turnover, return on investment, and current and quick ratios (see tip #309). If a company has gone public (that is, issued stock), this information is available on the Internet since the Federal Trade Commission requires published financial statements. A financial snapshot of your company in industry context can show if something is wrong but not how to fix it. Finding a way to correct the problems requires a second type of benchmarking, a qualitative evaluation.

2. *Qualitative evaluation*

   "How am I doing and how can I do better?" are the questions to ask in a qualitative benchmarking effort. You need to look at practices in your own industry and in other industries that use processes similar to yours. The effort can be handled in-house or contracted out to a consultant. If you are using customer questionnaires in a benchmarking effort, keep them short (three or four questions) or you will have a poor response rate.

The following is a list of benchmarking resources published in *Business Week* (April 27, 1998).

- The American Society for Quality offers a best-practices data repository and a registry of consultants. www.asq.org.

QUALITY MANAGEMENT

- The American Society of Training & Development Benchmarking Forum provides a forum for benchmarking training processes against those used by other companies, as well as statistics on training and development costs. www.astd.org.
- The American Productivity & Quality Center International Benchmarking Clearing House provides articles, lists educational programs and studies, and offers research services for benchmarkers. www.apqc.org
- Dun & Bradstreet Businesscope software provides statistical analysis of companies similar to yours ($99).
- The Management Roundtable provides online articles and a forum for giving and receiving advice and networking. www.trainingforum.com/MRT
- The Benchmarking Exchange offers surveys, market studies, and lists of best-practice companies. www.benchnet.com.
- The U.S. Inter-Agency Benchmarking & Best Practices Council provides a calendar of benchmarking events and offers an expansive list of benchmarking-related web sites and library resources. www.va.gov/fedsbest/index.htm.
- The U.S. Navy Best Manufacturing Practices site offers case studies from corporations. www.bmpcoe.org.

Success creates the illusion that everything is being done as well as possible. It can also lead to complacency about the business's long-term prospects. Constantly evaluating your company against other successful companies will provide a valuable reality check and will indicate areas where improvement can be made.

Zero Defects

Philip Crosby, an engineer from Wheeling, West Virginia, is one of the modern founders of the quality movement. In the 1950s he developed the *zero defects* approach to quality control that places responsibility for quality in the hands of the workers. By motivating employees to do their best and to eliminate errors in their work altogether, this approach forces them to pay close attention to detail, accuracy, and completeness.

The zero defects method is successful because it requires that everyone involved in a product or service take ownership for eliminating all errors. The message is very clear—do it right the first time. In addition, there needs to be complete buy-in and commitment from the entire team. In order for the process to work, everyone needs to believe in the concept. Everyone, from the top executive to the janitor, is encouraged to identify problems and find ways to solve them. Finally, the goal is to take immediate action to change behavior and to lessen conditions that cause errors. It is important for managers to have the authority to deal with most situations immediately while allowing top management to improve long-run conditions.

Some of Crosby's other important quality improvement concepts include:

- Encouraging individuals to establish their own goals
- Encouraging employees to let managers know about obstacles to goal achievement
- Supervisor training to support the quality improvement initiative
- Recognizing those who strive for excellence
- Recognizing that quality improvement must be a continuous process, not just a one-time effort

Zero defects was one of the first quality programs to instill a sense of pride in workers. The program is meant to be self-motivating and to put quality on a personal basis. Its goals are personal commitment and maximum participation by the entire company. To ensure success of the program, management must be an integral part of the commitment to quality.

QUALITY MANAGEMENT

141 Just-In-Time Inventory

Are you in a business where inventory is always inadequate to meet orders? Or is inventory so high that large amounts of liquid assets are tied up unnecessarily? The happy medium is just-in-time (JIT) inventory. JIT requires integrated management systems capable of delivering materials as close as possible to the time they are needed. This saves storage space and the expense of larger inventories.

Computerized technology, including computer-aided manufacturing and computer-aided managerial systems, are required to make JIT work. So are knowledgeable, motivated employees. Extremely good working relationships with your suppliers, and quality manufacturing processes that assure an adequate supply of components, are the other necessary ingredients.

The move to JIT by many industries has altered the geographic location of manufacturing facilities. Having suppliers closer at hand reduces transportation expenses. The pressures created by JIT have also encouraged the global expansion of industries.

The benefits of JIT include:

- Lower cost of inventory from current assets
- Decreased space requirements for inventory and production
- Decreased costs for carrying and handling inventory
- Decreased costs for obsolete inventory
- Possible lower accounting and manufacturing costs.

The Japanese pioneered JIT in manufacturing, and some American companies have refined it for retail merchandising. These companies require their suppliers to stock the shelves and carry the cost of inventory, thereby reducing overhead costs for the stores. JIT inventory is one of many techniques companies have found to maintain a competitive advantage and reduce costs.

The International Organization for Standardization (ISO)

The main purpose of the International Organization for Standardization (ISO) is to establish global standards that facilitate the international exchange of goods and services. Approximately 130 countries participate in this worldwide federation in an effort to develop cooperation in technological, economic, scientific, and intellectual activity.

Two of the most commonly referenced guidelines are ISO 9000 and 14000. These are both families of standards that relate to management systems. These standards fall into two categories—requirements and guidelines. Requirements are mandatory standards that dictate what a company must do. Companies become registered to or compliant with one of the requirements standards. Guidelines help a company interpret the requirements. ISO 9000 is primarily concerned with quality management, and ISO 14000 focuses primarily on environmental management.

In the context of ISO 9000, *quality* refers to all those features of a product or service which are required by the customer; and *quality management* means what the organization does to ensure that its products conform to the customer's requirements and expectations. The standards identify the general criteria by which any organization, whether it is oriented to manufacturing or service, can ensure that its products meet customer requirements.

ISO 14000 is targeted at how organizations minimize harmful effects on the environment caused by operational activities. Depletion of natural resources during production and pollution during disposal are both areas of key concern to the guidelines of the 14000 family.

Under both families of standards, a participating company must first document and implement its management systems and then verify, by means of an audit conducted by an independent, accredited third party, compliance of those systems with ISO standards.

Any organization can develop a quality management system based on the ISO requirements standards. Standards are intended to be generic and can accommodate the individuality of different companies and even different industries. It is simply up to each individual business to interpret the appropriate requirements standards in light of its own processes.

For more information, visit the official ISO website at: www.iso.ch

QUALITY MANAGEMENT

143 Benefits of ISO 9000

ISO 9000 family of standards specifies general criteria by which any organization can ensure that products leaving its facility meet the quality expectations and requirements of its customers. It outlines a comprehensive way to do business that provides measurable bottom-line improvements. The ISO 9000 family consists of three quality assurance models against which an organization can be certified: 9001, 9002, and 9003. The difference between them is merely one of scope.

Of the three, ISO 9001 is the most comprehensive. It provides a foundation for basic quality management and continuous improvement practices for organizations whose business processes range all the way from design and development, to production, installation, and servicing.

ISO 9002 does not include design and development standards and therefore applies to organizations that do not carry out these functions. The remaining standards are identical to those of 9001.

ISO 9003 is the appropriate standard for an organization whose business processes are limited to inspection and testing to ensure that final products and services meet specified requirements. Again, the standards are specific to the processes under quality control.

The ISO 9000 family consists of more than 20 standards and guidelines, and to make sense of them it is best to obtain more information directly from the Internationl Organization of Standardization. A brochure, *Selection and Use of ISO 9000,* is available from the sales department at ISO Central Secretariat. Visit their official website at www.iso.ch for more information.

Malcolm Baldrige National Quality Award

144

The Malcolm Baldrige National Quality Award was created to stimulate the growth of quality management in the United States. This award was named for Malcolm Baldrige, Secretary of Commerce under Ronald Reagan. It is the American counterpart to Japan's Deming Prize, named for the pioneering management expert W. Edwards Deming.

Each year, the award is given to one or two companies in each of the following categories:

- Manufacturing
- Service
- Small business (fewer than 500 employees)
- Universities and hospitals

The award is intended to:

- Stimulate quality improvement in U.S. companies
- Establish criteria that businesses can use to evaluate their quality improvement efforts
- Use companies that have been successful in quality improvement efforts as role models
- Help other organizations improve quality by sharing information about award winners' quality programs

Table 5, on the following page, gives a representative example of the weighted examination criteria for the Malcolm Baldrige National Quality Awards.

Winners and finalists have experienced positive outcomes including increased market share, improved employee relations, higher productivity, enhanced customer relations, and higher profitability. Many people believe that the winners of the Baldrige Award tend to consistently outperform the stock market. The award has also raised awareness of the importance and value of quality improvement programs.

Table 5
Sample Criteria for the Baldrige Award

Strategic planning	5.5%
Information and analysis	7.5%
Leadership	9.0%
Human resource development and management	14%
Process management	14%
Business results	25%
Customer focus and satisfaction	25%
	100%

Quality Control Tools

Talking about quality is meaningless without having some way of measuring and tracking the effects of quality management. The most common techniques for identifying quality problems and their causes are known as the *seven Quality Control tools,* or the *magnificent seven.* Figures 14–20 demonstrate each of these techniques.

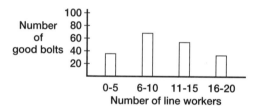

Figure 14. Histogram—*A diagram of data that relate to a quality issue.*

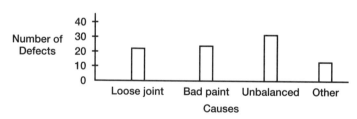

Figure 15. Pareto Analysis—*A diagram that tallies the number or percentage of defects resulting from various causes. It usually indicates that the majority of the problems are caused by one or two elements.*

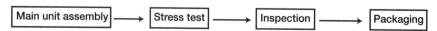

Figure 16. Flow Chart—*A diagram showing the steps in a process that can help to identify a particular step that may be causing quality problems.*

Figure 17. Scatter Diagram—*A graph showing the relationship between two variables in a process, used to identify patterns that may be causing quality problems.*

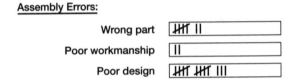

Figure 18. Check Sheet—*A tally of the number of defects by cause.*

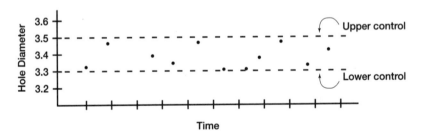

Figure 19. Process Control Chart—*A chart with upper and lower limits; if the process stays within the limits, there is no immediate problem.*

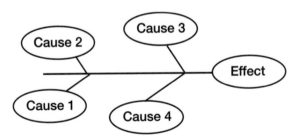

Figure 20. Cause-and-Effect Diagram—*A diagram that divides the causes of a quality problem into categories, also known as a "fishbone" diagram.*

Recruiting Potential Employees

146

The first step in the hiring process is to attract qualified people. After all, a manager is only as good as his or her employees. When recruiting for a position, be familiar with your company's hiring procedures. If your company has a human resources department, work closely with it throughout this process. Take advantage of what the HR department has to offer:

- Do they have an in-house recruiter?
- Can they provide standardized applications and checklists?
- Will they do preliminary screening for you?
- Will they help advertise?

To help them fulfill your needs effectively:

- Justify the need for the position.
- Fully explain the job requirements.
- Let them know exactly what you are looking for in an employee.

Smaller companies without HR departments can publicize openings through newspaper ads, trade journals, job fairs, university postings, faculty, and the Internet. As you seek out potential employees:

- Check with competitors who have recently downsized.
- Consider interviewing past temporary employees, interns, and summer help.
- Ask colleagues if they know anyone they would recommend for the job.
- Decide to whose attention responses to the job opening should be sent.
- Consider the most convenient way for your potential applicants to respond, and which method will be best for you. You might ask applicants to respond via e-mail, telephone, post office boxes, or toll-free numbers.

Make time for the recruiting process. Putting in the initial effort will help attract qualified applicants from the start and will make your management job easier down the road.

147

Interviewing
Potential Employees

When interviewing job candidates, the manager must ask questions that are strictly job-related. The mere suggestion of bias or infringement of equal employment opportunity laws can cause you and your company legal problems. Legally, you are forbidden to address areas of:

- *Race, color or national origin.* Never ask about race or national origin, or make racial or ethnic comments.
- *Religion.* Do not ask questions about religion or offer comments concerning the religious affiliations of the organization.
- *Sex.* Do not ask questions or make comments of a sexually biased nature.
- *Age.* You are only allowed to ask if the applicant is over the age of 18. Otherwise stay away from the subject of age, including indirect questions aimed at estimating age, such as "When did you graduate?"
- *Marital status.* Do not ask about spouse or children.
- *Address.* You can ask whether the applicant is an American citizen and how long the applicant has lived at his or her current address. However, questions beyond these are illegal.
- *Criminal record.* You may not ask an applicant if he or she has been arrested. You can ask if the candidate has ever been convicted of a crime, and if so when and where. You cannot deny an applicant employment based on a criminal record, unless it can be proved that the record would damage the employer's company.
- *Physical capabilities.* You cannot ask the candidate how physically able he or she is. This type of question may be viewed as sexist. You can require a physical exam and can explain the physical nature of the position. The applicant has the opportunity to withdraw the application if the job appears to be too physically demanding, but it would be illegal for the manager to make that decision during an interview.

Questions concerning education and experience are allowed as long as the question is relevant to the job for which the applicant is interviewing. It is a legal requirement that the questions asked at an interview be relevant or connected to a "bona fide occupational qualification." Experienced man-

agers will ask open-ended questions that begin with one of the *five W's,
who, what, where, why, when* (and *how*). An open-ended question—such as
"How do you feel that your past work experience will help you in this
job?"—gives the candidate a chance to talk and gives the manager an opportunity to understand the person's character.

148

Making the Most of Interviewing

The interview process is a critical part of your role as a manager. Successful interviewing is a skill you need to develop. Be aware that the interview may be a stressful situation for both you and the applicant. Careful planning and preparation are key to a successful interview.

If your company requires one, make sure applicants provide a completed and signed employment application. Be familiar with the applicant's resume and qualifications before the interview starts. Some other aspects of the interview to consider are:

Atmosphere

- Pick an appropriate site that is comfortable and free from interruptions.
- Pick a time that is convenient for you.
- You may consider sitting next to the person, not behind an intimidating desk.

Introduction

- Introduce yourself and offer a refreshment if available.
- Develop a rapport with the applicant and make him or her feel welcome.
- Provide an overview of the interview structure, the company, yourself, and the job.
- Use the opening to set the ground rules and subtly establish control.

Interview Process

- Request a brief oral summary of relevant work experience and education.
- Devise a series of questions to test how the applicant would respond to situations he or she will likely encounter in the job.
- Ask how the applicant has handled conflict in the past and what he or she learned from the experience.

Use the interview to get a feel for the applicant's personality and to assess whether this person would fit into the culture of your organization. Remember that you spend as much time with your coworkers as you do with your family—and you can't pick your family.

Employee Background Checks

Managers know that background checks on potential employees can supply vital information. The laws covering background checks include the Fair Credit Reporting Act, the Americans with Disabilities Act, equal employment opportunity laws, and privacy laws. Knowing what you can and cannot do when performing a background check on an employee will help you select the best candidates and will afford you legal protection.

During background checks you should:

- Verify all important information and carefully document the process. Talk to the references and previous employers personally. Ask them specifically if they would hire this individual again.
- Customize the background check based on the position. High-risk positions—such as ones involving driving or handling money—require greater diligence.
- Routinely check on all employees including part-time, temporary and volunteer workers. Any staff member is a potential liability if due diligence is not performed.
- Do not assume that temporary agencies perform background checks. Most agencies do not routinely do so unless that clause is part of the contract between employer and agency.
- Update application forms annually and replace generic forms with ones specifically designed for your business.
- Recheck employees in high risk-positions periodically. Employee theft and fraud cost billions of dollars each year.
- Ask references about the candidate's honesty and inquire if there was ever any violent or threatening behavior. More and more former employers realize the need to be forthright in communicating the potentially criminal behavior of former employees.
- Do not ask for personal information about the applicant. Stick to job-related questions to help avoid defamation suits.

You want to hire the best people, not workers who are going to steal, engage in violent behavior, or present disciplinary problems. Your employees represent you and the company. Conducting reference and background checks, in accordance with state and federal laws, can help assure that your employees will be good performers.

150

Documenting the Reference Check

How can you demonstrate that you acted reasonably when you hired your newest employee? How can you show your boss that you performed due diligence if the new hire turns out to be unsatisfactory?

According to the Equal Employment Opportunity Commission, companies with 15 or more employees must keep reference check records for at least one year. To standardize your hiring methods, it is prudent to create a reference check policy. This policy should include the following:

- A list of all the references checked
- The name of the person who contacted the references
- The method of request for reference, preferably written
- Name and title of all references contacted, with notes taken if telephone conversations occurred
- Copies of all records received, including credit reports, driving records, and conviction records
- The references on the applicant's list who did not respond

To ensure that the documentation will be available in case of a lawsuit, keep these records as part of the employee's personnel file. Even if the employee leaves the company, it is wise to keep his or her personnel file for seven years. The Equal Employment Opportunity Commission also requires that you keep the records of your reference check on unsuccessful applicants for a period of one year after the determination not to hire. Of course, if a discrimination suit is brought against you, you must keep the records until the matter is concluded.

You should not keep confidential reports or medical records in the employee's personnel file. This type of information may be viewed as prejudicial and is not meant for a supervisor's review.

There is no guarantee that the next employee you hire will be a winner. If you hire carefully, however, and systematically check references, you will increase your opportunity of picking a successful candidate. If that candidate does not turn out to be a good fit with your organization, or perhaps even sues you for wrongful termination, then at least the problem is not that you did not perform due diligence in hiring. Likewise, this type of documentation will help protect you against any unsuccessful candidates who file discrimination suits against you.

How People Learn

The *American Heritage Dictionary* describes learning as (1) the act, process, or experience of gaining knowledge or skill; (2) knowledge or skill gained through schooling or study.

As today's business environment changes faster and faster, an organization must actively support learning to remain competitive. Everyone has his or her own way of learning, but there are several qualities that must be present in order to learn. Individuals need to be:

- Motivated
- Interested
- Open to new ideas
- Able to listen to others

An authoritarian, or hierarchical, organization does not usually encourage a learning atmosphere. These organizations tend to establish rules that people must follow, and this does not encourage a sense of trust or belonging for employees. Mandated programs do not usually foster trust, curiosity, or team spirit. Employees need to be seen as knowledgeable, honest, and committed individuals who can learn from each other.

About 85 percent of our learning comes from visual stimuli. Enhanced learning can occur with the addition of verbal communication to visual communication. Table 6 shows the difference that this combination makes.

Table 6
Retention of Verbal and Visual Information

	Percent Recalled After Three Hours	Percent Recalled After Three Days
Verbal Information	70	10
Visual Information	72	35
Verbal + Visual	85	65

(From J. Penrose, R. Rasberry, and R. Myers, Advanced Business Communication, *Wadsworth, 1993.)*

152 Training Programs

Today, more and more companies are offering their employees training programs. Many experts believe that companies are providing employee education and skill upgrading in part as compensation for the disappearance of job security. A survey of fast-growing businesses by Coopers & Lybrand found that, over the past two years, more than half had sponsored training programs or had created plans for new training initiatives. The survey also indicated that most established internal programs rather than using outside sources.

Nonetheless, there are many companies that specialize in offering training programs for large organizations. Training may focus on job-specific tasks or may cover broader topics, such as working in groups, assisting troubled coworkers, or managing time effectively. It may take place in a classroom, or take the form of a computer-based program that employees can use at their convenience.

The government has established tax incentives to encourage worker education and training efforts. Employees can receive up to $5,250 in compensation, tax-free, for undergraduate or graduate courses that are job-related. This tax act has been extended to courses that start by June 1, 2000.[5]

In weighing the costs associated with training programs, keep in mind that employees are the most valuable assets a company has. Investing in employees will help maintain a mutually beneficial relationship between the company and its employees, and will contribute to the company's long-term competitiveness.

---

[5]*Business Week,* April 27, 1998.

Making Training Work

Training is costly. Offering training to your staff makes sense only if you can demonstrate that the training is job-related and will result in measurable payoff.

To determine the costs of training, include direct costs such as materials, space rental, and consultant fees. You also must include indirect costs, such as time off from work during training. If the training isn't well thought out, there can be the additional costs of retraining.

Less formal approaches to training include having new employees work alongside more experienced ones. Seasoned employees can serve as role models and help new hires succeed. When this is planned, the manager needs to prepare the chosen preceptors so that they can be more effective trainers.

High-quality training leads to improved product and service quality. In addition, the manager who can successfully train his or her employees will:

- Be rewarded with a more cooperative staff
- Have a workforce of highly trained personnel
- Have employees prepared for advancement or intradepartmental transfers
- Have more time to spend on other supervisory tasks

There is no question that effective training will reflect well on your managerial skills. A manager looking for a promotion needs to demonstrate that he or she can train a workforce that produces quality work. The trick is to prove that the training has produced positive, measurable results. One way to show improvement is to evaluate the productivity of the staff prior to training and after the training. Another measure might be to compare performance of trained employees to that of untrained employees and to forecast the result of that difference over the next year. In this way, you will be able to demonstrate the improvements made by training and justify the associated costs.

Ultimately, training is only useful if it is transferred to the job. In order to increase this probability, you should discuss the objectives of the training with your staff in advance. Then monitor your employees' performance after the training and offer feedback. Training is one of the most important supervisory objectives, and effective managers should be skilled at implementing, monitoring, and evaluating it.

TRAINING

154 Taking Advantage of Video Training

More and more businesses are taking advantage of video training. Recorded presentations can be used repeatedly to train new employees and refresh skills and knowledge for long-term employees. This saves instruction time and allows for the recording of a well-prepared and illustrated presentation.

Many firms distribute videotapes regarding their products (for example, computers, software, and health care products). These are often available at little or no cost.

Internet sources of training programs include:

- VIS Development, a leader in the creation of PC-based interactive videotraining and education. To date, VIS has delivered more than 250 interactive video applications for major publishers and corporations. www.visdev.com
- L&K International Videotraining, Buyers' Guide Company Index for L&K International Videotraining. www.powermag.com/buyguide
- An index of videotraining is available at: www.aa.net/videotraining
- Executive Introduction to The Internet, Video Training Edition. www.videoed.com
- Quality Assurance Videotraining Program to Support Your Company in ISO-9000. Module 1—Why Quality Assurance? (Tape is available in Spanish.) www.sidecom.com.mx/calidad/quality.htm

Distance learning networks are developing on the Internet and indicate a bright future for videotraining. They will allow a business to offer continuing education to all employees, thus enhancing their skills and making them more valuable both to their employer and in the larger job market.

Unconventional Training to Become a Better Manager

155

You went back to school to complete your MBA. You signed up for and attended all the workshops you could on leadership, management, finance, and marketing. You went through all of your company's training programs and you've learned all the on-the-job lessons you can about your work. But you still aren't the corporate executive you aspire to become. What else can you do to fully equip yourself for a leadership role?

The additional focus and discipline that are necessary for successful business leadership may indeed originate from unconventional sources; how you spend your leisure time may be instrumental to further developing your managerial skills. For example, activities such as karate or martial arts may help increase your concentration, while honing your chess skills may help you to strategize better. Are your presentation skills weak? Do you secretively fear speaking in front of your employees? Perhaps becoming involved with a debating club or amateur theater group will make you more comfortable at public appearances.

Experts agree that leisure time is important to help relieve stress and revitalize the spirit. However, some after-work activities can offer even more advantages by helping you improve managerial skills, even activites that don't at first appear relevant to work.

A manager confided that she began making intricate beaded jewelry to fulfill her creative side. What she soon realized was that she needed infinite patience to learn and complete the process. At her job, patience with her employees had not been her strong point. Her jewelry-making experience helped her to realize two pearls of managerial wisdom. The first is that learning new tasks requires time and support, and the second is that achieving quality goals requires patience and attention to detail.

Another activity that teaches work-related lessons is coaching children's sports. Anyone who has coached Little League or similar sports knows the challenge of getting kids to pay attention and work as a team toward a common goal. Yet yelling, scolding, and threatening hardly work with these vulnerable athletes. Just as challenging is dealing with the parents, who can be seen as external customers. A successful coaching season can add confidence and sensitivity to your everyday managerial role.

Today's managers have little time for after-work activities and must choose wisely how to spend leisure time. Certainly, activities such as sports, hobbies, and family vacations lead the list of choices. However, if your managerial skills are of major concern, you may want to add some activities that can help improve your leadership qualities.

Why Conduct an Appraisal Interview?

Many employees and employers view the appraisal interview as an excruciating experience. Yet in these days of downsizing or "rightsizing," it has become crucial to do more with fewer workers, and it is therefore critical that those workers continue to be the optimal ones for your company.

The traditional purpose of the performance appraisal has been to identify areas where improvement is needed and to determine pay raises. But the performance appraisal is an important opportunity for communication between manager and employee and, conducted correctly, can play a significant role in motivating and developing staff.

- It is an opportunity to give feedback, direction, and leadership.
- It is a time to show support and encouragement.
- It is a time to open a discussion about areas that need improvement.
- It is an opportunity to evaluate accomplishments and to set goals.

The appraisal interview may be the best tool a manager has for positive interaction with his or her employees. It will be easier to make the experience a successful one if you prepare for the review throughout the year by working with your employees on goals, strengths, and weaknesses.

EVALUATIONS AND REVIEWS

157

Conducting an Appraisal Interview

The performance appraisal meeting is no more than a summary of the feedback and communication that should have been occurring regularly throughout the year. This meeting should not present any surprises.

The following is a list of some of the things to include in the meeting:

- A discussion of the employee's value to the organization and an expression of gratitude
- Encouragement for good behavior and accomplished tasks
- Consideration of the areas of performance that need to be improved, with specific suggestions or goals for achieving improvement
- A discussion of the opportunities for growth within the company that exist for the employee
- A pleasant, positive environment with sufficient time and no interruptions
- A review of the self-evaluation tool with the employee
- A systematic approach, based upon a tool for rating performance against established standards
- A focus on the employee's behavior, not on his or her personality
- Time for feedback from the employee or for other issues the employee wants to discuss
- Establishment of new targets

End the meeting on a constructive note, with firm commitment to follow up in one or two days if the employee requests additional time before signing or completing the evaluation form. Remember that the performance appraisal is not a presentation but a dialogue. The manager needs to be an active listener and is responsible for keeping communication flowing in both directions.

The Role of Discipline

The goal of discipline is to encourage employees to meet job performance standards and to help maintain a safe and efficient working environment. A positive discipline policy will do more than punish the employee who performs poorly. It will improve behavior and establish self-control across the entire workforce.

While most employees accept that disciplinary actions are necessary to preserve order and to ensure that everyone is working toward common organizational goals, the best discipline is still self-discipline. When self-discipline and coaching are not effective, then disciplinary actions must be taken to restore a secure working environment.

The most common situations that result in disciplinary action are absenteeism, fighting, insubordination, dishonesty, alcoholism, drug use or possession, and negligence. Fortunately, only a small percentage of workers will pose disciplinary problems. The manager can avoid problem employees by hiring candidates who appear to be well adjusted and to have positive attitudes. It is much simpler to teach skills than it is to teach attitude.

What else can managers do to avoid workers with disciplinary problems? Managers who are good leaders have fewer employees with disciplinary problems. Workers who enjoy coming to work are less likely to be late or sick. When employees feel they have a boss who is understanding and who will listen, they will be more comfortable discussing personal issues that can impact job performance. While it is never appropriate to snoop, managers who are insightful can help employees through difficult personal times with creative solutions, such as flextime (see tip #34).

Supervisors need to be just and equal in their treatment of employees. A manager who is soft or who overlooks poor performance and gives repeated chances to wrongdoers will become unpopular among his or her staff. No one likes to be punished, but dedicated workers find it more upsetting to see other workers go without punishment for doing a poor job. Remember too that employees do not want to see discipline administered selectively. A manager must make sure the disciplinary policy is put in writing and distributed to the staff, and he or she needs to enforce it fairly and quickly when infractions occur.

159

Administering Discipline

Effective discipline must always be handled in a positive and a progressive manner. A positive approach uses discussion and constructive criticism, while a negative approach would be simply scolding or suspending the wrongdoer. Progressive discipline means incremental steps, such as oral warning, written reprimand, second written warning, suspension, and termination. Also important to progressive discipline are the following principles:

- Advanced warning—"If you do that, you will be disciplined."
- Consistency—"Everyone who demonstrates that kind of behavior will be disciplined."
- Immediacy—"Every time you do that, you will be disciplined."
- Impartiality—"No one is exempt from disciplinary actions if he or she demonstrates that behavior."

Supervisors normally feel that discipline is an unpleasant task. However, it will seem less unpleasant if the supervisor views discipline as a consequence for poor performance or behavior and not as a cure for a personality or attitude problem. One way a manager can discipline constructively is with a process aimed at behavior modification. This process would:

- Define the problem. "You failed to get those important contracts out by the deadline."
- Ask the employee for his or her input on the problem. "Can you explain to me why this happened?"
- Ask the employee for a solution. "What might be a solution for this problem?"
- Agree on the plan for resolution. "We will get the copier checked and serviced."
- Give the employee a warning. "You should have come to me if there were equipment problems. If this kind of behavior continues, I will need to place a written warning in your file."
- Set a date for review. "Let's recheck your deadlines in a month."

Behavior modification is effective because it involves the employee in the process. If the employee still performs poorly, the manager must continue with the progressive discipline process at the next review date. Even if the process eventually leads to termination, the employee has a better chance of accepting the outcome if the process was conducted fairly and without condemnation of him or her as a person.

160

Possible Fallout from the Disciplinary Process

Managers must ensure that their disciplinary process conforms to legal requirements and is supported by documentation for just cause. The law requires managers to have a policy that informs employees of the kinds of performance and behaviors that will trigger disciplinary action. Since employee handbooks cannot possibly cover every situation that may result in the disciplinary process, managers must communicate regularly to their staff a definition of acceptable performance. Likewise, the law requires that the staff be made aware of the penalties for unacceptable performance. Again, although having a written policy describing the disciplinary process is important, the manager needs to clearly communicate what the consequences are for unacceptable behavior.

To prevent legal action by an employee terminated as a result of the disciplinary process, a manager should avoid the following:

- **Lack of positive evidence.** The manager does not witness the breaking of the rule but relies on what others tell him or her. This means there is no hard evidence of the infraction.
- **Inadequate warning.** Having an employee handbook that describes rules and policies is not enough. A manager needs to warn an employee when behavior is unacceptable.
- **Prejudice.** A manager who shows favoritism by allowing one worker to get away with unacceptable behavior but punishes another one for the same behavior is looking for legal trouble.
- **Poor record keeping.** A documentation of warnings and agreed-upon solutions is imperative in the disciplinary process.
- **Punishment that doesn't fit the behavior.** It is unwise to terminate an employee for minor infractions, especially without evidence that the employer had already warned the employee about the potential consequences of these infractions.
- **Violation of union contracts.** The manager must heed the company's established contracts and policies in the formal disciplinary process. Labor representation is often required during the coaching sessions.

Careful planning with supportive documentation will help protect your disciplinary process from legal scrutiny. Your actions must be based upon firm evidence without bias or prejudice. A manager who is spiteful or impulsive in disciplining employees will leave the door open for lawsuits.

Avoiding Lawsuits from Departing Employees

Employers should always use written job descriptions, performance appraisals, coaching, and one-on-one disciplinary sessions to help direct employee behavior. But despite your best efforts, some employees are apt to sue upon termination.

The following employees may be more likely than others to sue:

- Employees who are unwilling to accept constructive criticism. They suffer from the belief that they are right and everyone else is wrong. They do not grow in their roles, nor do they accept responsibility.
- Employees who have been with the company for five or more years. These employees feel that they have given more to the company than they have gotten in return. If you let them go, they feel wronged and revengeful.
- Below-average employees with good written performance appraisals. These employees have managed to receive positive written evaluations, perhaps due to inexperienced or non-confrontational managers.
- Employees who are opportunists. They look for the easiest, not necessarily the most correct, solution. When terminated, instead of seeking additional training or searching for a new job, they may take the path of least resistance and sue the former employer.
- Employees who have always found fault with every new idea or concept. These people are usually unhappy and disgruntled in both their work and personal lives.
- Employees who have no initiative. They appear helpless and do not act on their own behalf. They fear the idea of searching for a new job and would rather sue than face their fears.
- Employees who have been doing the same jobs for a long time without taking advantage of opportunities to update their skills. They are not good enough to promote and not bad enough to fire. When they are terminated, perhaps because of a reorganization, they are quick to seek legal advice.
- Employees who, when faced with a new boss and additional duties, are unable to perform satisfactorily.

Keep an eye out for the employee who feels he or she has nothing to lose by initiating a lawsuit. There are many employment attorneys who will accept contingency cases. Terminated employees may not have to pay up-front attorney fees and therefore feel they have nothing to lose.

162 Coping with Stress

Managers tend to be workaholics. They enjoy the challenge of impossible projects and are entitled to reap the rewards of a job well done. But they also face the stress of accountability and ultimate responsibility. What can a manager do to lessen the impact of stress?

Whether you are a manager or just starting out in your work career, there are constructive steps that you can take to help relieve stress. You can:

- **Try to be realistic about your capabilities.** Everyone has limitations, and to help avoid undue stress, you must learn to live within your mental and physical means. Most people would rather accept a position or project in which they can succeed than take on a job that is beyond their capabilities.
- **Take a break.** Even ten or fifteen minutes away from a problem can give you a new perspective. Learn to meditate, listen to music, or simply think and relax.
- **Exercise.** Everyone can participate in some form of exercise, and exercise does reduce tension and stress. Find a coworker to take a half-hour walk with you during lunch. If you are more athletically inclined, find a fun activity and commit to doing it at least every other day.
- **Find a hobby.** The purpose of a hobby is to divert your attention away from the stress of work. Diversions help to give your mind a rest and to recharge your mental batteries.

People who are victims of stress tend to concentrate only on themselves. Many would alleviate their stress simply by taking the time to appreciate the world around them. A simple way to start might be taking the time to watch the sunrise or sunset. More advanced steps would be to start helping others.

Managers are expected to counsel their employees and are usually skilled at giving advice. But are they equally skilled in the art of active listening? Listening to others discuss their problems can be helpful in lifting your own stress. Can you listen to someone worse off than you are without interrupting? Are you always trying to top his or her story with one of your own? An effective stress eraser is active listening, with the goal of helping others.

Like all skills, stress reduction steps require practice. Managers who learn techniques to keep stress in check early in their careers can look forward to longer and more productive professional and personal lives.

Stress Management Techniques

Being a manager is by nature a stressful job. In fact, most managers feel that the stress of their job is part of what makes it so invigorating, challenging, and even downright fun. Yet there is a definite difference between a stimulating amount of stress and an unbearable amount.

The basic goal of stress management is to eliminate annoying, persistent, and unnecessary stress. The correctable types of stress that you should eliminate are:

- **Unclear expectations relating to your job.** Check your job description and review it with your supervisor. Make sure your responsibilities are clear and that you both agree upon them. Do not accept performance expectations that are vague. Expected outcomes should be measurable and quantitative. And by no means allow the "rules of the game" to change midstream without your knowledge and consent.
- **Inadequate resources to accomplish the job.** You need to pay close attention to the resources that are required for the jobs assigned to you. You cannot assume that your supervisor has thought out all the details. He or she will depend upon you to know what labor, equipment, and materials are needed for the completion of the job. If you are not paying close attention to what it will take to get the job done on time, then you will be adding unnecessary stress by trying to accomplish a job without the necessary support.
- **Playing two roles.** Often managers are asked to work on projects from different departments or from different supervisors. Many times the jobs or requests come with ambiguous instructions. When faced with this stressful situation, it is best to approach all parties with the dilemma and work through the problem jointly. An experienced manager will confront the problem and not try to please everyone, which is not only stressful but also impossible.

Managing stress at work is sometimes easier than managing sources of stress outside of business. However, those sources of stress greatly affect your professional performance. Some helpful stress-reducing techniques that you can apply in your personal life include:

- Trying to change your personal environment. For example, you can't sleep, or perform well, with neighbors who stay up partying loudly every night.
- Being realistic in your goals, strengths, and weaknesses. Pushing yourself without careful self-appraisal will set you up for failure.

Sometimes, tackling unmanageable amounts of stress may require professional guidance. Many companies offer employment assistance programs that can help. There is no weakness in seeking professional help for stress. In fact, it shows courage and insight.

Employee Assistance Programs

Managing a business is often mostly about managing people. An employee assistance program (EAP) offers a way to help employees resolve conflicts, improve relationships, and address issues that may hinder them from working effectively and cooperatively. It is estimated that 20 percent of all employees have problems that can reduce job performance by as much as 25 percent. A comprehensive EAP is designed to counteract such problems.

An EAP is designed to assist employees *before* their problems negatively affect job performance. It offers confidential counseling to address problems, whether they are problems at home or conflicts with fellow workers.

Consider the following statistics:

- Of employer health insurance costs, 10 percent are spent on unresolved mental health and substance abuse problems.
- The accepted average cost of replacing an impaired employee is $19,000.
- More than 80 percent of managers rate themselves as ineffective in managing employee conflicts.
- Nearly 20 percent of management time is consumed by employee conflict problems.
- An estimated 65 percent of job performance deficiencies result from ineffective relationships, not ineffective employees.
- Employee assistance programs have proven to be 70 percent to 80 percent successful in restoring the workplace productivity of employees who use them.
- Of more than 100 companies surveyed, 71 percent reported that their employee assistance programs were responsible for reducing employee accidents and injuries.

Employee assistance programs are commonly available to both employees and their families. While an EAP offers its services to workers, it also provides distinct benefits to employers by helping to possibly lower health care costs, turnover rates, liability, and absenteeism.

THE PERSONAL SIDE

165

Change and the Grieving Process

The grieving process has long been misunderstood. As originally described by Elisabeth Kubler-Ross in her classic book *On Death and Dying* (Macmillan, 1969), patients diagnosed with a terminal illness went through five stages of "receiving catastrophic news":

- Denial
- Anger
- Bargaining
- Depression
- Acceptance

As the grieving process was further studied, it became clear that this process not only applied to receiving catastrophic news but also to dealing with any perceived loss to the individual. In 1984, Dr. Terese Rando, a grief specialist, described grief as a "process of psychological, social, and somatic (physical) reactions to the perception of loss." In 1991, the Grief Resource Foundation of Dallas described the grief process as "the total response of the organism to the process of change." Notice how the emphasis now includes not just catastrophic news but more generally the process of change. Many changes result in loss and in the grieving process.

Researchers have also found, consequently, that not all of the steps of grieving occur in each case or in the usual order. But psychological problems may occur if major or unpleasant changes are not accompanied by some version of the grieving process and are instead simply blocked out.

Understanding the grieving process will be helpful when dealing with changes in your life or in your employees' lives. These might include work assignment changes, job changes, or family changes such as divorce. You must keep in mind the possible effects of any changes in peoples' lives.

Counseling for Alcoholism

The employee with poor performance related to a drinking problem presents a special type of counseling challenge for the manager. These problem employees frequently require more than just a manager's counseling; they often need professional help.

The manager must first recognize the employee who is drinking. Frequently alcoholic workers will have a high overall rate of absences. These absences may be spread out throughout the workweek if the employee is trying to avoid a pattern. There may also be partial absences, in which an employee shows up in the morning but leaves in the afternoon. Look for frequent short absences during the day. Pay attention if behavior and performance deteriorate as the day progresses. Tardiness does not seem to be a typical element of these patterns.

Counseling the alcoholic employee requires training. Managers should discuss the necessary steps with their supervisors or human resource representatives prior to the counseling session. The following is a guide to the counseling process:

- Since your responsibility is to maintain acceptable performance on the part of all employees, do not apologize for confronting the troubled worker.
- Ask the employee to explain why performance or attendance is poor. The employee may confide the drinking problem at this point.
- Don't enter into a moral conversation concerning alcohol. Present a medical perspective instead. Experts agree that alcoholism is a progressive and debilitating illness that, if left untreated, will lead to illness and death.
- Don't be distracted by the employee's excuses for drinking. Clearly state that you are concerned with the way the problem affects work performance.
- If the employee tells you that a personal doctor has the problem under control, point out that if the matter were in fact under control it would not be creating problems at work.

- Emphasize that you are concerned with job performance and that the decision to seek help is the employee's responsibility. End by stating that if the performance does not improve, progressive discipline will continue and may lead to discharge.

Many times a manager is more successful in getting the alcoholic to seek help than even a well-meaning friend, spouse, or clergyman can be. The reason is that the threat of losing your job is a powerful stimulus for change.

Managing Diversity

Today there is increased awareness of diversity in the workplace. We are all multidimensional and complex people. Workers bring a diversity of languages, origins, education, religious beliefs, and sexual orientations with them to their jobs. It is the manager's legal and moral responsibility to manage this diversity. Most people understand what is meant by diversity in the workplace, but many do not understand what diversity is not. Diversity is not:

- A problem, but an opportunity. Diversity presents the opportunity to use workers' different skills and thinking styles to grow and improve business.
- Limited to race and gender. Diversity encompasses more than issues concerning minorities or women. It also involves cultural differences between internal and external customers. The goal is to create a corporate culture in which each individual can contribute to the organization.
- A human resources department responsibility. Managers must train their workers to understand that they all have a key role in the acceptance of diversity in the workplace. It must be clear that the goal of the organization is to create a multicultural climate.
- A concept of exclusivity. Diversity is inclusive. It is not about favoring one group over another but about increasing sensitivity to and knowledge about individual differences, and using that knowledge to create a corporate climate that respects and embraces those differences.

Embracing diversity is the right thing to do and is also good business because your staff and customers will demand it. Diversity training needs to begin with an assessment of the current corporate culture. Managers can gather this information by looking at exit interviews, customer surveys, attitude surveys, and hiring tendencies. Ask employees what diversity means to them and how they would define success. Explore the origins of prejudice, intolerance, and other obstacles that might threaten a successful diversity program. There are consultants and seminars that can assist in creating an effective diversity program.

Your company must resemble the community it serves. The customer population is diverse, as are the applicants for jobs. In order to retain top talent and to perpetuate success, managers need to take the lead in championing successful diversity programs in the workplace.

THE PERSONAL SIDE

168

Cross-Cultural Management

Now that advances in technology, such as the Internet, have made world business just a click away, managers need to become skilled in global management. Global management recognizes that workers from different cultures exhibit different behaviors. The role of the global managers is to understand the cultures that affect their companies to help their workers understand these different cultures and behaviors for the purpose of creating a more effective workplace.

The following are some examples of what the global manager may need to learn.

- Many cultures do not like to say "no" or do not express it as directly as Americans do. Managers will need to understand when they are being told "no" in a fashion so polite that it may sound like "maybe" or even "yes." They will also need to learn to say "no" themselves in a manner that does not come off as rude.
- A tendency toward personal ingratiation or toward pleasing outsiders. Ways of presenting oneself or a situation positively, or of appeasing a boss or client, may be considered appropriate in one culture but be misleading to someone from another culture.
- Pressure for social desirability. Other cultures may emphasize behaviors that meet social norms regardless of the individuals' agreement with those norms.

Doing business across cultures is not easy. To succeed at being a global manager you must educate your staff to:

- Keep an open mind when dealing with a multinational team.
- Accept that people are different and encourage them to speak about these differences.
- Learn and appreciate the strengths each member has.
- Recognize that in dealing with cultures there are no right or wrong perspectives, just differences.

Being a global manager implies that you have, in addition to the skills needed for domestic management, the ability to bridge the gap between different cultures. Success depends upon your belief that different attitudes and behaviors bring new opportunities and your ability to foster this belief in others.

Must-Have Company Policies

The employee handbook should present company policies. It is a reference guide that clarifies benefits and procedures. However, manuals provide only summary information. The manager remains the best source of information for the employee and he or she should therefore be thoroughly familiar with company policies and benefits. If you also have the responsibility of determining what these will be, here are some guidelines:

Overtime Pay

The Industrial Wage Commission and Federal Labor Standards Act defines overtime based upon the employee's regular rate of pay. Overtime pay is usually 150 percent of the regular rate for hours worked in excess of eight hours per day, or forty hours per week, and is 200 percent of the regular rate for hours worked in excess of twelve hours per day. Flexible work schedules usually waive overtime requirements, although some shifts may be worked only in accordance with state laws. Non-productive hours, such as vacation or sick time, do not count as hours used for overtime purposes.

Categories of Employment

Companies hire full- and part-time employees depending on their needs and on the employee's choice of work commitments. Be sure to discuss assigned work hours and relevant benefit plans with each employee.

Paydays and Pay Periods

While some companies prefer a biweekly payday resulting in 26 pay periods annually, others may elect bimonthly paydays. It is important for the employer to provide a schedule of the pay periods in advance so that the employee can plan accordingly.

Time Cards and Time Clocks

Federal and state laws require that an employer keep accurate records of time worked for employees. While some businesses rely on time cards, others expect the employee to keep track of time spent on various assigned duties. Time cards, when used, must be signed. Most organizations will view tampering with time cards as grounds for immediate suspension and possible termination.

Bereavement Leave

Company policy usually entitles employees who have completed an introductory period to bereavement leave. This is a paid leave of absence of three to five days, taken after the death of a parent, step-parent, spouse, domestic partner, child, step-child, sibling, parent-in-law, legal guardian, legal ward, grandparent, grandchild or other member of the employee's immediate family. Supervisors have the ability to grant bereavement leave upon the deaths of other family members as well. Employees are usually allowed to extend bereavement leave by using sick or vacation days.

Holidays and Personal Days

Companies may give their employees holidays off as part of a paid-leave accrual system or as an automatic part of the benefit package. Some companies allow employees to work on holidays and then compensate them with overtime pay or additional vacation days. In addition to paid holidays, some companies will allow personal days so that employees may take time off to celebrate individual holidays or events. On the average, companies allow seven paid holidays and three to four paid personal days a year. Those businesses that do not recognize personal days may give more generous vacation packages.

Jury Duty

Companies should allow employees time off for jury duty with pay. Full-time employees are usually allowed a maximum of 80 hours in a 12-month period. Grand jury service is a long-term commitment and allowing an employee to participate will depend on department needs.

Vacation Time and Sick Time

Vacation time can be granted up front as part of a benefit package or earned as part of a paid-leave plan. The number of annual vacation days often depends on salary grade and years employed. Similarly, some companies require employees to accrue sick time, while others start with an allowable number of sick days annually. Companies may also give "well days" or grant bonuses for sick days not used. Many employers will allow payment for unused vacation days. However, state laws govern the way employees are compensated for such unused time, and a manager needs to be familiar with the applicable regulations.

Education and Training

Most companies will have a budget set aside for training and some will offer compensation for education related to job activities. The manager is ultimately responsible for determining the educational and training needs of his or her workers and budgeting for them. The employee must be able to offer a sound proposal about the benefit that additional training and or education will offer to the company.

Medical Leave of Absence

Employees are granted medical leave for serious illnesses, as defined by law. The leave usually begins on the eighth consecutive day of illness and cannot exceed a defined limit, usually 16 weeks per 12-month period. If the employee's serious illness becomes a disability as defined by law, the employer must make reasonable accommodations for the disability if these would allow the employee to return to work.

Family Leave

The law allows an employee to take 16 weeks of leave in a 12-month period to provide care for a child, legal spouse, or parent. Family leave can be combined with pregnancy disability, but the total cannot exceed 28 weeks in a 12-month period.

170

Insurance and Employee Benefits

Medical and dental insurance may be offered to employees as pre-tax contributions. Many companies will allow the employee to waive medical coverage with minimal reimbursement or some type of credit to salary. Many companies offer more than one type of medical coverage, such as membership in a preferred provider organization (PPO) or a health maintenance organization (HMO). The manager should understand the company's benefits and be able to explain the differences to employees.

Other types of benefits that may be offered include life insurance, personal accident insurance, and long-term disability. These benefits are usually offered at the employer's expense, with the employee contributing only if above-normal coverage is desired. Optional spousal and family life and disability insurance may be offered as well. Some companies offer employee stock plans, retirement plans, and tax shelters as well. A manager must be able to explain the benefit package in detail to any prospective employee.

Employee Retirement Plans—Vesting

Many companies offer retirement plans to their employees. The Employee Retirement Income Security Act of 1974 (ERISA) is the most important legislation concerning private employee retirement plans (see tip #266). This act was prompted by cases of employees who had contributed to a retirement plan for many years, only to find that they had nothing when they retired. This is exactly what happened when Studebaker closed in 1963 and left more than 8,500 employees without any retirement benefits.

Vesting Requirements

The law establishes vesting requirements and guarantees that plan participants will receive some retirement benefits after a reasonable length of employment. Notice that the law does not define the amount that will be received or define a reasonable length of employment. The law does state that all full-time employees over the age of 25 who have worked for a company for one year are eligible for participation in the employee benefit plan. This means that if an employee is fired or quits after one year, he or she does not lose all retirement benefits.

ERISA also established mandatory vesting, in which an employee becomes the owner of retirement proceeds. The percent of vesting is the percentage of the total retirement funds set aside for an employee that he or she is entitled to receive at a given time. Employers have three options:

1. They can provide 100 percent vesting after ten years of employment.
2. They can provide 25 percent vesting after five years, then five percent additional vesting per year for five more years.
3. They can provide vesting under the "rule of 45." Under this rule, if the age and years of service of the employee total 45, or if an employee has 10 years of service, there must be at least 50 percent vesting. Each additional year of service then provides 10 percent more vesting, so that the employee is fully vested within 15 years.

You must understand what retirement provisions are available to you. Ask questions regarding the plan and your options. Make sure you understand the vesting plan your company has adopted. If you will be 50 percent vested after five years of employment, you would not want to leave your job after 4.5 years of employment to take another position. It might be better to stay the additional six months so you will be entitled to 50 percent of your retirement funds.

The amount that is not vested will be turned over to the plan and be distributed to the accounts of the other members of the plan after you leave. You would then lose your right to the remaining funds in your retirement account. When you leave your place of employment you can transfer your vested amount into another plan at your new employer or to an IRA rollover account. If you take out the retirement funds, you will be taxed on the funds as income for that year.

Don't make the mistake of ignoring your retirement benefits—you will regret it in the future!

Types of Retirement Plans

You need to start your retirement planning sooner or later, and the sooner you begin, the more your funds will grow with time. Do you know what type of retirement plan your employer has adopted? Do you understand your options and benefits? You need to ask these questions and find out what retirement coverage you have. You may have to sign up to participate in the plan. You also may have the options of putting additional funds into your retirement plan. Often your employer will match this amount in whole or in part. The funds you put into your plan give you an additional tax deduction, and interest compounds tax-free.

Your employer may offer a pension plan, a 401(k), or a 403(b), all of which either put away a specified amount or up to a maximum percentage of each employee's earnings for retirement each year. If your employer provides a 401(k) or 403(b) plan, you can make what are usually voluntary pretax contributions to the plan and management may match the amounts deposited in whole or in part.

If your employer provides a pension plan, a profit-sharing plan may also be available. A profit-sharing plan allows up to 15 percent of your salary, or a specified maximum dollar amount that may be less than 15 percent, to be placed in your retirement plan. Management can vary the amount each year according to the company's profits. It may be that no deposits are made in a bad year. As with the pension plan, the same percentage must be contributed for all employees, including owners. Sometimes a company will also match voluntary contributions to your plan.

The funds may be managed by a retirement fund investment committee in-house, by an outside fund manager, or may be self-directed by each employee. You should receive annual reports stating the actual amount that you have in the plan. These funds should be left alone until you retire. Profits that accrue each year are not taxed. The funds are, however, taxed when you take them out of the plan.

By law, if you take any funds out of your retirement plan before age 59, tax penalties will apply. Most retirees begin taking out funds at age 65 either in a lump sum or in annual payments. You will be taxed on the funds you take out at a rate proportional to your income that year; therefore, it is frequently better to take out smaller annual payments.

173 Cafeteria Plans

Does your business offer a selection of health care coverage? If so, it may include a so-called *cafeteria plan* as a choice. A cafeteria plan allows each employee to be paid an amount specified by the employer, which can be applied toward health care expenses. How much of this amount to spend and how to spend it is up to each employee. The funds can go toward medical insurance or expenses, dental care, disability insurance, life insurance, and adult and child care. The amount spent on these expenses is not taxed as income. Any of the funds not spent on health care will be taxed as income.

Why would you as an employee prefer a flexible cafeteria benefit plan to other health care plans and a dental care plan? What are the benefits to the business of providing a cafeteria plan? By offering a fixed sum for health care, the employer avoids having to offer several health plan options, a dental plan, a life insurance policy, disability insurance, or child care funds or facilities. This can amount to substantial savings. The crucial questions for the employee are how the sum provided by the cafeteria plan compares to the employee's actual health care costs, and how they compare to that of a flexible healthplan.

Understanding Employee Stock Ownership Plans

174

Employee stock ownership plans (ESOPs) are designed to distribute the ownership of a corporation into the hands of employees. There are estimated to be more than 10,000 ESOPs in the U.S., involving more than 10 million employees. ESOPs grew largely from the observation that having a stake in ownership of a company serves as a strong motivator for the employees. Why are employees motivated by ESOPs? An employee with an average income may be able to acquire hundreds of thousands of dollars in stock!

In addition to motivating employees, ESOPs also provide potentially significant tax and financial advantages. They typically operate through a trust that distributes tax-deductible contributions from the company to the employee participants. ESOPs also enjoy special benefits in regard to borrowing money and are often used as a method for corporate finance.

If a few major shareholders run a business, the future of the business is a major concern when a prominent owner retires. In such a closely held company, an ESOP purchases shares from the retiring shareholder and subsequently distributes them to the employees. The retiring owner may receive certain tax advantages on stock sold to the ESOP.

Establishing an ESOP is a fairly involved process, and the needs of a small, privately held organization will be different than those of a larger corporation. Consultants specializing in the creation of ESOPs offer advice tailored to the circumstances and desires of each corporation. More information can be obtained from the ESOP Association:

www.the-esop-emplowner.org

175 Managing Payroll

If you are responsible for managing the payroll, you must be familiar with all the relevant federal and state tax obligations. As an employer, you must pay the taxes and file supporting documentation that show how the taxes were computed. You must also have a federal employer identification number.

The following are your federal tax liabilities:

- Federal income tax
- Employee Social Security tax
- Employee Medicare
- Employer's Social Security contribution
- Employer's Medicare contribution

For federal income tax, Social Security, and Medicare, it is the employer's obligation to accurately calculate and deduct the sums and pay them to the federal government on time. Employers also contribute a portion of the Social Security and Medicare taxes. Again, it is the employer's responsibility to be sure that the entire tax is paid regardless of the amount actually withheld from the employee.

Income taxes and Social Security and Medicare taxes are due semiweekly or on a monthly basis. They can be deposited with a bank or financial institution that is authorized to accept federal tax deposits or with the Federal Reserve Bank. The federal government has a lookback period to determine whether you must pay semiweekly or monthly. If you paid $50,000 or less in taxes during the lookback period, you can make your tax deposits monthly. Otherwise, the deposits must be made semiweekly. There are strict rules governing when these taxes must be paid in relation to your company's payday. If these payments are not made on time or are lower than the amount due, you may be assessed a penalty. Mandated electronic payment began for certain employers on January 1, 1997.

The federal government provides formulas for the amount of income tax to be deducted from an employee's pay. The Federal Insurance Contributions Act mandates that you collect the Social Security tax, which for 1998 was 6.2 percent of an employee's gross wage for both employee and employer (for a total of 12.4 percent), and the Medicare tax, which was 1.45 percent for both employee and employer (for a total of 2.9 percent). If an employee earns more than $68,400 there is no further Social Security tax. The Medicare tax has no upper limit.

The employer is also responsible for the Federal Unemployment Tax (FUTA). This tax funds the federal unemployment program and cannot be taken out of an employee's wages.

If one of the following conditions are met, the tax obligation begins on January 1 of that year:

- One or more persons are employed, for at least part of a day, in each of 20 or more calendar weeks during the current or preceding taxable year, or
- Wages of $1,500 or more are paid during any calendar quarter in the current or preceding calendar year.

FUTA taxes are usually due on a quarterly basis (use an 8109 coupon to pay them) unless your FUTA tax liability is $100 or less. If this is the situation, you can carry it forward and add it to your FUTA liability for the next quarter until the total exceeds $100. If there is unpaid liability of $100 or less at the end of the year, you can either deposit the tax or send it with your annual return.

This overview of tax obligations may not provide all the information you need. Seeking advice from legal and accounting professionals is always a good idea.

176

Keeping Payroll Records

After providing the government with all required reports and forms, you also must keep your own copy of records. The federal government requires that records be kept a minimum of four years. Most states have similar laws but Minnesota, for example, requires that records be maintained for eight years.

Information that should be stored for each employee includes:

- Name
- Address
- Social security number
- Date and amount of wages paid
- Period of time the wages cover and the portion of wages that were taxable
- Copies of the W-4 form
- Dates and amounts of tax deposits
- Copies of returns that were filed
- Copies of any W-2 forms that were not distributed.

Surprisingly, the various governmental agencies do not specify a format for keeping these records. The records must, however, give tax agencies enough information to allow them to determine if the correct amount of taxes were paid, and, if not, what amount should have been paid. These records must be easily accessible, available to the agencies at all times, and stored in a convenient and safe place.

Meeting Payroll— Rules, Regulations, and Deadlines

If you manage payroll and taxes, there are certain obligations you must meet. Not only do you have to make deposits on time but you must also use and file the correct forms on time. Example of these forms are:

- Form 8109-940: Deposit of Unemployment Taxes
- Form 940: Quarterly Federal Unemployment Tax Return
- Form 941: Quarterly Federal Tax Return
- Form 1096: Annual Summary and Transmittal of U.S. Information Returns
- Form 8027: Employer's Annual Information Return of Tip Income and Allocated Tips; if required, Form 8027-T Transmittal
- Form W-2: Wage and Tax Statement
- Form W-3: Transmittal of Income and Tax Statements, to be filed with form W-2 (copy A)

After meeting all filing obligations, you also have a reporting obligation to your employees. They must be told their total taxable compensation for the year and the amount that was withheld from their salary for federal, state, and other taxes. The W-2 form is the acceptable method for reporting this information. You must give these forms to each employee who worked for you during the calendar year, by a date no later than January 31 of the next calendar year. If employees are terminated before the end of the year they may ask to receive a W-2 form sooner. You have 30 days from the date of the request to provide the form. The government requires that you file a copy of the W-2s of all employees with the Social Security Administration by the end of February of the following calendar year using form W-3.

The Personal Responsibility and Work Opportunity Reconciliation Act of 1996 (see tip #270) took effect on October 1, 1997. It requires employers to report all new employees to the appropriate state agency within 20 days of employment. The states will use the information to help locate parents for child support payments and to identify others who might have filed fraudulent worker's compensation and unemployment claims.

LABOR MANAGEMENT

178

Deciding to Use Payroll Services

Each year the rules and regulations for payroll taxes become more and more complicated. Consequently, the costs of payroll processing are climbing yearly. If one of your duties is the supervision of payroll, it might be worth the effort to compare the costs and benefits of processing payroll in-house and outsourcing the work. Consider the following aspects of each option:

Doing It Yourself

- You can use either a manual process or a software program. (Calculate the cost of the software.)
- Someone must calculate wages, payroll deductions, and payroll tax obligations.
- Checks have to be written.
- Payroll information must be recorded and maintained.
- Taxes must be filed.
- W-2 forms must be prepared and filed.
- You must keep track of tax deposit dates to avoid penalties.
- Consider the amount of time you or your employees spend preparing the payroll.

Outsourcing

- By handling this task for you, payroll services allow you to concentrate on your business.
- They keep abreast of current tax law rules and regulations.
- They can prepare W-2 forms quickly and accurately and provide them to the employees.
- They increase the confidentiality of payroll information.
- They provide quick turnaround after receiving payroll information.
- They can provide additional services, such as handling payments into retirement plans and direct deposits of checks.

- Some firms will pay the penalties incurred if they make any errors in processing your payroll.
- If you outsource the handling of retirement funds and the money disappears, your company is still financially responsible.

Ultimately, the decision whether to manage payroll yourself or outsource it depends on the size and resources of your firm. Many organizations feel that they are not in the business of managing payroll and prefer to leave the task to a specialized service. Large companies, however, are likely to have the internal resources to run their own payroll division.

179

Labor Laws

The National Labor Relations Act allows employees to organize into unions. Since its passage, supervisors have learned to work with union employees and their representatives. The National Labor Relations Act, also referred to as the Wagner Act, comes under the jurisdiction of the National Labor Relations Board. The NLRB is an independent federal agency created by Congress in 1935 to enforce employee rights to:

- Self-organize
- Form, join, or aid unions
- Bargain collectively for wages, hours, and working conditions
- Engage in activities for mutual protection
- Refrain from any of these activities

The Taft-Hartley Act of 1947 amended the Wagner Act by clarifying and increasing the list of unfair practices against management. The act forbade unions from certain activities. For example, they cannot:

- Force employers to discriminate against or terminate unpopular union members
- Force employers to pay money for services not performed
- Force employees to join or not to join a union
- Charge excessive fees to discourage union participation
- Discourage employees from bargaining directly with management, providing that any settlement does not violate the union contract

The Taft-Hartley Act, also called the Labor-Management Relations Act, clearly protects both management and labor unions. In addition to ensuring rights for employers and employees alike, it permits activities such as 60-day notice of contract termination, an 80-day injunction should a dispute endanger the health and safety of the nation, and the right of either party to sue for damages. Labor laws provide the legal framework for management to work with union employees. Managers willing to work collaboratively with union representatives will become more effective with their staff, as well.

Modern Labor Laws

The Taft-Hartley Act (see tip #179) outlawed the closed shop, which forced workers to join a union to be hired. Likewise, the act allowed states to pass laws making the union shop illegal. The union shop differed from the closed shop in that the former allowed for a trial period of 30 or 60 days before requiring workers to join the union.

Many states have enacted right-to-work laws that make forced membership in a union illegal. Today either open or agency shops are the norm for union organization. In an open shop, participation and payment are not required. In an agency shop, all employees pay union dues, but they are not required to join the union.

Another important labor law is the Fair Labor Standards Act. Also known as the Wages and Hours Law, it sets the minimum wage, describes conditions for overtime pay, and addresses employment of children for companies engaged in interstate commerce. It also defines exempt and nonexempt employees, especially as this status relates to paid overtime.

The Walsh-Healey Public Contracts Act addresses standards for safety and health, establishes a minimum wage, and discusses child labor for companies that work on government contracts in excess of $10,000.

The Labor Management Reporting and Disclosure Act, also known as the Landrum-Griffith Act, requires employers to report payments to:

- Labor representatives when the payments are not related to work performed
- Outside consultants on labor union issues
- Employees when the payments are not related to work performed but are related to union matters

The law also requires that unions disclose the sources and disbursement of their funds. Any payments for reimbursed expenses must be reported as well. It is the intent of the law to prevent unethical collusion between the company and labor union as well as to prevent misuse of union funds.

Labor laws help define the framework in which management and labor unions should function. It is the supervisor's responsibility to become familiar with these laws so that he or she can be sure to operate within them.

181

Contract
Administration

Managers play key roles in the implementation of labor contracts. They must maintain positive relationships with union representatives while protecting the rights of management. Their interactions with staff may have vital consequences in terms of the relationship between management and union. Managers, therefore, must be well acquainted with the labor practices of the company and should follow procedures as outlined. Inconsistent or unfair practices by a manager could result in consequences that reach far beyond his or her department or even the company. Potentially, the employer could be charged with breaking the labor contract or even breaking the law.

The Wagner Act (see tip #179), which prohibits unfair labor practices, clearly defines pitfalls for the manager to avoid when interacting with employees. The most frequent charges filed against managers are interference and discrimination.

Interference is a danger during union organization drives or elections. At these times, managers should avoid all actions that affect employees' jobs or pay. Supervisors should take care that any interaction with union officers is in line with senior management direction. Finally, supervisors should avoid arguments over union questions or the appearance of threats directed toward union representatives.

Discrimination applies to any action management takes against an employee as retaliation for that employee's union membership. These actions include termination, demotion, or reassignment to a more undesirable type of work. What the manager must do is avoid negative talk about the union or union members. Remember that nothing is off the record and that a manager who socializes with employees after work must not express any negative feelings about the union. A manager who evaluates his or her staff solely on ability, performance, and attitude, and not on union activities, will be safeguarding his or her company against a serious charge of discriminatory behavior under the Wagner Act.

Union stewards have the authority to let the manager know how the labor contract limits his or her actions. The steward's job is to protect the rights of the union members. The manager must protect the rights of management. While the two will and should never co-manage employees, the manager's job will be made easier if he or she tries to cooperate with the union steward on labor contract issues. A manager who appears genuinely interested and fosters a constructive approach to problem solving with the union steward will do much to improve working relationships between union and management.

182

Understanding Employee Rights

Today it is expected that a good manager will understand employee rights when handling sensitive issues such as privacy, drug testing, and AIDS.

The legal right to privacy at work varies from state to state. However, in general employees are entitled to know what information is contained in their personnel files, and employers are prohibited from obtaining confidential information about their staff. Examples of activities viewed as an invasion of employee privacy are:

- Recording or monitoring of an employee's telephone conversations without his or her knowledge or consent
- Enlisting the aid of an outsider to validate an employee's absence or off-the-job behavior
- Searching an employee's workspace for information unrelated to work
- Commenting on the employee's work performance to someone outside the company without the consent of the employee

Testing for drug use is only acceptable if it can be clearly demonstrated that the test is meant to protect customers from damage or theft or to protect employees from harm. Companies are encouraged to have a written policy on the use of drug testing, and it is the managers' responsibility to educate and enforce such a policy.

Legally, employees' right to privacy concerning the sensitive issue of AIDS is still uncertain. Managers must rely on company policy when dealing with employees who have AIDS or are HIV-positive. A prudent manager will also become familiar with the various statutes that address AIDS and follow them carefully.

There is a strong body of law that protects the rights of employees (see tips #179 and #180). Sometimes supervisors feel that these laws make managing difficult, but they must remember that they maintain the right to manage. Managers must deal consistently and fairly with employees whose performance is unsatisfactory. They must also keep in mind the importance of the equal employment opportunity laws. Awareness of the laws and excellent managerial skills will win the respect of employees and help the manager retain his or her right to manage.

What Constitutes an Employee?

Did you know that there are two categories of employees, *common-law* and *statutory*? It is important to know which classification covers your employees, since different tax and withholding rules apply to each.

Common-law employees are any employees who perform services that you, as the employer, assign and define. A statutory employee is an employee who works for you but does not meet the common-law rules for federal withholding tax. Examples of statutory employees are officers of corporations who render nominal or minor services and receive no compensation, agents or commission drivers, full-time life insurance salespeople, home workers, and traveling salespeople.

The Fair Labor Standards Act (FLSA) is a federal law that sets two other categories for classifying employees and provides certain employee protections. The law regulates minimum wages, overtime pay, equal pay, record keeping, child labor, and handling of tips. The Department of Labor is responsible for the FLSA, administers the regulations and interpretations of the act, and monitors compliance.

There are certain employees who may be exempt from parts of this act, such as executives, administrators, professionals, computer software professionals and outside sales personnel. The FLSA has two lists of requirements, called the "Short Test" and the "Long Test," that determine whether the employee qualifies for the exemption. These requirements deal with the primary duties and authority of the employee and other aspects of his or her job.

Exempt employees are normally required by their jobs to use discretionary judgment, spend at least 80 percent of their time working on their exempt duties, and receive their full salary each pay period. They are exempt from the minimum wage and overtime requirements of the FLSA.

Minimum wage laws apply to nonexempt employees. They are also entitled to 150 percent of the normal pay rate for all hours worked over 40 hours within one work week. Nonexempt employees cannot give up their rights to overtime pay.

184

Employment Categories

Employees are categorized in order to make sure they receive the proper wages and benefits mandated by law. Federal, state, and local laws define the statutory benefits employees must receive. Managers should know all the categories and benefits associated with each type of classification.

Full-Time Employees

- Work a designated number of hours
- Receive statutory benefits (benefits mandated by federal, state, and local law)
- Are eligible if the company has fringe benefits

Part-Time Employees

- Work a designated number of hours each week
- Receive fringe benefits as determined by company policy
- Receive statutory benefits

Seasonal Employees

- Work a specified number of hours
- Perform a specific job
- Receive statutory benefits only, unless company policy states differently

Per Diem Employees

- Work on an as-needed basis only
- Receive statutory benefits only, unless company policy states differently

Managers should avoid using the term "temporary employee" because this might imply that all other employees are permanent. This in turn could cause problems with an employment-at-will relationship.

What Constitutes an Independent Contractor?

185

As a manager, why would you want to hire an independent contractor? The answer is that there may be substantial payroll savings in doing so. Independent contractors do not receive company benefits like pension plans, health insurance, life insurance, worker's compensation insurance, paid vacations, holidays, or retirement plans. In addition, Social Security, Medicare, unemployment insurance, and state and local taxes do not have to be paid for these employees and none of the forms associated with theses taxes have to be filed. The only tax form needed is the 1099-MISC form, which must be filed if the independent contractor received more than $600 in one year.

The question of whether someone is an employee or an independent contractor usually depends on the control over the person's performance. An employee receives direction from an employer while an independent contractor determines this direction on his or her own. Independent contractors usually have special education, licensing, experience, or skills for a particular job. They provide what is needed to get the job done, even if it means they must hire more help. There is normally a contract between the employer and independent contractor. Therefore any disputes are governed by contract law.

Independent contractors are responsible for paying their own payroll taxes. There is a 20-factor test that the IRS uses to determine if an employee is an employee or an independent contractor. Form SS-8 may be helpful in determining the employee's status. For more information, explore the IRS web page at www.irs.gov.

The Fair Labor Standards Act has its own test to determine whether someone is an independent contractor. Both the IRS and FLSA requirements should be satisfied. If you intentionally misclassify an employee, stiff penalties could be incurred; if you do so unintentionally, penalties are not as severe. Congress has established safe harbors to help employers who have misclassified employees. This is an area in which you may need professional help from your attorney and accountant.

If you have any doubts on how to classify a worker, classify him or her as an employee. Also, remember that people who work for independent contractors are employees of the contractor, not your employees.

LABOR MANAGEMENT

186

Using Temporary Employees

It is estimated that up to 98 percent of businesses use temporary workers at some time. Managers are responsible for establishing guidelines for using temporary workers and for establishing relationships with reputable temporary staffing agencies.

Temporary staffing is appropriate for a special project or a position that has a high turnover. If your business is experiencing an unusually busy period, you may want to use temporary employees to ease the extra workload. Or you may just want to take advantage of trying out an employee before you commit to long-term employment.

When selecting a firm to assist you with your temporary staffing needs, there are several key questions to ask:

What is the recruitment strategy? Does the agency use employee referrals, newspaper or radio advertisements, or recruitment techniques at technical schools or community programs? Recruitment strategies determine the applicant pool the agency has.

Does the agency conduct preliminary interviews? It should screen applicants for skills and attitude.

Does the agency pay a visit to your business to determine company needs and to view processes? Site visits can help the agency better prepare applicants for the job.

Will the agency make recommendations and evaluations? Based upon the preliminary interview and the needs of your business, the agency should be able to match the right applicant to your staffing need.

What type of billing procedure is offered? Most agencies will prepare statements on a weekly basis and expect payment within a negotiated time period, usually 30 days. The statement should include employee name, standard hours worked, overtime hours, standard pay rate, and standard billing rate.

What is the policy on permanent hiring and on benefits offered? Know what can be expected if you should choose to hire the employee permanently. If the agency offers a competitive benefit package, it demonstrates commitment to employees and in return will receive greater loyalty.

Building a relationship with a quality temporary staffing agency can ensure that you have dependable temporary workers available when needed.

Employee Retention

It is costly to hire and train new employees. Sometimes, however, it is cheaper in the long run to replace an employee who is not performing up to his or her potential. As a manager, you must make sure that you let employees know what you expect of them, and you must let them know when their performance is not up to par. You must document these evaluations; otherwise, firing an employee, regardless of his or her incompetence, can leave you open to legal action.

The first and most important step in keeping good employees is hiring them. Make sure you use an interview process and application forms that tell you as much as possible about the prospective employee while keeping within the guidelines for non-discrimination (see tip #147). Check references personally, especially previous employers. You may obtain very helpful information. Ask "Would you hire this person again?" Sometimes what isn't said is as important as what is said. For example, if you inquire about the prospective employee's abilities with customers, and the reply is "She didn't fight too often with them," then they may be giving you a valuable clue to the candidate's personality.

Also, be sure that both you and the new employee understand the job description, salary, and benefits. An employee who begins a job unhappy will never be happy in that job. You must develop a mutual trust with the employee, and your actions must demonstrate this trust and respect. If the employee feels that you do not trust or value him or her, you will not have a long-term employee.

Find out what benefits are most desired by your new employee. Your employee may want time to go back to school, time off to care for small children or elderly parents, or the ability to work at home sometimes. If your company allows some flexibility in work hours and times, you may retain valuable employees who would otherwise leave.

If you show your employees that you care about them, and review their performance regularly, you stand a much better chance of retaining them. When you give them projects, it is sometimes better not to dictate how every step should be handled. Let them work out the details; just make sure that they are making progress, and give them help when they request it. Finally, show your appreciation for a job well done or for a valuable employee. A simple thank you, or formal recognition in front of other employees, will go a long way in keeping an employee happy.

188

Employee Compensation

How is your salary determined? Most employees are paid using traditional job-based pay systems. Other systems of compensation include skill-based pay, broad banding with salary ranges (also called pay grades), team-based pay, variable compensation, and executive compensation.

The traditional system determines the knowledge, ability, and skills necessary for the job. Each job is then ranked relative to other jobs in the organization. The traditional system has several problems, including the unspoken message to lower-paid employees that they aren't being paid to think. Also, since the pay is tied to a specific job, managers have less flexibility in using the work force.

Skill-based pay gives workers an incentive to improve their skills in order to increase their pay. This system allows more flexibility in using employees where they are most needed. With a broader range of skills, the employee also has greater job security.

Broad banding refers to the use of salary bands or pay grades. There is a salary range within each band, allowing employees to receive pay raises without promotions.

Team-based pay rewards members of a team for reaching their shared goals. This tends to aid cooperation among team members and is common for research and development teams.

Variable compensation links a portion of the employee's wages to performance measurements. It may mean the use of bonuses or the reduction of base pay by making it at-risk. This form of compensation ties the employees' wages to the company's profits or losses. It gives the company better control of labor costs. Xerox and Westinghouse are among the companies that use this system.

Executive compensation may be the most crucial factor in tying strategy to performance. Whatever approach the organization rewards in the top executive positions will filter down into the approach the entire organization takes.

Employee compensation systems can set the tone for the organization. Employees can be encouraged to solve problems, develop a broader range of skills, improve company performance, decrease labor costs and increase competitiveness, or efficiently operate as teams. Does your organization use this tool to improve company performance?

Forecasting Workforce Requirements

The size of the workforce you need depends upon the nature of the work, work schedules, unplanned absences, anticipated time off, and vacations. To estimate the necessary workforce for a given period of time, you can use sophisticated time studies and labor standards, but a good prediction can be achieved with the help of some simple math.

The first step is to evaluate what the expected workload or production is for the next week, month, quarter, or year if possible. Next, you will need to determine what the work schedule means in terms of total worker-hours. Sometimes these estimates are available from the various departments in the company; otherwise, you will have to make your own estimates. To do so, record the time required for each job or check the average time spent on similar jobs. Make sure to take into account startup times, breakdown times, and other delays.

Total these times, convert them to worker-hours, and divide the figure by eight hours. The result is the number of worker-days it will take to complete the workload for the period selected. To find out how many employees you will need, divide the number of worker-days by the number of working days during the given period.

Next, include your indirect workers, such as housekeeping employees. Adding these indirect employees to the direct number will give you the total number of employees needed on the workforce for that period.

This figure is not final, however, until you consider absences. On the average, how many days do your employees miss each month? If you run a large department, this number could be substantial. If, for example, these absences approach 15 worker-days per month, you may need even more help during this period.

Even if you are careful and adhere to a well-thought-out forecast of workforce needs, you can fall prey to a shortage of employees when unpredictable absences or production emergencies occur. One way to ensure that you do not overstaff or understaff is to pool the workforce estimates for each manager. In this way, you will maintain an workforce of optimum size as a cushion against unforeseen occurrences.

The term "workforce balancing" refers to the matching of employees to the workload. All companies will experience waning and waxing of their workforce needs. When mismatches are measured in hours or days, the discrepancy usual doesn't affect the success of the business. However, when these shortages or abundances of employees add up to weeks or more, they are costly and inefficient. Using the tools of forecasting, based on the manager's knowledge of the job and the worker-hours needed to complete it, will help you to balance the workforce and produce a more efficient and productive department or company.

Markov Analysis

Do you know how to forecast your employee needs for the future? How many employees will be available to promote, how many will leave for other employment, and how many will retire? Being able to plan your staffing will improve performance and morale, since vacancies will be very short-lived. You can do this using Markov analysis. While determining the data for the Markov model can be somewhat difficult, the model is relatively easy to understand, and the results can be very useful.

The model takes the distribution of employees across various jobs at a certain time and changes it into a forecasted distribution at a designated future time. The main weakness of Markov analysis is that it is inaccurate with a small number of employees. Also, a baseline of three to five years should be used to provide more stable data. The model also assumes that conditions such as downsizing have not occurred to affect the data. Markov analysis is used mainly for predicting supply but it can also forecast future demand for employees.

As a human resource tool, Markov analysis can determine the flow of employees in and out of the organization, including the flow of minorities and females. This can be very useful for affirmative action programs. An organization can adjust promotion and termination rates using Markov analysis to achieve the desired distribution of employees.

The Weyerhaeuser Company first developed this model during a growth phase to forecast the number of employees available for the internal labor supply. Since the forecast was that the supply would fall short, the company instituted training programs to qualify current employees for the positions where shortages were forecast. Later, a recession meant Weyerhaeuser needed to reduce the number of employees. Information obtained from a Markov analysis revealed that the company could achieve its goal within 15 months through attrition and that layoffs were unnecessary.

Markov analysis is a powerful tool for forecasting employee supply and demand, but it can be fairly complicated and is usually left to specialists in a human resource department.

191 Employee Demand Forecasting

Along with those already discussed, employee demand forecasting methods include:

- The rule of thumb approach, which relies on simple guidelines a company develops internally.
- The heuristics method, which forecasts needs using conceptual diagrams based on previous guidelines. An example might be opening a new store using the same number and positions of employees as an existing store.
- The Delphi technique, which involves a judgment based on expert opinion. This qualitative method does not require historical data and is almost as accurate as a quantitative method.
- Operations research and management science techniques, which are expensive and take into account various factors such as training requirements, or the time in a position necessary for promotion. Complicated computer programs are necessary.
- Regression analysis, which is a complex technique for forecasting demand used mainly by organizations with large human relations departments.

Table 7, on the following page, shows the percentage of companies studied that use various demand forecasting techniques.

Table 7
Usage of Demand Forecasting Techniques

Demand Forecasting Techniques	Percent of Companies Using Technique
Succession planning or replacement charts	66.7
Personnel (HR) inventories	66.7
Supervisor estimates	48.5
Rules of thumb or non-statistical formulas	27.3
Computer simulation	12.1
Renewal models	9.1
Regression analysis	7.6
Markov or network flow models	6.1
Exponential smoothing or trend analysis	6.1
Operations research techniques	4.5

From C. Greer, D. Jackson, and J. Fiorito, "Adapting Human Resource Planning in a Changing Business Environment," *Human Resource Management, Vol. 28, 1:110, 1989.*

192

Employee Supply Forecasting

Employee supply and demand forecasting is essential to prevent either an oversupply or an undersupply of employees. Either situation can be detrimental to an organization.

The following are some common employee supply forecasting methods:

- Replacement charts show the organizational structure of the company and each individual occupying a managerial or professional position. The chart lists each employee's skills so that he or she can be considered for lateral or upward moves in the organization.
- Succession planning concentrates on the training and development of potential replacements as a pool rather than as individuals. This approach applies more to long-term than to short-term planning.
- Markov analysis (see tip #190) accounts for the flow of all employees in an organization.
- Renewal models are easy to understand and involve using cohorts of employees, divided, for example, by age, gender, and ethnicity. This method determines attrition rates for these cohorts and allows for planning, such as hiring and training for replacement.
- Computer simulations are becoming more popular because they present a range of future possibilities and allow the user to change the parameters of the forecast.

Some employee forecasting tools are more complicated than others. The key is to pick an approach that you are comfortable with and that enables you to adequately predict the workforce you will need.

Rewarding Employees

Do you recognize and reward outstanding employees? If you don't, you should. Everyone enjoys receiving a compliment or being acknowledged for exceptional achievement. Most employees begin with a willingness to go the extra mile for their company, but they may not repeat such efforts if they do not receive recognition. The following are events and achievements that may need special recognition.

- Superior customer service
- Increased productivity
- Meeting a deadline early
- Solving a problem
- Saving the company money
- Noteworthy length of employment or attendance record
- Retirement
- Personal successes

Recognition must be given with sincerity and thoughtfulness. Your job as manager is to make the employee feel special. The recognition can be given at your weekly presentations, a yearly awards ceremony, or, if the recognition is very special, a dinner with significant others.

Some employees do not like being in the limelight and may in fact shy away from endeavors that would bring public attention. The method of recognition should be tailored to suit both the individual and the accomplishment.

194

Choosing Employee Rewards

There are many types of rewards that can be bestowed upon employees for a job well done. Here are some ideas:

- Plaques or trophies
- Pens or watches
- Tickets to movies, plays, or sporting events
- An evening on the town
- Lottery tickets
- Cash bonuses
- Extra time off
- A weekend away
- A company picnic that includes family members
- A contribution to the employee's favorite charity
- A major vacation

If your company has a limited budget, you can still make the reward meaningful. Take the employee to lunch. Bring in something special like a cheesecake and have a few moments set aside to make a presentation recognizing the employee's accomplishments. Present a suitable gift, such as a portable radio. If there is a company magazine, make sure a photograph and/or an article appears to thank the employee. Some companies have special parking places for the employee of the month. There are many ways to thank someone; the important point is to remember the importance of doing so.

Promoting Employee Self-Esteem

Encouraging employees to be proud of their jobs and accomplishments can generate an extra amount of zeal in their work every day. The better employees feel about themselves, the better their performance and productivity will be. Surprisingly, it does not always take much for a manager to produce such results.

- The easiest, simplest, and least expensive way is to say "thank you" for a job well done or for extra time and effort put into a project.
- Listen to employees' complaints and use some of the solutions they suggest. When projects are often delayed because a copier keeps breaking down, for instance, the employee who uses it most may know whether or not it is beyond repairing.
- Allow employees to increase their skills. Send them to training courses that will further enhance their knowledge on a particular subject. A secretary may know a particular word processing system or spread sheet program, but an advanced course will not only advance his or her skills but may also save you time and money because of new efficiencies.
- When employees possess special skills, have them teach it to others.
- Some employers promote and pay for fitness programs, which can boost employee energy, health, and self-esteem.

Finally, take an interest in your employees' outside activities and be sure to compliment or congratulate them on accomplishments. Take time to celebrate the birth of a child, the completion of a marathon, or the receipt of an advanced degree.

196

Understanding the Grievance Process

A manager faces additional challenges from an employee with a grievance when a union contract exists. Fortunately, most union contracts have formal grievance procedures that provide an objective manner of dealing with employee complaints. This process helps add consistency for the manager when he or she is faced with the task of coordinating labor and personnel practices across business units.

A formal grievance process affords the employee assurance that his or her concern will be handled in a systematic and timely fashion. The grievance procedure will vary from business to business but will be written down and described in the labor contract.

An example of a formal grievance process after an employee voices a concern either to a labor steward or manager is that the manager discusses the grievance with the employee and labor steward. If the employee is still dissatisfied, then the manager's supervisor and the labor relations manager discuss the concern with the union grievance committee.

If there is still no resolution, then representatives of senior management and the labor relations manager should discuss the grievance with the union grievance committee. If necessary, senior management will also discuss the matter with the national union representative and the union grievance committee.

If there is still no resolution after these well-intended steps, then the dispute will be referred to an arbitrator for decision. Both union and management representatives should prefer to settle employee grievances among themselves rather than use an outside arbitrator. Therefore, it is advantageous for the manager to try to resolve employee conflicts quickly and successfully to avoid bringing in an outside arbitrator. However, peaceful settlement by arbitration is still more desirable than a personnel strike or a lockout.

Managers must face the reality that sometimes their decisions concerning employee grievances will be overruled by their supervisors. One reason may be that the manager did not follow company policy or acted on insufficient evidence when making the decision in question. However, another reason may be that management wants to avoid arbitration, which can lead to more difficult labor negotiations and labor contracts in the future.

Relocating Overseas

Millions of dollars are spent each year on overseas relocations. It costs a minimum of 3.5 times an average employee's salary to relocate him or her overseas. Unfortunately, about 40 percent of these transfers do not work out and the employee returns home early. Failed transfers are both costly to the company and employee, costing an estimated quarter of a million dollars, although it is much more difficult to estimate the impact on the company and its global plans.

Many companies now hire specialists to help employees prepare for international relocation. Cross-cultural training is probably the most important preparation the transferee and family can receive. Learning about the new culture and being able to accept the differences will allow you to succeed in your new environment. It is important to show respect for your host country's values and customs. Remember that what you consider correct or important may not have the valuation there. You must be cautious not to appear condescending either by actions or words, or your tenure will be doomed to failure.

The following are some tips for making overseas relocation a rewarding experience:

- Learn about your new destination.
- Explore the area and surrounding countries.
- Bring essential medications; check first to see what medications are legal.
- Learn what vaccines, injections, or medications are needed before arriving in your new country.
- Learn where to get medical help before it is needed.
- Learn if there are any special laws or rules that cannot be broken in the host country.
- Learn about the schools that are available.
- Learn about the various housing possibilities.
- Make contact with the American Embassy and discover the services it makes available.
- Learn how to communicate with the people back home via telephone, fax, or e-mail.

International experience can be a wonderful opportunity for you and your family. Be sure to take advantage of everything you can. In today's global market multicultural and multilingual employees are key employees.

198

Dealing with Relocation

Relocation is never a simple process. The costs can be personal as well as financial. If you have been offered a position that involves relocation, consider the following points:

If you are married and your spouse has a job, will your company offer spousal employment assistance? These services may include resume preparation, paying search firm fees, compensation for lost income, paying for job hunting trips, or even hiring the spouse. By meeting the needs of dual-career couples, a company can help ensure a successful transfer.

Couples with children or elderly parents face other problems. Child care, schools, or health care facilities become overriding factors in relocation decisions. Companies can provide extra financial assistance when the cost of living will be significantly higher in the new location. Allowing families to bring older children along on house-hunting trips can ease the burden of starting new schools, making new friends, and becoming part of a new community.

Home ownership poses other problems. Will your company help you sell your present home? Will they buy it from you if you are not successful in selling it? Will they help make up the difference in price if the housing markets are not similar? Are selling costs covered, including brokers' fees, escrow, or inspections? What closing costs are covered? Is a mortgage assistance program available? How long will the company pay for temporary housing until your new residence is ready and will they pay for a trip back to close on your old home? What moving expenses will they cover?

Will the company provide a lump-sum relocation allowance? This means the company makes a single payment for all expenses, and the employee decides how the money will be spent. Or will the company want expense reports and receipts for the move?

Does your company have a temporary relocation assistance plan for employees who will be moving on a temporary basis and will still maintain their own residences? What arrangements can be negotiated if the transfer does not work out, if the company is sold or downsized, or if the transferred employee leaves the new position within the first 12 months?

These are just some of the questions you should investigate before accepting a new position requiring relocating. Companies vary in their policies, but they all want the relocation process to go as smoothly and quickly as possible.

Apprenticeships

Apprenticeships are a combination of on-the-job training and related classroom instruction. They are common in Europe, especially in Germany where apprentices make up 6 percent of the workforce. In the U.S., the figure is approximately 0.16 percent.[6] While these programs are rare in this country, an apprenticeship may allow you to advance at your place of employment, enter the job market if you don't have a job, or change careers.

In an apprenticeship, you can learn the practical and theoretical aspects of highly skilled occupations. Individual employers, joint employer and labor groups, and/or employer associations may sponsor apprenticeship programs, as may training schools and secondary educational institutions. Your employer may offer such a program or reimburse the cost of participation.

The Bureau of Apprenticeship and Training (BAT) lists apprenticeship for 23 states. The purpose of BAT is to safeguard the welfare of apprentices, monitor the quality of and equality to access of apprenticeship programs, and provide integrated employment and training information.

Applicants for apprenticeship programs must be at least 16 years old and meet the program sponsor's qualifications. An excellent source of information is the Department of Labor Employment and Training Administration (DOLETA) web site at www.doleta.gov.

Check with your local educational facilities and find out what training is available. If you are interested in a specialized career, investigate opportunities at companies within that industry. If opportunities in your present position look bleak, an apprenticeship either at your present place of employment or elsewhere can help move you to a better career path. Apprenticeship programs can help you develop relationships and networks which will improve your prospects.

LABOR MANAGEMENT

---

[6]Margaret Hilton, "Shared Training: Learning from Germany," *Monthly Labor Review,* Vol. 114, No. 3, 1991, pp. 33–37.

200

Recognizing an Employee's Hidden Costs

Many managers underestimate the cost of hiring a new employee. Before you hire a new employee, understand that the cost of doing so will far exceed the employee's hourly rate. In 1996, for example, the minimum wage was $4.75. Across the country, however, the average hourly cost per employee was $18.82 (U.S. Department of Labor, 1996). Table 8 lists payroll items you must consider before you hire an employee.

Table 8
Factors Contributing to an Average
$18.82 Per-Hour Cost of Compensation

Factor	1996 Dollar Amount	Percentage
Total compensation	$18.82	100.0%
Wages and salary	$13.48	71.6%
Legally required benefits	$1.59	8.5%
Insurance	$1.29	6.9%
Paid leave	$1.24	6.8%
Retirement	$0.75	4.0%
Supplemental pay (overtime)	$0.44	2.4%
Other	$0.13	0.6%

In addition, within a business office, productive workers normally require a desk, chair, a phone and phone line, a computer, a printer, and other office equipment. Other costs include additional administrative costs (payroll processing, reviews, and personnel files), and training and startup costs.

In order to budget correctly, a manager must take into account the hidden costs per employee.

The High Cost of Absenteeism

Employee absenteeism is costly to the entire organization. Each day an employee with a salary of $24,000 is absent from work will cost you roughly $100. Even an hourly worker who doesn't get paid when he or she is absent can still create costs through absenteeism. To fill the gap, a manager might need to offer overtime to other workers or even hire temporary help so the job can be accomplished. There is also the time and aggravation of counseling the employee who frequently misses work. In fact, experts agree that absenteeism is one of the biggest obstacles to efficient workforce planning.

Calculating your workforce absenteeism rate and comparing it to national benchmarks will help you plan better for workforce needs. The comparison will also help you to understand if you have a problem with absenteeism. Two recommended calculations are

- Absenteeism rate = $\dfrac{\text{Total days absent}}{\text{average size of workforce}}$

  = Average days absent per employee

- Absenteeism rate = $\dfrac{\text{Total days absent x 100}}{\text{worker-days worked plus worker-days lost}}$

  = Percentage of scheduled worker-days lost

National averages for days lost per employee range from 9 to 36 days a year. Controlling absenteeism depends upon good supervision. As with any other undesirable employee behavior, a manager needs to monitor, coach, and counsel employees who display repeated absences. However, time is better spent on other work responsibilities, and, by screening applicants and hiring wisely, a supervisor may be able to avoid the problem of absenteeism to a large extent.

A key to avoiding absenteeism is by hiring those applicants best suited for the job. Also, there are some workers who display undesirable characteristics in any job situation, and it is important to recognize these traits during the interview process. Many times managers make the mistake of hiring workers with excellent skills but poor attitudes, thinking that the attitudes will improve under good supervision. Managers who have learned through experience will tell you it is more important to hire for attitude than on skills alone.

202

Reducing the Risk of Turnover

Turnover is the number of people working for you who leave for one reason or another. The term includes employees who are laid off, who leave and then are rehired, who quit or are fired, or who retire or die.

A manager can reduce the risk of turnover by carefully selecting suitable workers. To do this, decide in advance exactly what kind of employees you want and interview enough candidates to ensure that you will find the best ones. Besides a thorough interview, you may want to administer simple performance tests to potential candidates. But remember that current laws restrict psychological testing. While personal references usually are not valuable, checking with former employers is essential in ensuring the candidate has the skills your company needs.

Experts note that employee turnover is probably the best measure of morale. When there is a positive attitude in the workplace, the turnover is low; with poor morale, you find high turnover. If you have selected the right employees and you still experience high turnover, then chances are that there is poor supervision or that good employees tend to be given the wrong jobs.

The cost of turnover to an organization is substantial. For example, it costs as much as $5,000 to add an unskilled worker to the payroll, and it will cost as much as $20,000 to keep that worker on the payroll for a year. Wages for a skilled employee are $25,000 a year or more. It costs an average of $2,000 a year to train a new employee and another $3,500 in benefits. Add to this a minimum of $2,500 in depreciation on the capital investment that makes the job possible, and a worker must return at least $33,000 in productive efforts to justify the position.

Further, absenteeism, which comes with its own costs, is often more prevalent in a workplace plagued with turnover. Turnover rates vary from job to job and company to company. The national average for all companies is 7 percent a month or 84 percent a year. This rate is calculated as follows:

$$\frac{\text{Number of separations x 100}}{\text{Average size of workforce}} = \text{Turnover percentage}$$

This national benchmark can help you understand how well your organization is doing. However, very few managers would be satisfied with an annual 82-percent turnover rate. Turnover is too costly and can be prevented. Commit to hiring wisely, placing candidates in appropriate jobs, and, supervising effectively, and you will be setting your own benchmarks that others will strive to meet.

203 Recognizing Employee Theft

According to studies by the Department of Commerce, employee theft and dishonesty cost U.S. companies anywhere from $60 billion to $120 billion per year. This means that employers are losing more than a billion dollars a week. Experts agree that no business is immune to this problem. In fact, smaller companies may be more susceptible than larger ones because of the way duties are combined. As a manager, you must always be aware of this problem.

What is stolen? Almost anything. Theft can range from pilfering of products, inventory, cash, stamps, and supplies, to stealing trade secrets or embezzling on a grand scale. Who may steal? Almost anyone, including executives, trusted long-time employees, customers, vendors, family, or friends.

One of the reasons this problem continues is management's inability to understand the magnitude and nature of employee theft. Most managers do not want to recognize that inventory shortages, decreasing profits, or rumors of dishonesty may be warning signs of theft.

The following are some reasons why employees may steal:

- The opportunity presents itself.
- Most employee theft is not detected.
- Drug abuse can drive theft.
- Honest employees will often not report problems.

In addition, poor managerial supervision may lead to employee theft:

- Employees may retaliate for unreasonable discipline or favoritism.
- Management may steal by adding expense accounts or abusing perks.
- An employee may have been passed over for a promotion or may feel cheated by the company, and wants to get even.
- Competitors may find it cheaper to steal a trade secret than to develop the product or idea themselves.

As a manager, you must be vigilant for possible signs of theft. Look out for the following:

- Inventory found near employee exits, loading docks, or other areas frequented by employees
- Restricted documents found in the copy machine first thing in the morning
- Essential employees refusing to take vacations.
- Files containing only photostatic copies instead of original copies of important documents

Some of these problems may just be signs of carelessness, inexperience, or incompetence, but they may also be signs of theft. Keep in mind that over 95 percent of thefts are committed by less than 10 percent of the workforce.

204

Preventing Employee Theft

What steps can be taken to cut losses from employee theft? Most companies have some kind of loss prevention or security program. This in itself does not ensure that the program will be successful. Your company must first take an inventory of all its potential problem areas. In addition, each potential loss should be ranked according to the likelihood it will take place and, in that event, the economic consequences.

Every employee must learn about the impact that theft-connected losses have on the company and workforce. These losses may prevent raises, promotions, and company growth. Gaining employee acceptance for theft prevention programs may help to eliminate hostile feelings they might otherwise provoke. An effective loss prevention program requires that everyone work together. Set realistic goals and definitive guidelines that spell out how to deal with prevention, investigation, and possible action against those who may have committed a crime.

Your company needs an ongoing loss prevention and security program that includes constantly updated policies and procedures, good pre-employment screening, periodic audits, security awareness training, and the development of new preventive measures to counter any new problems exposed during an audit.

Pre-employment screening is essential. If done properly, it should detect undesirable job applicants. Companies that do not screen applicants are more likely to find themselves with employees prone to theft, violence, and workers' compensation fraud. An additional reason to hire desirable employees is that they tend to recommend others like themselves when additional help is needed.

Teaching employees to report potential security problems allows many of these problems to be prevented. It is not easy to encourage employees to report thefts and to show them how this benefits everyone in the company, but this step is necessary. By offering an anonymous reporting system, you allow employees to avoid the "tattletale" label. When employees know that management is concerned and will take action, an effective loss prevention program will eventually develop.

If employee theft is left unchecked, it will continue until management decides to stop it, the guilty party leaves, or the company goes out of business.

Detecting Embezzlement

Detecting embezzlement is often difficult and taking action against the embezzler, who is sometimes a trusted employee, may be even more difficult. The number one cause of embezzlement today is substance abuse.

Embezzlement usually takes place when there has been a relaxation of existing internal controls. The checks and balances that prevent or detect theft are gone. Opportunity for embezzlement also occurs when an individual has been granted more authority than is necessary.

The following are some of the warning signs that embezzlement may be occurring:

- Collection of accounts receivable appear to have slowed down.
- The company's checks are bouncing.
- There are inventory shortages.
- Financial records are not prepared properly or are not current.
- There is an increase in returned merchandise.
- There is an increase in write-offs of bad-debt.
- Increasing expenses are coupled with declining profits.
- An employee is unwilling to take a vacation, transfer, or promotion.
- An employee lives beyond his or her means.
- Collectors or creditors are calling an employee at work.
- There are signs of gambling beyond an employees' means.
- Records are redone to make them neat.

Embezzlement occurs every day. Management cannot become complacent and must have a good system of checks and balances in place in order to prevent it.

206

Preventing Embezzlement

Even the smallest businesses can institute measures to prevent embezzlement, such as creating an internal audit system and dividing up critical financial responsibilities. Some additional tips to protect against embezzlement are:

- Cross-train personnel and have them alternate in sensitive positions.
- Do not let one employee control every step of a transaction.
- Require double signatures on checks.
- Keep checks locked up.
- Do not sign blank checks.
- Review bank statements and canceled checks.
- Pre-number checks, invoices, billing statements, purchase orders, or receipts. Account for any missing numbers.
- Review payroll records and watch for unknown names.
- Perform spot checks on inventory.
- Review the list of suppliers.
- Review each employee's work or expense reports.
- Make employees take vacations, and have someone else perform the vacationing employee's duties.
- Be sure that the employees who receive supplies and goods are not the same ones who order them.
- Examine bank deposit slips, if you did not make the deposit, and get duplicates or other documentation from the bank of the amount deposited.
- Have an outside accounting firm verify your accounting system and check it for possible weak areas.
- Be sure there is proper computer security. For example, ensure that employees cannot access financial data from home. If an employee is terminated, immediately lock him or her out of the computer system.

Senior executives, managers, or owners should set a good example. Employees imitate what they see. If senior executives pad their expense accounts, employees will be able to rationalize theft on their parts.

Common Embezzlement Schemes

207

Embezzlement is usually a crime of opportunity. Normally it is a trusted employee who commits the crime. Embezzlers feel that they can outfox management. The schemes they develop can be very simple or amazingly complex. The following are some common methods of embezzlement.

One of the easiest schemes is pocketing proceeds from a simple cash transaction. The employee simply takes the money and makes no record of it. Another method involves opening up a bank account with a name similar to that of the business name and depositing checks into this account. To cover this transaction, the customer's account is issued a credit. An employee may issue checks to a fictitious vendor with a name similar to a real vendor's. Or someone in payroll may issue checks to non-existent employees and then cash them.

More complicated schemes have their own names. One is *lapping*, using current cash collections to replace other cash collections that have been previously stolen. It is a continuous scheme that starts with small sums of money but can grow to involve large amounts. The embezzler receives a payment from customer X on an open account on a given date and pockets the money. To conceal this loss, he or she then falsely credits a payment from another customer to the account from which the original theft occurred. A third account is then used to cover the second account. This scheme is repeated over and over again. One way to prevent lapping is to be sure that the employee who records transactions is not the same person who handles the cash. The loser in a lapping scheme is usually the business from which the money was stolen.

Kiting uses the float period in which financial transactions are processed. The embezzler needs to have the authority to write checks and make deposits in two or more banks.

An example of kiting is the following: A customer deposits a check in Bank B. The check was written on Bank A. Bank B has not yet received the actual funds but allows the customer to write a check on those funds. This scheme continues through "kiting" checks that are drawn on non-existent funds from bank to bank. The victim in a kiting scheme is usually the bank that paid out on the uncollected deposits. A business or bank can prevent kiting if it allows enough time for the check to clear.

LANDMINES

208

Avoiding Fraud

Managers must sometimes make critical ethical and legal decisions about what constitutes fraud. Fraud is an intentional misrepresentation of a material fact, designed to induce the person or company receiving the miscommunication to rely upon it to their detriment. Fraud can be a benefit for an individual or a company. An act of fraud involves the following steps: An individual or business must intentionally make a false statement about an important piece of information. The victim must believe and act upon this false information, suffering the loss of money or property as a result.

There are specific federal and state statutes that protect against fraud. Fraud may also come under other statutes dealing with embezzlement, robbery, or bribery. The federal government handles fraud as a felony and prosecutes it through the Department of Justice. If a telephone, telegraph, or the U.S. mail system is used in conducting this crime, the perpetrator can be prosecuted for felony mail fraud and/or wire fraud. If collusion occurs, the perpetrator may also face conspiracy charges. Failure to report fraud committed against the federal government to the proper authorities, along with concealing information, obstructing justice, or providing misleading information are crimes that carry a prison sentence of up to three years.

The following are specific crimes that fall under the auspices of fraud:

- Bribery
- Receipt or payment of illegal gratuities
- Conflict of interest
- False statement or claims
- Extortion
- Mail and/or wire fraud
- Conspiracy
- Breach of fiduciary duty
- Embezzlement
- Failure to report a federal felony to the proper federal authorities

As a manager, you have the responsibility to always remain vigilant to possible problems in your department or company and to act appropriately. If problems should arise, you may want to check with a legal advisor.

Discrimination and Sexual Harassment

Discrimination and sexual harassment issues can significantly affect job performance and employee morale. They may also lead to legal problems. As a manager, you cannot ignore any such situation and must act promptly; you are legally responsible for recognizing and resolving these issues. Your human resource department should have established guidelines that all personnel must read and acknowledge in writing. If you don't have an HR department, be sure that you and your employees are aware of all federal and state guidelines. Read and understand Title VII of the Civil Rights Act.

The Supreme Court has established that Title VII is violated when the workplace is permeated with "discriminatory intimidation, ridicule, and insult" that is "sufficiently severe or pervasive to alter the conditions of the victim's employment and create an abusive working environment."[7]

Sexual harassment is a form of sexual discrimination involving unwelcome sexual advances, requests for sexual favors, and other physical or verbal conduct affecting job, pay, or career. It may take the form of "quid pro quo" (a request for something in exchange for something else), hostile work environment, or sexual favoritism (including relationships with customers).

Unlawful discrimination relates to unlawful or unjust actions related to race, color, religion, national origin, sex, age, and handicaps. Any of the following may constitute discrimination or sexual harassment. The issue lies in how the action or comment is received, not in how it was intended.

The following are potential sources for sexual harassment:

- Physical contact or gestures
- Jokes or comments
- Pictures
- Terms of endearment, such as "honey"
- Questionable compliments, such as "nice legs"

Failure to abide by these guidelines may result in prosecution, fines, and/or loss of employment. Make sure you treat others with the respect you desire for yourself.

---

[7]*Harris v. Forklift Systems, Inc.*, 114 S. Ct. 367 (1993), quoting *Meritor Savings Bank v. Vinson*, 477 U.S. 57 (1986).

210

Avoiding Discrimination— Guidelines for Behavior

Our communities and workforces consist of people of varied backgrounds, races, cultures, and religious beliefs. It is important that you respect others for their differences and strive to understand your coworkers. Embracing diversity will result in a happier, more productive environment.

To foster the spirit of diversity, you should keep the following in mind:

- Relationships with employees should contribute to work performance and accomplishment of goals.
- Treat people equally. Don't pick favorites or scapegoats.
- Avoid actions that can be misinterpreted as offensive or harmful.
- Actions should not intentionally or unintentionally condone inappropriate behavior by others.
- Actively listen to all employees.
- Make it clear to employees that you will not tolerate inappropriate behavior and insist that such behavior be reported directly to you.
- If there is any suspicion of discrimination, take immediate action. Document all the facts and consult your supervisor or HR department so that the appropriate actions can be initiated.

If you observe or are approached with information regarding discrimination, take action immediately. Depending on the situation, it may be appropriate to advise the offended person of his or her right to seek legal advice or to advise the offending person to stop immediately. Inform your supervisor; if the offender is your supervisor, report the incident to someone at a higher level or encourage the offended employee to do the same. It is your legal and moral obligation to take action and report the incident. Keep records including the date, time, and location of the incident, what happened, what was said, how you felt, and the names of witnesses or others victimized by the offender.

Nepotism

Nepotism is defined as patronage or favors bestowed on the basis of family relationship and not of merit. Many companies hire family members of the owner and provide them with higher pay and faster advancement than other employees receive or give them other special favors such as country club memberships and extra vacation time. Some companies take the reverse tack and refuse to hire any relative of employees to avoid any questions of favoritism.

Anti-nepotism policies are legal as long as there is no hint of discrimination on the basis of sex, age, race, ethnicity, religion, or marital status. These policies also cannot violate employees' right to privacy or attempt to regulate their personal conduct.

If you are developing an anti-nepotism policy, make sure that the policy is put in writing and that it is consistently and fairly applied to all employees and prospective employees. Be sure the policy is gender-neutral and that there is a written justification of the policy on the basis of issues such as favoritism or conflict of interest. Specify the relationship that a prospective employee would have to have to a current employee to trigger the policy. The policy may prevent hiring of the prospective employee, or may state that this employee and the current employee cannot work in the same department and that one cannot supervise the other. Be sure to check with your HR department or legal department regarding state and federal laws that may cover this issue.

212

E-Mail Etiquette

It is always important to understand your company's e-mail policies and to keep in mind that e-mail is *not* confidential. It may be monitored and used as legal evidence. Here are some general guidelines for effective and professional use of e-mail.

- When forwarding an e-mail message, include only the most relevant portions.
- Forwarding a message to a large group of people is not always appropriate. When in doubt, ask the sender.
- When you use a reply function, check to see whether the recipients who are listed automatically all need to receive the response.
- E-mail may take seconds or hours to deliver, depending on the systems involved. A telephone call may be more suitable when time is a concern.
- E-mail is for informal correspondence and communication and should not be used for the more formal business purposes.
- E-mail delivery is not 100 percent certain. Confirm delivery by telephone or fax if the matter is urgent or important.
- Avoid using e-speak (acronyms) or symbols (emoticons) in business e-mails.
- If you don't have time to make a detailed response to a message, make sure you acknowledge receipt of the message and establish a time frame for a response.
- Sending unnecessary e-mail takes attention away from important messages.

Finally, when composing e-mail messages, avoid writing messages entirely in capital letters. WOULD YOU RATHER READ THIS? Or would you rather read this?

E-Mail Techniques

E-mail provides a powerful tool for communication, but it comes with pitfalls. People are inundated with junk e-mail (also called "spam"), chain letters, and jokes—and genuinely important messages can easily be lost in the clutter.

- Make a conscious effort to organize e-mails. They can accumulate and cause clutter just like papers on a desktop.
- Keep your e-mail secure by taking advantage of password functions. Log off when you leave your office.
- Prioritize each e-mail immediately. If it is not important, delete it and move on.
- Make functional folders to help organize e-mail messages, filing them like letters.
- Avoid sending e-mail that is not related to work. Keep any such e-mail you receive separate from work-related e-mail.
- If your e-mail system does not come with an address book function, have a folder that doubles as an address book. Archive one message from each sender so you can just use the reply function rather than type the entire e-mail address when sending a message.
- Save your address list on a disk or somewhere else safe in case something happens to your e-mail program. Address books are incredibly valuable, something often realized only after an unforeseen glitch occurs.
- Give the same attention to detail and spelling in your e-mails as in your letters. An e-mail message is a reflection of both you and your company.

Keep in mind that even if you check e-mail frequently, others may not. Also, remember that it is possible for an e-mail message to carry a virus, so make sure you use an anti-virus program to scan your computer regularly.

COMMUNICATION METHODS

Reach Out and Talk to Someone

A telephone call is often the first form of contact with a customer or client, and it should make the right impression. Your company or department must determine who will have primary responsibility for answering the main phone. Make it clear that if for some reason this person is unavailable, everyone should make sure that this phone ring does not go unanswered.

- Answer incoming calls quickly. The phone should never ring more than three times.
- If call screening is necessary, have an assistant or voice mail system take the calls. Otherwise, answering your own phone will prevent time wasted on telephone tag.
- Never use a speaker phone without permission from the party on the other end of the line.
- For optimal customer service, put a smile in your voice that people can hear.
- Always be prepared to leave a message on a machine. If you don't know what you will say, call back when you are more organized.
- At the end of a conversation, summarize the significant points and establish the next step you and/or the other party will take.
- Before making a call, prepare the points you want to discuss. Have relevant materials handy and jot down notes. This will help prevent follow-up phone calls in case something was forgotten or unclear.
- Keep your cool when faced with a rude or nasty caller. This is easier said than done, but maintaining a professional composure will reduce potential conflict.

Finally, misdirected calls frustrate everyone. Do your best to forward the caller to the person he or she is trying to reach; you would appreciate someone doing the same for you. Before transferring a call, give the person the number or extension in case the call is disconnected. This will save everyone time in the end.

Written Messages

What is the best way to deliver information to your employees, superiors, customers, and suppliers? Many times, messages are best delivered verbally or face-to-face, but there are often circumstances when a written message is best:

- When you want the message to be documented
- When the message is complex
- When you need to deliver the message to many individuals
- When it is difficult or inconvenient to deliver the message in person

Written messages are often necessary to document a verbal exchange. For example, if you discipline an employee, a letter to document the incident should be placed in the employee's personnel file. Remember that written messages, whether they are letters or e-mail messages, are usually recoverable. Even when you have deleted a message or file from your computer, you may be able to recover it if it has been backed up.

Written messages can take the form of a letter or memorandum, and can be sent via interoffice mail, U.S. mail, fax, or e-mail.

A memorandum is more streamlined than a letter. Headings include "To," "From," "Subject," and "Date," and there may also be titles such as "Facts," "Discussion," and "Recommendations." Memos are more informal than letters and are usually intended for a company's internal communications.

A letter is more formal. It is frequently meant for only one reader, while a memorandum may be sent to many employees, departments, managers, or teams.

No matter what you are writing, be brief. A longer message does not necessarily contain more useful information. In fact, writing a concise letter is often more difficult than jotting down a stream of thoughts. Mark Twain once said, "I would have written a shorter letter, but I didn't have the time."

216

Writing Direct and Indirect Messages

Whether you are writing a memo, a fax, an e-mail, or just a good old-fashioned letter, the tone of the message can have a tremendous impact on the reader. A message can be written in either a *direct* or *indirect* style, depending on how the reader is likely to react to the information. For example, you might write a message differently if you were sharing good news rather than bad news.

Indirect Messages

Writers often use an indirect style when they expect to encounter resistance to the message, whether because it contains negative information or because it tries to persuade the reader to take some action he or she may be reluctant to perform. The writer is transmitting negative information while at the same time maintaining a positive tone.

> "We would like to thank you for your application with our company. We had many outstanding applicants and it was very difficult to narrow our choice down to only a few. We regret to inform you, however, that we are unable to offer you a position at this time. Your qualifications are impressive and it is apparent that you offer a great deal of knowledge in your field."

The delayed opening presents general statements without referring directly to the upcoming news. The bad news is usually followed by some sort of positive note or sign of appreciation.

Direct Messages

A direct message immediately states your most important information; other information is then presented in order of importance. Writers most often use this style when they expect the reader to agree with the message. Direct messages concern positive, neutral, or negative matters.

Positive: "Congratulations! We are pleased to offer you a position with our company. We look forward to working with you in the near future . . ."

Neutral: "Enclosed is the information you requested. Please return the extra copies at your earliest convenience . . ."

Negative: "My sincere condolences on your recent loss. Please let us know if there are any arrangements . . ."

While an indirect letter is often used to break bad news, it is sometimes better to state negative information directly, as in the last example. Each situation is different, and you must decide what the most appropriate and effective style and tone will be. A good general rule is to consider the reaction you want to generate, and then write your letter accordingly.

Preparing an Effective Presentation

Almost everyone needs to do some public speaking at one time or another. And almost everyone gets a little nervous in front of a group, especially when the audience consists of top executives or key clients. If you have not had much experience making speeches, the following are some tips for giving an effective presentation.

Plan and organize the presentation well in advance; this cannot be emphasized enough. Set your goals. What do you want to tell the audience and what message do you want listeners to take home? Think about the purpose of each of the speech's three parts:

Introduction: Get the attention of the audience, state the purpose of the talk, and preview the main points if appropriate.

Content: The talk may present new information, report on the status of a project, or, like a sales talk, be intended to persuade the listeners. Each type of talk will require a slightly different approach. But, in any case, you should cover no more than three to five points. If you try to cover too much, no one will remember the most important points.

Conclusion or *Summary:* Be sure you leave your audience with a positive impression.

Arrive early and check out the room and equipment. Be wary of equipment you have never used before, and be sure you have some type of backup if your equipment fails. For example, if you have your slides on a computer for projection, have transparencies for the overhead projector in case you have problems with the computer. It is usually best to keep special effects and razzle-dazzle to a minimum.

Since the purpose of a presentation is to share information, always keep in mind the message that you want the audience to take away. Follow these three tongue-twisting pointers:

1. Begin by telling listeners what you are going to tell them.
2. Then tell them what you have to tell them.
3. Finally, tell them what you told them.

Giving an Effective Presentation

A skillful presentation will impress the audience with your knowledge and ability. But it takes preparation to give a good presentation that stays on track. Do not cram too much information into your allotted time. Also make sure that you leave time for questions.

Remember to tailor the presentation to the audience. You will give a different talk to new employees than to 15-year veterans of your department. If you are presenting to a group of CPAs, you would present financial data differently than you would to other employees. Make sure your audience will understand the language you use as well as the concepts you will be discussing. It is better to concentrate on a smaller subject than to try to cover too much. Repetition is important for learning and communicating. If your message is important, make sure you repeat it in different words.

High-quality visual presentations require planning. The presentation should be well prepared and clearly presented. Moving text, flashy graphics, and multiple colors may be entertaining, but they also frequently distract the audience.

Try to use white or a light color for the background of your slides. Words should be in a dark color so they will be easy to see. Pastels are difficult to see. Some lights should be left on during the presentation so the audience can write notes and so that no one will fall asleep.

Plan to spend at least one minute discussing each slide, and keep the amount of information on each slide limited. Studies have shown that three or four points are the maximum an audience will retain.

Practice your presentation several times until you are comfortable with the information. Do not read from your notes, but have notes at hand if they will help you stay on track. Make sure you practice using your visual aids. You will not make a good impression if you arrive for your presentation to find that the overhead projector, computer, or projector is not working. Using a laser pointer can be helpful, although overuse of a pointer is distracting.

219 Using Visual Aids Effectively

Visual aids may be videotapes, slides, or overhead projections. The information they present may take the form of graphs, tables, charts, drawings, photographs, diagrams, or text. Choose the form that presents the material most clearly. The most important rule is to keep it simple. Presenting too much information is distracting and will result in poor retention.

You may print out visual aids from your computer onto transparent sheets for use in an overhead projector, or you can print them on paper and use a copier to transfer them to transparent sheets. You can also give a presentation with a projector connected to a computer. If your audience consists of only a few individuals, the material can be shown on a computer screen. You can prepare visual materials with a software program, save them on a disk, and have your local copying and duplicating shop turn them into slides. Programs such as PowerPoint or Harvard Graphics create visual aids ranging from charts and graphs to simple lists. Videotapes, VCRs, and televisions have made it easier to give high-quality, professional presentations. These presentations, along with question-and-answer sessions, enhance learning, understanding, and retention.

Keep in mind, however, that integrating video into a presentation involves planning. Make sure the necessary equipment will be present (VCR and TV or video projector and screen, videotape, blackboard, pointer, and chalk or colored pens) and that the entire audience will be able to see and hear the presentation. This may require several screens or TV sets located around the room.

A presentation that is planned and prepared can be an effective tool for educating and communicating. It can also enhance your image. Take the time to prepare properly.

Honing Your Public Speaking Skills

220

The way you present yourself to your audience is important. You want to be perceived as:

- Confident
- Knowledgeable
- Credible
- Interesting
- Personable
- Sincere
- Professional
- Competent

There are certain speaking techniques you should practice to achieve these ends:

- Face your audience.
- Observe them.
- Make eye contact with all areas of the room.
- Project your voice. If ranked on a scale of one to ten, your volume should be approximately seven.
- Use your hands appropriately. Do not keep them clasped or folded behind or in front of you. Use them to help make your point, then drop them.
- Watch your feet. Try to keep them balanced and the same distance apart as your hips. Do not pace.
- Speak from notes. Do not read your slides verbatim.
- Speak to the audience—not to the blackboard or screen.
- Use handouts.
- Try to interject some personal experiences into the talk.
- Be ready to field questions. Establish at the outset whether you wish to be interrupted or will take questions at the end of the talk. Leave time for questions at the end if you took the latter approach.
- Use humor if appropriate for the audience.
- Be enthusiastic. This will show your passion for and confidence in the subject matter.

After the talk is over, be sure to thank your audience, check that materials are available, ask for questions, let the audience know if you will be available at a later time, and get feedback on the lecture. This is obviously a lot to keep in mind, especially considering the normal level of anxiety most people experience before a group presentation. Practice, practice, and more practice is the best way to improve your speaking skills and to build confidence.

Using Feedback Effectively

Learning and practicing the different forms of feedback will lead to more effective communication. Improving your questioning skills, becoming an active listener, and being aware of nonverbal communication are all ways of becoming a better communicator. Additional guidelines include:

Start with Definitions

Words and phrases may mean different things to different people. During the process of communication, use feedback to make certain that the employee understands exactly what you mean by the terms you use.

Do Not Make Assumptions

Similarly, do not assume you understand what the employee is feeling or saying. The seasoned manager depends upon feedback skills to determine employees' thoughts and feelings and shies away from making any assumptions.

Use Questions

Get into the habit of using questions to generate feedback. Questions that clarify, identify or echo phrases you or the employee have used are appropriate and necessary in effective communication. In return, invite questions from your staff without encouraging questioning of your authority.

Avoid Jargon or Unfamiliar Terms

Always remember the degree of training and experience your audience members have had. Try to keep your language simple and clear. For example, company abbreviations or acronyms would not be appropriate for new hires.

Be Observant

Look at your audience and read the nonverbal communication. Are people bored, are they uncomfortable, have they tuned you out? More importantly, respond appropriately to the feedback. If the audience has lost interest, change your approach. Nonverbal feedback is a powerful tool, and you should gratefully accept and learn from it.

Direct Feedback at Behavior

When you need to provide feedback to an employee, always address the behavior rather than making personal comments. Examples are "Your reports are first rate," or "This is the second time that you didn't keep your appointment with the customer." Finally, if the goal is to improve communication and interpersonal relationships, remember that there is no place for abusive or counterproductive feedback.

222

Forms of Feedback

Feedback is most often thought of as being verbal, but it can also take nonverbal, factual, and feeling forms. Each type of feedback is an important part of the communication process, and the proficient supervisor will use all types as essential management tools.

An example of *oral feedback*, or interactive feedback, is a manager asking an employee for clarification. "Did I make myself clear when I described the assignment?" Managers also use the verbal form of feedback when they give negative or positive criticism to their employees. "That was a superb job you did on the account." Managers should also encourage their employees to use verbal feedback, instructing them to use clarifying statements such as "My understanding of what you just said was. . . ." It is important for the employee to present his or her interpretation of what was said and not just to repeat the words of the original message.

Unspoken feedback can be a conscious or an unconscious activity. Our bodies, eyes, faces, and posture can relate negative or positive attitudes. An insightful manager must be aware of this form of nonverbal communication. Employees may display pleasure or displeasure in this way. Likewise, a manager must take care that his or her nonverbal communication sends the right message. Many managers are caught saying one thing while their bodies or facial expressions are saying something different. This mixed message forces employees to choose between the verbal and nonverbal statement and creates confusion or mistrust in the employee/manager relationship. Also, some managers feel that being stone-faced or unemotional displays strength, but this demeanor in fact makes their staff feel that they are not interested or are not listening.

Substantiated feedback is a tool used when accurate and specific data is essential. This kind of communication relies on precise information being disseminated to employees and back to management. Fact feedback answers questions like how, who, where, and when. When a clear expectation needs to be presented, a manager relies on fact feedback to keep the message from being misunderstood.

Perceptive feedback is an understanding of the message behind the words. This type of communication should flow in both directions. It is important for the manager to understand why the employee said what he or she said and what the employee really thinks. On the other hand, the employee must believe that the manager feels strongly about the words he or she uses, or that the manager really cares about the employee as well as the matter at hand. There is unspoken empathy involved in this kind of feedback. The manager who uses it effectively will strengthen his or her rapport with employees.

223

Communicating Effectively

For communication to be effective, there must be a completed cycle. That is, the sender must transmit information to the targeted audience, and the audience must confirm reception and comprehension of the message. Without a process to ensure clarification and verification, there is monologue rather than dialogue. Dialogue is an interaction between individuals with the goal of reaching a shared meaning.

Positive and respectful communication requires that each party listen to the other. There are many forms of listening, and understanding how you listen and modifying your listening technique will help you communicate more effectively.

One form of listening is an *understanding* style. People who tend to listen in this style want to be entertained or inspired. They relax and enjoy the dialogue, latching onto points that interest them and frequently missing points that do not.

Some listeners use a *consoling* style. These people connect with what is said by relating it to experiences of their own. They are supportive and non-judgmental but can become so absorbed in one aspect of the conversation that they miss other equally important aspects.

Another form of listening is to be *perceptive*. These listeners do not want to miss a single idea or fact conveyed. They also try to make connections between their past experiences and those being related. But they frequently miss the nonverbal messages that are communicated.

Some people are *discriminating listeners*. These people listen carefully to all information. They focus on receiving accurate and complete details and on detecting the main message. Often this focus on processing information will cause them to disregard other critical aspects of the dialogue.

When a listener attempts to fit the dialogue into a bigger picture, he or she uses a perceptive form of listening. Such people tend to look for hidden meanings behind the dialogue and to question the motives of the person speaking. If the message conveyed doesn't fit into their personal beliefs, they will reject it.

Receiving a complete message is key to successful communication. It may be necessary to adopt other styles of listening to make sure that you fully hear what is being expressed.

Giving Assignments

Managers are more likely to be successful when giving assignments and orders if they are clear and confident, and if they follow up to make sure that the assignments were understood and carried out. More importantly, managers will be more respected if they present orders as requests and explain why the tasks are necessary. Workers will accept assignments with less resistance if managers:

- **Avoid playing the boss.** Inexperienced managers often use their new authority to force employees to do tasks. Experienced supervisors are more confident and know that pushing their weight around often backfires.
- **Choose words carefully.** Employees accept the fact that managers give assignments. Their gripes tend to be with the tone and choice of words used in conveying the order. Managers should be truthful and clear when assigning tasks.
- **Provide enough detail but not too many orders.** Workers differ in their need for details. Experienced workers are frequently bored with too much information and new employees can be overwhelmed by it. Do not be guilty of communication overload. Keep your orders brief and, when possible, assign one job at a time.
- **Distribute work evenly.** Frequently a company will have its share of both willing and less cooperative workers. Inexperienced supervisors will overwork the willing employee and neglect the less cooperative ones. A manager must learn how to work with all members of the staff and avoid the appearance of unfairness.
- **Avoid power struggles.** Focus on the goal and avoid an "I am the boss, you are the employee" approach. Remind employees that the purpose of every assignment is success for the company.
- **Solicit feedback.** If you sense that an employee is unhappy with an assignment, seek out feedback immediately. It is better to discover the problem at the start when there is time to solve it.
- **Convey messages professionally.** Assignments should be thought out seriously and treated with importance. This approach spurs employees to take assignments seriously as well.

These guidelines can help managers prevent unpleasant situations. However, there will still be occasions when employees are displeased with assignments and may show this displeasure. In these cases, a manager must remain calm and review the assignment with the employee. Give the employee an opportunity to discuss his or her objection. But if you feel you have been fair and defiant or insubordinate behavior still continues, your only recourse may be to take disciplinary steps.

Less Formal Styles of Communication

In addition to everyday forms of communication such as memos, e-mail, telephone messages, and meetings, you may want to consider other ways of communicating effectively with your staff. Some communication ideas that may work for you and your company include:

- **On-site communication.** If you actively engage in day-to-day business activities, then you may be able to increase communication just by walking around the department. Spend a portion of the day in employee offices or work areas. Let your staff know that you will be available to discuss issues. Since your employees will need some time to adjust to this walk-around style, make sure you engage in the activity on a regular basis.
- **Brainstorming communication.** Brainstorming works when you need to obtain as many ideas as possible to solve a problem. This form of communication helps build a sense of teamwork among your employees, because everyone can participate and there are no wrong or bad answers. During brainstorming sessions, many ideas will lead to other ideas, and the end result is often a solution to the problem. Again, this is a technique that, once adopted, should be used frequently to build employee confidence in speaking freely.
- **Communicating with suggestion boxes.** Suggestion boxes have gotten a bad rap in the past because employee suggestions were rarely enacted or even considered seriously. But it is still possible to use them as an effective form of communication. A manager can set up periodic meetings to discuss the ideas that have been deposited. In this way, employees will feel that their input is valuable and they will have an opportunity to participate in a discussion with fellow employees and management.
- **Off-site meetings.** Another idea is to hold informal lunch or breakfast meetings with employees on a regular basis. Attendees could be selected through a lottery or raffle and, at the meeting, be encouraged to discuss openly issues that affect their departments or themselves. The manager would have the responsibility of taking these "beefs" back to the office and to work on solving them.

Whether you use formal or informal means of communication with your employees, remember that the simple act of listening and responding is essential to your company's success. In addition, effective communication will result in employees who are more highly motivated and who have been encouraged to think more creatively and strategically.

Quality Communication

226

Effective managers quickly learn that quality communication is crucial to achieving company objectives. Quality communication will lead to positive interactions between workers and will indicate that the company respects the individual and appreciates the value and contributions of its employees. Try providing your employees with basic exercises in quality communication. For example, on Mondays they can only engage in behaviors that are productive for the business. On Tuesdays, when employees are engaged in conversation, they should allow the other person to complete his or her full thought before responding. On Wednesdays, employees will practice rephrasing the information just heard to assure that effective communication has taken place.

Other simple ways to achieve a positive communication strategy are:

- Help your staff to succeed. Managers should make sure they notice their employees doing something good and share that achievement with the rest of the staff.
- Be enthusiastic. Enthusiasm is contagious, and a manager who behaves enthusiastically will encourage the staff to do likewise.
- Encourage new ideas, be bold, and act with initiative. Allow your staff to take chances by taking them yourself.
- Don't be afraid of having fun. The workplace should be non-threatening and supportive; going to work should not be an unpleasant experience.
- Do not allow gossip. It blocks the development of a supportive and productive team. Gossip should be discouraged and never repeated.

These strategies will help both you and your staff learn the elements of quality communication. The key to successful communication is consistent application of these tactics.

227

Using Feedback— Employee to Employer

Most employees expect to get feedback from management, but is management willing to take feedback from its employees? It should be—employees can provide superb insights into work environment, effective job procedures, potential problem areas, and performance of their superiors up to and including the CEO or chairman of the board. Remember that most people want to have a role in shaping the things that affect them.

Unfortunately, employees may feel threatened when asked for feedback and may not respond honestly. They may feel that their job might be lost, that management might retaliate, or that nothing is likely to come of their feedback. In addition, they may have anxieties about talking to management in person. How then do you get employee feedback? The following are suggestions.

During performance reviews, ask employees directly what they like or dislike about their job and working conditions, or what they like and dislike about your management style and that of other supervisors. If they are reluctant to open up, there are other methods such as:

- A suggestion box
- Employee forums
- Employee surveys
- Small informal meetings within a department or with representatives from each department
- Problem-solving groups
- An open-door policy (schedule times when you will be available and adhere to them)
- A walk-around management style (see tip #225)

Employees are your company's most valuable asset and can greatly influence the company's culture, and the level of customer satisfaction, as well as the bottom line.

Using Feedback— Employer to Employee

Most employees expect to receive honest, constructive feedback from their managers about their job performance and potential and about management's expectations of them. They often feel that they do not get enough feedback, whether good or bad. But most managers say that when they try to give feedback, employees become defensive and argumentative. Managers have a responsibility to provide this evaluation. If they do so productively, they can help shape employee development and make the evaluation as positive an experience as possible.

Employees should be evaluated on the following points:

- Are they good workers?
- Do they get along with other employees?
- Do they get along with customers?
- Do they need specialized training to help them improve performance?

To make sure you are giving useful feedback:

- If discussing employee behavior, use specific examples.
- Deliver feedback as soon as possible after the event in question.
- Give honest feedback.
- Discuss the effects both good and bad behavior has on management, on coworkers, and on the employee.
- Tell employees exactly what is expected of them.
- Reinforce good behavior.
- Have the employee contribute ideas on how to improve.

Be sure both you and the employee understand what has been discussed. Usually employees receive appraisals in their yearly performance review. But for feedback to be more effective, it should take place more often and should not be just a review of performance but a look at the total employee.

Using Employee Opinion Surveys

Some employees do not communicate well in a one-on-one situation and the feedback they provide will not be of much value. In this situation an employee survey may be useful. If you have a large number of employees and cannot conduct enough employee forums to involve them all (see tip #230), an employee survey may be a valuable way of getting feedback. You can either hire an expert to design and administer a survey for you, or you can create your own.

If you design your own survey, be sure to keep your questions clear, concise, and easy to answer. Consider using true/false or multiple-choice questions. You may leave room for written answers, but if the number of employees is small, they may not want to respond out of concern that you will recognize their handwriting.

A written survey gives employees time to think about their answers. If the survey is well written, it can be completed in a relatively short time. In a large organization, you may get back more honest answers, since the fear of recognition will be gone. Be sure everyone completes the survey, or your results will be skewed. Make sure all responses are confidential. Most importantly, be sure that there is some response to the employees' concerns.

In interpreting the surveys, keep in mind that 10 percent to 30 percent of employees will be dissatisfied with their jobs at any given time. If negative responses are higher than this, you may need to investigate. If a large percentage of respondents answer any one question negatively, you should also investigate the matter. Once you identify a problem or problem area, do not hesitate to involve your employees once again in helping to find a solution.

If an employee opinion survey is done correctly, it can give valuable insights, help refine management skills, and improve motivation, quality, productivity, and profitability.

Conducting Employee Forums

Employees may be reluctant to talk openly about problems, but this feedback is essential if management wants to know what is really going on in the company. One way to obtain feedback is to organize an informal meeting or forum. The group should be small, involving five to seven representatives. The employees may all come from one department or be a cross section from several departments. After selecting the participants and the time of the meeting:

- Be sure to give advance notice of the meeting.
- Set the tone of the meeting. Keep it relaxed and casual.
- Prepare in advance ways to spark the discussion.
- Try to make sure everyone talks.
- Keep speakers from interrupting each other.
- Prevent employees from griping about each other.
- Try to keep the discussion on matters that you can influence.
- Do not get upset if you receive harsh criticism; remember that you asked for this meeting.
- Ask the group, "What could we all do better?"
- Take good notes.
- Do not ridicule.
- Try to give participants a date when they can expect some follow-up from the meeting.
- Thank everyone for his or her input.

After the meeting, be sure some type of action is taken. Employees want to know that their input was taken seriously by management and has made a difference.

231

Conducting Effective Meetings

As a manager, you may spend up to 50 percent of your time in meetings, whether you are planning, participating in, or chairing them. A considerable amount of work needs to take place in advance if your meetings are to be effective. Remember that meetings cost the company money (multiply the number of employees involved by their average hourly rate by the length of the meeting, and add in the costs of equipment and materials used). The following are some steps to take in planning an effective meeting:

- What do you plan to accomplish at the meeting? What needs to be on the agenda? Establish priorities. The most important items should be covered first.
- Should the meeting be social, informal, or formal?
- Who should attend the meeting?
- What if any information needs to be circulated before the meeting? The agenda should be written and distributed in advance to all attendees so they can come prepared.
- When should the meeting take place?
- Where should the meeting take place?
- What equipment, for example, audiovisual equipment or blackboards, is needed at the meeting? Do pens, pencils, or paper need to be provided? What kind of room arrangement, such as a circular table or square table, would work best?
- How will the events be recorded?
- Are refreshments needed?
- Do you need to hold pre-meeting briefings?
- Try to start and finish the meeting on time.

Meetings have the potential to be a waste of time if not conducted correctly, but proper planning can help you accomplish important tasks efficiently. Preparation is the most essential ingredient.

Participating at Meetings

Since meetings will invariably occupy some or much of your time, knowing how to participate is important. Active participation involves three main areas: listening, speaking, and disagreeing.

Listening

Listening is a basic skill that many people forget to use, but it is one of the most important aspects of participation. Listen attentively to what is being said, rather than paying only partial attention or being preoccupied with your own ideas. Let the speaker finish before you respond. Do not interrupt.

Speaking

In order to contribute to the meeting, you will need to actively participate. You need to voice your concerns or opinions. Present your ideas in a concise way. It is helpful to practice speaking well, neither too slowly nor too quickly. Do not dominate the conversation, and try to incorporate other speakers' views in your remarks. Be sure you are not presenting misinformation.

Disagreeing

You will not always agree with everyone else. This is expected and is often a necessary part of reaching a well-considered conclusion. If you disagree, do so with respect and without becoming emotionally involved. Remember not to attack the person presenting the idea, only the idea. Make sure you understand the plan or idea you are disagreeing with, and have another suggestion available.

Come to the meeting prepared and interested. Ask for background information, if necessary, and try to sit near the action. Following these general guidelines will help make meetings more productive and will help you get more value out of them.

MEETINGS

233 Chairing a Meeting

As a manager, you may find that it is your job to chair many of the meetings you attend. This gives you an excellent opportunity to make sure the meetings run smoothly and accomplish their goals. As the chairperson, you can maintain the enthusiasm and interest from the other participants. You will have the ability to encourage participation, solicit input, and urge good listening habits. Be sure to:

- Start and stop on time.
- Allow enough time for each topic, and avoid the reading of overlong reports.
- Have an agenda, preferably available ahead of time so everyone can be prepared.
- Make sure each member can participate without interruption.
- Keep the meetings focused.
- Record and distribute meeting minutes.
- Be able to summarize the information presented.
- Assign tasks, topics, and/or deadlines for the next meeting.

Conducting meetings should be an enjoyable experience. Try to keep them lively and productive, and no one will dread attending them. If the only conclusion you reach at a meeting is when to hold the next one, then the preceding suggestions are worth heeding.

Reasons for Meetings

Meetings occupy a great deal of time that could otherwise be spent doing your assigned work. Why are they necessary? Couldn't you spend that time more effectively if you were left alone? The 3M Meeting Management Team has developed a list titled "The Thirteen Most Common Reasons to Hold a Meeting."[8] These reasons are:

1. **To accept reports from participants.** Meetings frequently take place weekly or monthly to provide updates on the activities of departments or divisions. This allows the information to be passed upward to superiors, downward to employees, and horizontally to managers of other departments or divisions. Ad hoc meetings may also be necessary to inform participants of new developments.
2. **To reach a group judgment or decision.** Decisions may be made by the leader of the meeting, by a plurality of participants (the largest number of participants, even if it is less than a majority), by a majority (more than 50 percent), by consensus (all support the decision, although some may have reservations), or by unanimity (all agree).
3. **To analyze or solve a problem.**
4. **To gain acceptance for an idea, program, or decision.** If you anticipate resistance to a new program or development (such as a new computer system), holding an educational meeting can head off such a reaction.
5. **To achieve a training objective.** At meetings, younger executives can observe how more experienced managers plan and conduct meetings and achieve their objectives.
6. **To reconcile conflicting views.** Airing differences often leads to a compromise that is acceptable to all. This sometimes requires an outside consultant specializing in conflict resolution.
7. **To communicate essential information to a group.** The meeting will include presentation of the information and an interactive session to resolve questions.

---

[8]3M Meeting Management Team, *How to Run Better Business Meetings: A Reference Guide for Managers* (New York: McGraw-Hill, 1987), pp. 8–13.

8. **To relieve tension or insecurity by providing information and the management's viewpoint.** When the company is facing a major change or crisis, this will help to quell rumors and distrust of management.

9. **To ensure that everyone has the same understanding of information.** Highly complex or controversial written messages should usually be complemented with a face-to-face meeting, at which feedback can be provided and questions answered.

10. **To obtain quick reactions.** Such input may be helpful or necessary as management makes decisions or plans.

11. **To address a stalled project.** There may need to be an administrative decision to discontinue or reactivate a project that has stalled.

12. **To demonstrate a product or system.** The demonstration may be internal, made to employees or management; or external, made to customers or suppliers.

13. **To generate new ideas or concepts.** A brainstorming meeting can be extremely productive when managed correctly.

No matter what the reason for a meeting is, always try to keep it focused and productive. Plenty of preparation and clearly defined objectives are two key ingredients. Nobody wants to attend a disorganized meeting, and it's worth putting in the time to ensure that yours runs smoothly.

State-of-the-Art Meetings

Teleconferencing or videoconferencing is proving to be an important new means of communication. It can enhance your ability to gather and review information, communicate with employees quickly, and make decisions in hours rather than days. One of the advantages of videoconferencing is that it allows two or more people to conduct a meeting simultaneously and to share information from various locations. This can save considerable time and expense while keeping employees informed and motivated.

Videoconferencing can be part of almost any kind of meeting, including weekly staff meetings, presentations to prospective clients, training sessions, bargaining sessions, and strategy sessions. In addition, the meeting can incorporate other technologies or materials, such as computer files, documents, spreadsheets, or products being demonstrated.

There are currently four major systems that provide videoconferencing:

1. *Network videoconferencing*
   This allows you to connect with one or more sites anywhere in the world.
2. *Portable videoconferencing*
   This is a system that travels with the employee and is usually reserved for executives who need to be able to hold a meeting at any given moment and place.
3. *Group or room-size videoconferencing*
   These meetings are controlled by one person in a very formal manner. They usually require extensive and expensive equipment and arrangements.
4. *Desktop videoconferencing*
   This method is rapidly becoming the standard. It allows equal participation, informal communication, and a relaxed setting.

The cost of videoconferencing used to be out of reach for the average business. Now many personal computer manufacturers are starting to include desktop video with their PCs and servers. Just as e-mail began as a fad and has now become commonplace, so will videoconferencing.

236 Videoconferencing

Videoconferencing can eliminate travel costs while maintaining the benefits of a face-to-face meeting. Knowledge of videoconferencing will put you on the cutting edge. But, as with traditional meetings, preparation is the key to success. Take the time to make sure everything is in place before the lights, camera, and action start.

First, you must be sure that all the equipment works. Then make sure you are using the proper high-quality technology in as unobtrusive a manner as possible, so that all participants will have the feeling of being in the same room. Next, you must provide ways for everyone to participate. More and more videoconferencing meetings have laptops available for each participant in addition to a large screen. This allows private messages to be sent or everyone's thoughts to be displayed anonymously at the same time. The use of laptops can be productive, allowing participants the opportunity to voice their opinions in a more private manner.

Here are some tips to keep in mind when setting up and running a video-conference:

Preparation

- Prepare well in advance and consider your equipment needs.
- Distribute material needed for the meeting ahead of time.
- Have your presentation material ready in advance, so that there are no last-minute glitches.
- Prepare an agenda.
- Choose a discussion leader or chairperson for each site.
- Dress appropriately and keep in mind that some clothing does not look good on video. For example, reds run, and stripes or plaids may "vibrate" on screen.

Camera Etiquette

- Identify yourself.
- Identify the site you are representing.

- Try to be as natural as possible; remember that this is replacing a face-to-face meeting.
- The microphone amplifies noise, so do not tap your fingers, rattle papers, or talk to others near you.
- Look at the camera as often as you can. This simulates eye-to-eye contact.

Conducting the Meeting

- Start on time.
- Keep to your agenda.
- Introduce participants and, if the numbers are relatively small, have them appear on screen. If there are many participants, introduce the moderator for each site.
- Be sure you know which camera is live and, when possible, vary camera positions so that the meeting is not visually monotonous.
- Learn to use laptops to keep everyone involved in the meeting.
- Try to give a ten-minute warning before the meeting comes to a close.
- Review the various assignments that have arisen from the session.
- Set your next meeting time.

237 Resolving Conflicts

Misunderstandings and conflicts can and will arise in the workplace. While most situations resolve themselves without intervention, a manager will often be called upon to help mediate disputes. The best way to resolve conflicts is to prevent them from happening in the first place. But they are sometimes inevitable, and so it behooves you to master the art of resolving them.

Some important points to keep in mind:

- Deal with difficult issues sooner rather than later. Delaying intervention only allows hurt feelings and resentment to increase.
- Do not ignite conflict through behavior that causes defensiveness or counterattacks. Supervisors who threaten, degrade, lack patience, or behave unprofessionally invite conflict. Avoid hot-button or demoralizing words and phrases such as "constantly," "never," or "I hate it when you. . . ."
- Take notice of nonverbal cues that indicate people are upset. Sighs, tense body posture, or sarcasm may mean trouble is brewing.
- People feel less threatened when treated with respect. They become defensive when they are not given the benefit of the doubt. Managers must know when the other party needs to save face and when a conflict is simply not worth provoking or lengthening.
- Avoid arguments. Sometimes employees need to vent, and their concerns and comments are not necessarily meant to be personal. Experienced managers will acknowledge the areas of concerns and help steer the discussion to a productive action plan.
- Sometimes it helps just to listen and to help guide a troubled employee in solving his or her own problem. Simply lending an ear can often diffuse the strong emotions associated with frustrating problems that, if left without an outlet, can grow into major conflicts.

Perhaps the least recognized way of dealing better with workers' conflicts is to lower your own tension level. Make a habit of both mental and physical stress-reducing exercises. Sometimes it helps to vent your frustrations to a trustworthy confidant outside the organization. When you have rid yourself of your own baggage, you are better prepared to hear and talk about tough issues.

Causes of Conflict

Many times conflicts arise because individuals or groups are trying to control resources in pursuit of their own goals. Some ways in which supervisors can ward off conflict within the organization are to:

- **Allocate resources fairly.** Most businesses have a shortage of some supplies or materials. Managers will avoid conflicts if resources are distributed fairly without any appearance of favoritism. If supervisors must allocate resources to one worker versus another, the decision must be made openly, with an acceptable explanation based upon business need.
- **Clearly state company expectations.** Many conflicts arise because workers judge that their contributions to the company are more important, or viewed as less important, than those of other workers. Sometimes supervisors spark these types of disagreements by stressing the goals of one department over another, rather than focusing on the goals of the entire organization. A manager's role is to set priorities but also to ensure that all workers understand the value of their roles and their importance within the team.
- **Avoid sudden unexplained changes in processes.** Workers become comfortable with routines and avoid change, especially change without explanation. When change is necessary, managers must offer explanations and provide training to help prevent undue stress and the development of conflicts.
- **Address workers' fears.** When there is change in an organization, many workers become fearful. Even with explanations, many workers will feel threatened. Managers may not be in control of all the changes, but they should be willing to openly and honestly discuss workers' concerns. Reassuring your workers will alleviate potential conflict.

It is up to the manager to clearly state the purpose of the organization as a whole and the role of each worker in achieving the company's vision. A manager who openly discusses the challenges of the organization, who manages consistently and fairly, and who is available to alleviate rumors and fears will do much to limit employee conflicts.

239

Handling Personality Conflicts

Personality conflicts are most often responsible for unrest in a workplace. The manager must promote better relationships among employees to avoid conflicts. There are four ways in which someone can view a relationship. Eric L. Berne, a psychiatrist and author of the bestselling book *Games People Play* (1964), developed a method to analyze relationships in social situations. This method is called "Transactional Analysis" and, to illustrate, let's suppose:

- A worker comes in late every day and, when confronted by his supervisor, comments that the supervisor is also late for work daily. In this case, both worker and supervisor have a negative view of each other.
- A worker cannot complete an assignment without continuous guidance. This worker has a negative view of his own abilities, but places a positive faith in his supervisor to guide him. This person lacks self-esteem and needs continuous guidance, reassurance, and supervision. His supervisor should help him to become more independent.
- A worker is given an assignment and questions his supervisor about its purpose. The supervisor responds with, "Because I said so." The supervisor's attitude toward his subordinate is like that of a parent toward an immature child. The worker may resent this supervisor's attitude and lose enthusiasm for the projects at hand. This scenario shows that the supervisor thinks positively of himself, but has a negative view of his workers. A manager, however, must strive to instill a sense of pride and accomplishment in his or her workers. It is a costly error to treat staff as if they are children who can't understand the company's goals.
- Finally, a supervisor might say to a worker, "You've requested the next holiday off but I need to explain why I can't give it to you at this time." The employee might respond, "I understand and I'll work that day, but I'm disappointed since I expected that day off." They both might then agree to a compromise, such as the employee receiving the next two holidays off. In this type of relationship, both the employee and employer have a positive attitude toward each other.

The first three approaches are negative situations that will only serve to keep conflicts going. The last example, however, encourages honesty, respect, and compromise.

Leadership Qualities

You may have heard that leaders are born and not made, but leadership qualities can in fact be learned. With practice and feedback, managers can and will become successful leaders. The following are several characteristics that separate leaders from mere managers:

- Leaders are agents of change.
- Leaders are original, while managers copy.
- Leaders develop, while managers maintain.
- Leaders embrace change proactively.
- Leaders focus on things they can control and dismiss the things they cannot.
- Leaders focus on people, while managers are busy focusing on systems and structure.
- Leaders inspire trust, while managers rely on control.

Managers who become competent leaders will be rewarded with employees who work proficiently and excel at their jobs. Managers who become extraordinary leaders will find their departments' productivity, quality, and savings to be far above average.

241 Understanding Your Team Leadership Style

Although businesses today often take a team-based approach, leadership still remains necessary if a group of people are to work effectively toward a common goal. There is no one correct method for leading teams. Each situation will dictate the most appropriate tactic, and time and experience will help you create the style that works best for you. Figures 21–24 illustrate general team leadership styles .

The most effective leaders strive to evolve toward the "hands-off" leadership style, but this is only possible once trust and open communication are well established with the group. Eventually, all teams should be able to take more responsibility for day-to-day activities and decisions, enabling the leader to focus more on strategic and global issues.

This type of leader receives little or no input from team members and maintains a strong hierarchical structure, much like a dictator. Team members are considered strictly as subordinates.

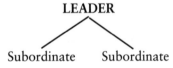

Figure 21. *Leadership is direct and dictatorial in nature.*

In this situation, the leader is a central figure who receives input from all team members.

Figure 22. *Leadership is participative.*

This type of leader functions more as a member of the team. Team members are recognized as valuable sources of both information and suggestions. They are not considered to be simply subordinates; they are considered integral members of the team.

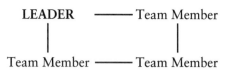

Figure 23. The leader is open to receiving input from all team members.

This type of leader functions primarily outside the everyday functions of the group. Leadership is mostly "hands-off" since the group is able to monitor its own activities. The group receives input and guidance from the leader when necessary.

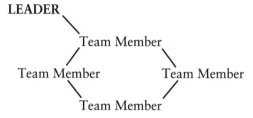

Figure 24. The group operates autonomously from the leader.

242

Striving to Succeed as a Leader

It is useful to consider the differences between leadership and management in order to determine how best to perform as a leader and not just as a manager. Leaders achieve success because:

- They are innovators while managers are administrators.
- They look toward the future while managers have a short-range view.
- They challenge the status quo while managers accept it.
- They do the right things while managers do things right.
- They have their eyes on the horizon while managers are looking at the bottom line.

Managers are charged with the task of managing people, processes, and systems. They must predict and plan for the future, and must motivate, guide and direct their staffs. Their jobs will become easier if they understand the differences between managers and leaders and if they choose to act and think like the latter.

> The leader of the past was a person who knew how to *tell*. The leader of the future will be a person who knows how to *ask*.
>
> —*Peter Drucker, in a talk given to the Drucker Foundation Advisory Board in 1993.*

An effective leader must consistently ask for and receive feedback, ideas, and information. Sources should include customers (past, present, and potential), suppliers, team members, peers, managers, and experts.

What Type of Leader are You?

Different business organizations, depending on their type—start-up or mature organization, small informal business or large hierarchical organization—require different types of leaders. Among these types are visionaries, administrators, and implementers.

Visionaries communicate their ideas and enthusiasm and inspire others to follow them. They speak in positive and confident terms, use nonverbal communication effectively, show personal conviction in the ideas they advocate, find common goals and dreams to appeal to in others, and can make their visions for the future seem real.

Administrative-type leaders are able to keep track all at once of many different departments, projects, and employees, the competitive environment, and the company's vision, and integrate these factors together into plans and strategies. This type of leader is best suited to run a large, growing company and keep it profitable.

Finally, an implementer is able to assign work, monitor it well, and inspire his or her staff to get it done. This type of leader empowers employees to work efficiently, productively, cooperatively, and innovatively.

Traits most admired in leaders include honesty, competency, and an ability to inspire. Leadership abilities seem to be innate in some people, but everyone can develop them. You need to examine your leadership style, and learn ways to enhance it from experience and from the example of others. You must create an atmosphere of trust and encourage feedback from your employees. You must also learn to listen.

LEADERSHIP

244 Defining Delegation

Have your employees become stagnant in their growth, or is the department you head suffering from a severe case of organizational ineffectiveness? These are often signs that you are keeping too much work for yourself—perhaps more than you can handle—and that you need to delegate some of it.

Delegation involves three important concepts: responsibility, authority, and accountability. To delegate well, the manager must share responsibility and authority with the delegatees and hold them accountable for their performance. The ultimate accountability, however, must still lie with the manager.

Delegation:

- Is giving someone the responsibility and authority to do something that is normally part of the manager's job. Delegation is not a task assignment.
- Is not "dumping" problems on someone else. Employees should not feel that they are doing the manager's work but rather that they have received an opportunity for growth.
- Is not abandonment. The manager retains ultimate accountability for the project and needs to establish checkpoints to monitor progress.
- Is giving the employee the appropriate authority to act alone and providing the necessary tools for success. The manager should not dictate every detail of the way the job should be done.

Success in delegating work depends upon picking the right people. If you don't have the right people, maybe you need to reevaluate your workforce or maybe you should select another job to delegate, one that does not require talents only you possess. When you do delegate work, hand off only small pieces at first. If the project is handled well, then delegate more.

Delegation can free you up to concentrate on the matters most essential to your job. It can make you look good by increasing productivity, and help you groom a successor so that you can move on. But making delegation successful means giving the delegatee whatever time and hand-holding is necessary. It will only work if you practice excellent communication and effective coaching with all delegatees.

Delegating More Effectively

Delegating successfully is not a simple task, but developing the skills to do so will pay off down the road. Someone new to management may find delegation anxiety-provoking. If you are used to doing things yourself, will you be able to let go and trust others to do the work? You must understand that mistakes will be made and learn to guide employees in correcting or preventing those mistakes.

- Delegate when there is someone more skilled available or when the task can be completed by a subordinate whose time is less expensive.
- Do not give employees just menial tasks. Include tasks that offer opportunities for learning and growth.
- Distribute tasks with an understanding of each employee's job status, abilities, and total workload.
- Use benchmarks to monitor progress along the way. Having only a deadline can be overwhelming.
- Don't micromanage subordinates. Experienced employees likely have the skills to manage complex tasks on their own. They can also provide you with a wealth of information that will help you better understand the functioning of the department or even of the entire company.
- Establish *what* needs to be done, and then provide support for the employee as he or she determines *how* to get the job done.

Tasks should always be clearly defined. Use guidelines and concise instructions regarding *what* you want done within the context of available resources and potential limitations. Also, always remember to give credit for a job well done.

246

Keeping Your Workforce Motivated

Studies on employee motivation have found that 70 percent of employees find themselves less motivated than they once were. Up to 80 percent could perform better if they wanted to and, sadly, roughly 50 percent of workers only put in enough effort to keep their jobs. To motivate employees, the manager must discourage organizational problems that rob them of their natural desire to succeed.

Some pitfalls to avoid are the following:

- *Stagnancy.* Allow employees to challenge the status quo and to question ill-defined and outdated policies.
- *Unfairness.* Supervisors must manage all employees consistently and fairly.
- *Unnecessary rules.* Nothing stifles motivation more than needing to cross every "t" and dot every "i." Review rules and regulations to make sure they make sense for all employees.
- *Unconstructive criticism.* The old adage "Praise in public and criticize in private" holds true in every situation. If you must criticize, do so constructively and always one on one.
- *Tolerating poor performance.* Even highly motivated employees will not accept being asked to cover for poor performers. Use counseling, coaching, and even termination to make sure all employees pull their own weight.
- *Underutilized capability.* Help employees rise to their level of competency so that they feel challenged, not complacent.

By eliminating organizational factors that demotivate, and encouraging positive behaviors that do motivate, you can tap into an employee's natural drive to perform to the best of his or her ability.

Increasing Motivation

Most employees are self-motivated. Their motivation comes from feeling good about what they are doing, sensing accomplishments, and tracking their achievements. To encourage motivation in the workplace, the manager should use approaches such as the following:

- *Encouragement.* Compliments are very powerful, and employees appreciate them.
- *Input and choice.* Employees who feel empowered and accountable tend to perform better.
- *Measures of quality.* Employees are motivated when they can measure the outcomes of their work and track their performance over time.
- *Stake sharing.* When possible, allow employees to participate in stock holding programs. Ownership increases motivation to succeed.
- *Responsibility and leadership opportunities.* Employees are motivated by challenges.
- *Tolerance of errors.* A manager who nitpicks will rob employees of motivation.
- *Fun and variety.* All work and no play will make Jack a dull, uninspired employee. Schedule company picnics, parties, and pot lucks.

A forward-thinking manager realizes that it is not necessarily the group of unmotivated employees that needs to change, but rather the organization that needs to find ways to motivate the work force.

248 Maslow's Hierarchy of Needs

Managers can better motivate their staffs by understanding Abraham Maslow's concepts of human motivation. Maslow described a pyramid of human needs; each need must be satisfied before the next can be addressed. The five needs, in the order in which they need to be achieved, are:

1. Physiological (hunger, thirst, shelter, and sex)
2. Safety (security and protection)
3. Social (friendship, belonging, love, and acceptance)
4. Esteem or ego (self-respect, achievement, recognition, and attention)
5. Self-actualization (personal goals)

It is important for the manager to realize that a satisfied need no longer motivates. Therefore, if the employee feels well compensated, additional merit increases will no longer provide significant motivation. However, if the employee does not feel challenged and has not achieved recognition or self-esteem, he or she would be motivated by tasks that provide opportunities to fill these needs.

Maslow's needs are dynamic. Although an employee may be motivated at one time by tasks that appeal to the need for ego, it is possible that at another time, in the face of downsizing, for example, safety or job security would become the motivator. Perceptive managers know their employees well enough to use the hierarchy of needs to motivate each individual.

For an employee to reach the level of self-actualization and to achieve his or her highest potential, all of the lower needs must be met. The manager can help meet those needs with fair employment principles, pleasant working conditions, and positive feedback. According to Maslow, individuals do not move through the hierarchy of needs and reach self-actualization only because of roadblocks society has placed in the way. In the world of business, if you are not aware of what is required to satisfy employees' basic needs, you and your organization become the barrier preventing employee motivation.

Coaching Employees 249

While inexperienced managers view coaching as a euphemism for discipline, in reality coaching should be seen as a positive activity. Managers must see coaching as an ongoing communication between worker and supervisor. It is an opportunity for the manager to supply feedback and support that focuses on a specific professional goal or area of development. Through personal observation and appraisal interviews, managers can identify the coaching needs of individual staff members.

Following are some situations in which coaching is often useful:

- The employee possesses strong technical skills, but his or her poor interpersonal skills are interfering with the success of the department.
- The employee has a persistent problem with a specific area of responsibility.
- The employee is at the top of his or her salary range and desires advancement.

The successful manager knows that coaching is more than just feedback. Coaching goes beyond simply responding to actual performance and also anticipates the employee's future needs.

Successful coaching requires the manager to be:

- A role model with professional day-to-day performance
- An active listener who responds to employees' concerns and ideas
- A motivator and a developer helping employees set goals and priorities.

In addition, the manager must provide information about training and resources that can help employees succeed at their jobs. If you view coaching as merely disciplinary, you risk losing potentially valuable employees. On the other hand, if you understand that coaching is a way to develop and improve employee performance, you will likely be rewarded with a loyal, productive staff.

250

The Power of Empowerment

Employees lack the ability to act in many large companies. They do not have the tools to perceive a problem, find a solution, and implement the solution. Instead they must find a superior to handle the problem or leave it unresolved.

There are three other main reasons that problems remain unresolved:

1. The employee is not aware of the problem.
2. The employee is aware, but takes no action because he or she doesn't want to change the system.
3. The employee is too busy with other tasks. He or she does not have time to manage high-priority items or has not set priorities.

To help encourage employees to identify and solve problems on their own, some basic steps in the process of empowerment are:

• Minimize controls and provide resources.
• Provide education and training.
• Replace rules with guidelines.
• Empower employees, support them, and make them accountable.
• Make organizational units smaller and less dependent on other units for decisions and actions.

Guidelines do not, however, guarantee that an empowerment effort will be successful. Employees may fail to recognize the opportunity to make improvements, improvement may require excessive time and/or expense, or communication may remain poor. There may also be a high risk-to-reward ratio that creates a fear of making suggestions because of the risk of failure.

Getting Employees Involved

251

If motivating and encouraging employees is a new skill for you, it may feel awkward at first. But doing so can be highly rewarding to both you and your employees. Here are some tips to help get you started:

- Share your or your company's goals with your employees. If they understand what you are trying to achieve, whether it's increased sales, better customer satisfaction, or improved teamwork, it is much easier to get them involved.
- Identify problem areas. Seek employee feedback and solutions.
- Enable employees. Allow them to make decisions and to help determine how to improve productivity or customer service.
- Promote experimentation with new ideas.
- Reward your employees if things are going well. Let them share in the good times, since they will also have to suffer through the bad times. You might treat them to a breakfast, a ball game, or a dinner.

Remember that enthusiasm can be infectious; employees appreciate a motivated manager and have nothing to lose by following suit.

252 Must-Have Employment Policies

Employees can learn about company employment policies from the employee handbook. But managers need knowledge that goes beyond this summary to encompass a detailed understanding of company employee policies and an understanding of employee law. Topics you should know about, and your company's employment policies should cover, include:

Equal employment opportunity. Employees are assured employment and promotion on the basis of individual qualification for the job, without regard to race, religion, gender, marital status, sexual preferences, veteran status, age, or any other factors that do not affect the employee's ability to perform the job.

Sexual harassment policy. Employees must be provided with a working environment that is free from harassment of any sort. Sexual harassment is defined as unwelcome sexual advances, requests for sexual favors, or other verbal or physical conduct of a sexual nature. Employers have a legal obligation to respond to knowledge of sexual harassment immediately and professionally.

Post-offer physical. Many organizations will insist upon a post-offer physical, including drug testing, before finalizing the offer for employment. There is no charge to the prospective candidate for this examination. In addition, if the potential employment is in health care or other high-risk areas, other steps (a Hepatitis B vaccination or a screening for tuberculosis, for example) may be required.

New employee orientation. Depending on the size of the organization, there may be a formal new employee orientation program to acquaint new hires with the mission, history, and operations of the organization. In addition, the program will present information about employee benefits. This orientation is not designed to train the employee for his or her new job.

Introductory period. Most organizations have an introductory period for new hires or for employees who are promoted or transferred to different departments within the organization. This trial period is usually 30 to 90 days. During this period, the employee may not be entitled to any employment benefits. Both the manager and the employee use this period to evaluate the terms and conditions of employment. Successful completion of this period does not necessarily guarantee continued employment.

Safety and evacuation plans. The employee handbook should outline safety policies and required safety practices. Managers are expected to test new employees on their knowledge of emergency procedures. The company should conduct safety drills and review evacuation plans periodically.

Resignations and discharges. All employees who resign are encouraged to have exit interviews and are expected to submit notice of their resignation in writing. Usually a resignation clearance process follows, to allow employees to turn over company property and receive any compensation due them, and to inform employees about continuation of benefits.

Drug and alcohol policy. Employees are strictly prohibited from using, selling, or possessing alcohol and illegal drugs while on company premises, while conducting company business, or while operating business vehicles. Violation of this policy may result in immediate dismissal and legal prosecution. Use of alcohol or illicit drugs prior to or after work could affect performance on the job, and poor performance, regardless of the cause, can lead to disciplinary measures and ultimately termination.

253

Must-Have
Operating Policies

If you are responsible for helping set your company's operating policies, the following are some typical policies and procedures for you to consider.

Working hours. Supervisors determine the work schedule and the hours of the workday. Most state laws define the work week as 7 calendar days and 40 hours and the pay period as 14 calendar days and 80 hours. Your company may have weekly or bimonthly pay periods instead. A typical lunch break is 30 to 60 minutes, and employees typically receive two 10-minute rest periods in an 8-hour shift.

Promotions and transfers. Employees possessing the necessary qualifications are encouraged to accept transfers or promotions after discussion with their supervisors. However, new hires are usually discouraged from transferring to new positions until they have passed a certain probation period.

Attendance and tardiness. Employees are expected to notify their managers when they are unable to work. It is management's responsibility to establish a notification policy and procedure. Many companies will request a doctor's note if an employee is away from work for more than three days. Some employers ask that employees take a medical leave of absence for illnesses that extend past one week. Unreported or unauthorized time off may be subjected to disciplinary action. Tardiness is unacceptable behavior. Failure to notify managers of late arrivals may result in corrective action. It is also expected that employees will request time off in advance.

Confidentiality. The manager must be committed to ensuring that company and employee confidentiality is respected. Many companies will have policies restricting the business information that can be discussed in public areas. Some companies will require that employees sign confidentiality agreements before attending meetings, sales presentations, and discussions with customers. Company information cannot be disseminated, reproduced, disclosed, or removed by employees except to perform services on behalf of the business.

Conflict of interest. Employees must notify their manager of any potential or actual conflict of interest. Unreported conflicts of interest can lead to corrective action or termination. Managers have the responsibility of educating employees as to what constitutes a conflict of interest, which is typically anything that divides an employee's professional obligation between the interests of the company and those of a competitor.

Gifts and gratuities. Most companies do not encourage receipt of gifts, favors, tips, or entertainment from customers or suppliers, since they can be potentially misconstrued as bribes or other unacceptable exchanges. Some managers may wish to place a dollar limit (five dollars, for example) on gifts.

Inventions, patents, and copyrights. It is standard for businesses to consider any invention developed during company time the property of the business. This policy will generally apply to any resulting patents or copyrights (see tip #279).

Standards of conduct. Managers should introduce staff to the expected code of ethics for the company. Most standard codes of conduct define and have consequences for dishonesty, misconduct, breach of confidentiality, and failure to cooperate. In addition, this policy often addresses harassment, insubordination, substance abuse, threats, unethical behavior, and absenteeism.

Smoking. State laws often mandate where smoking is permitted. Many businesses have smoke-free environments and have designated outside areas where smoking is allowed.

Nepotism. Most organizations do not encourage employment of relatives if potential problems of supervision, safety, security, morale, or conflict of interest exist. Likewise, when two employees marry and one or more of these potential problems exists, one employee is usually transferred.

Referral of friends and relatives. Employees who recommend potential employees who are then hired may be eligible for financial reward. Many times, satisfied employees are the best source for new hires, and the use of incentives to find good workers is often much more cost-effective than the use of professional recruiters.

254

Information You Might Need to Post

Managers should be familiar with the many federal and state laws that govern employment. Companies are required to post notices that tell employees of their legal rights. The posters you must put up will depend on the number of employees you have and on whether you have any federal contracts. These posters must be kept up to date, must be placed in a prominent space, and cannot have any information omitted from them. Remember that each state varies in its requirements and you should consult with your local government, or with private companies that specialize in human resource requirements, to determine which posters are required.

Table 9
Labor Laws That May Apply to Your Company

Federal Employment Regulations	Number of Employees
Fair Labor Standards Act/minimum wage laws	1 or more
Overtime	1 or more
Social Security	1 or more
Medicare/Federal Insurance Contributions Act (FICA)	1 or more
Equal Pay Act	1 or more
Immigration Reform and Control Act	1 or more
Federal Unemployment Tax Act	1 or more
Occupational Safety & Health Administration (OSHA) Act of 1970	11 or more
Civil Rights Act (Title VII)	15 or more
American with Disabilities Act (ADA)	15 or more
Pregnancy Discrimination Act	15 or more
Age Discrimination in Employment Act (ADEA)	20 or more
Older Worker Benefit Protection Act	20 or more
Consolidated Omnibus Budget Reconciliation Act (COBRA)	20 or more
Family Medical Leave Act (FMLA)	50 or more
Worker Adjustment and Retraining Notification Act (WARN)	100 or more
Employee Retirement Income Security Act (ERISA)	100 or more

Establishing Work Station Standards

Managers have responsibility of maintaining a professional and agreeable office atmosphere. This responsibility includes regulating items that are used or placed in public or shared areas and in an employee's workspace.

Employees should also execute good judgment in their selection of personal items. Items must not be viewed as offensive or derogatory by coworkers. The following list will assist the manager in establishing work station standards:

Acceptable Desk Items

- Office supplies
- Recognition awards, photographs, knickknacks, or plants
- Approved electrical devices, such as fans or heaters

Radios and Tape or CD Players

- These are not acceptable in customer waiting areas, or in areas where employees regularly interact with customers over the telephone.
- They are only acceptable in work areas that do not have direct customer access.
- They should only be audible to the owner or, if played in a common area, to the employees in that common area.
- So that noise from these devices will not distract other employees, the use of headphones may be required.

Food and Beverages

- Beverages should be covered or in spill-proof containers.
- Odorless dry snack items are acceptable.
- Food may never be eaten in areas frequented by customers.
- Employees must not consume food while on the telephone.
- Food may never be stored at the work station overnight.

Special Occasions

- Birthday and holiday decorations should be confined to work stations. Decorations must be in compliance with fire and safety codes and must not leave marks when removed.
- Decorations outside of work stations must have management's approval.
- Holiday decorations are the responsibility of management or a management designee.
- Potlucks should be held in designated areas.

It is the responsibility of management to react to infringements of the work station standards, but try not to be overly strict. The work environment should be warm, friendly, and comfortable for employees, supervisors, and customers.

Employee Manual

An employee manual is a guide to personnel policies, procedures, and benefits. The manual should clearly state that it is to be used by the employee as a general guide, and that it is *not* a contract or promise of employment. Most companies require new employees to sign a document stating that they have read and understood the employment manual.

Here are some of the elements usually found in an employee manual:

- An introduction of the company to the employees
- A description of the company's compliance with and enforcement of labor laws, and information on company employment policies, covering harassment, diversity, unacceptable job performance, terminations, substance abuse, drug and alcohol abuse, and safety
- An outline of the company's compensation policies as they apply to job classifications, full-time and part-time employees, exempt and non-exempt employees, time sheets, overtime, employee performance reviews, pay periods, payroll advances, severance pay, unemployment compensation, wage garnishment, and payroll deductions
- A section on operating policies, addressing personal conduct, confidentiality, release of company information, personnel files, posting of notices and information, outside employment, solicitation for outside causes, political activity, telephone usage, security system and emergency and evacuation plans, electronic communication, employee privacy, absenteeism and tardiness, disciplinary action, at-will employment, work schedule, dress code, smoking policies, suggestion box, open-door policy, and ethics
- A description of company benefits including paid time off, holidays, sick or "well" days, vacations, accrual policies, paid personal days, and bereavement leave, as well as company policies on jury or witness duty, voting, and education and training
- Discussion of laws and company policies regarding family, medical, military, and personal leaves of absence

- A section on insurance and employee benefits describing medical and dental insurance, life and disability insurance, on-the-job accidents and benefits, flexible benefit plans, pensions, and profit sharing
- Forms such as an employee acknowledgment form, a security and confidentiality form, and a termination form

While the purpose of any employee manual is to serve as a guide to company policies, it also serves as a signed reminder that the employee is in an "at-will" relationship with the company.

E-Mail and Computer Usage Policies

As computers become more prevalent, stricter rules are necessary to ensure they are used correctly. More and more employers are monitoring computer and e-mail usage. The reasons for this are several-fold. The company may be held liable for inflammatory or defamatory remarks or sexual harassment on the part of employees using company computers. Additionally, such monitoring can safeguard against disclosure of information in discovery or regulatory proceedings. Employees must be able to notify their managers of any violations of these policies.

The following are some guidelines that can be used in formulating e-mail and computer policies:

- Decide whether e-mail can be used only for business purposes or also for personal messages.
- Decide what business documents can or cannot be e-mailed. Never send confidential messages via e-mail.
- Decide how long messages need to be saved.
- Remind employees of the company and personal liability risks involved in computer use.
- Only authorized employees should have access to sensitive files, databases, financial reports, or other classified information.
- Passwords should be closely guarded.
- Be aware that messages may remain on hard drives even after being deleted.
- Do not download files or programs without checking for viruses.
- Be careful of copying, sending, or downloading copyrighted material.

Inappropriate material such as offensive messages, jokes, or cartoons or sexually explicit images should never be sent via e-mail or in any other way. Spell out the disciplinary action that will be taken if these policies are violated.

258 Travel Policies—What Can Be Reimbursed?

If your company requires that employees travel for business, then business travel policies need to be made clear. Managers must be familiar with the costs that are covered and those that are not. The employee must be made aware that he or she is expected to exercise sound business judgment when incurring expenses. The company should provide travel expense reporting forms and training on how to complete them. Instructions on proper documentation will help make sure that employees are promptly reimbursed.

While companies may differ on the kind of documentation that is required (for example, original receipts versus photocopies) and the size of expenditures that require documentation, the following is a list of the usual reimbursable travel expenses:

- Forms of travel used to reach the destination (airline travel, taxi rides, shuttles, rental cars, and use of personal automobile)
- Hotel accommodations
- Meals, including alcoholic beverages in modest amounts
- Telephone or cellular phone calls
- Registration fees for conferences, expositions, and other events
- Entertainment expenses related to customer contacts
- Supplies, books, or other necessary business tools
- Photocopying, faxing, or other job-related expenses

Companies usually put dollar limits on meals, entertainment, and lodging. Many companies specify the hotels and rental car chains and even the airlines to be used. Larger companies may have travel arranged through an in-house agency or a travel agent with whom the company has a contract.

Travel Policies— What Cannot Be Reimbursed

It is not unusual for inexperienced employees to treat a business trip as a mini-vacation and to assume that items usually bought on trips are covered business expenses. The manager must explain in advance what expenses are not reimbursable. The list of these expenses will likely include:

- Items from the "honor bar" in hotel rooms
- In-room movies or video games
- Dry cleaning or laundry fees (unless travel time has been extensive)
- Excessive personal telephone calls
- Personal items
- Entertaining of non-business clients
- Expenses associated with side trips to visit friends or family

The manager should instruct the employee to spend corporate dollars as if they were his or her own money. Business travel is expensive and only justifiable if the employee is cost-conscious and provides a real return on the company's investment in the trip.

INTERNAL POLICIES

260

Using Company Vehicles

Your company should have a policy regarding vehicle use, covering both employee use of company-owned vehicles and the use of employee cars on company business.

If you are using your own vehicle for work assignments, your company will usually reimburse you at a certain per-mile rate. Check whether you are covered by your employer for accidents occurring while you are on company business.

Before letting an employee drive a company vehicle, it is a good idea to do a check on his or her driving record. There are numerous websites offering such services. Some organizations let their employees check out company vehicles for personal use. This may expose the company to tremendous liability, since it can be held responsible for any accident or damages caused. Insurance companies will want to know if employees can check out vehicles for their personal use, and they may raise the premiums accordingly. Additionally, checking out a vehicle is likely to be viewed as a privilege and it may be difficult to determine who should and should not receive it. There are companies, however, that report little or no trouble with checking out company vehicles. While they acknowledge that there is added risk, they say that as long as the employees are conscientious and respectful of the privilege, they see no reason to alter their system.

Writing Policies
and Procedures

As certain as death and taxes is the fact that a manager will be asked to write policies, procedures, and plans—tasks that can seem overwhelming at first. Fortunately, you can quickly become proficient in writing these important documents if you have an understanding of their purpose and a template to guide you.

The first concept to understand is that documents can be *policies, procedures,* or *plans.*

A *policy* represents a company's position on major issues.

A *procedure* is the operational steps taken to implement a policy.

A *plan* is a scheme or an action specific to a situation.

Regardless of the type of document you are creating, there should be a heading indicating the type of document, the departments impacted, the title and subject, the number of pages, and the document's originator. In many cases, the heading should also contain the signatures of the relevant department heads.

The body of the document should set forth its purpose. When necessary, concepts appearing in the text of the document should be explained; for example, a policy that deals with threats and violence in the workplace may need to define what constitutes "threats."

Next, the policy, procedure, or plan should appear in full. You may need to include cross-references to other policies, procedures, or plans, if applicable. Finally, include a history of the policy, procedure, or plan, stating the initial date of conception and any revision dates.

Following a boilerplate format for these company documents will not only save you time but will result in consistent policies for your staff. A template will make it easier for you to train qualified staff in writing these documents so that you can delegate such projects to them. The final step is to have some kind of system that will remind you to review and revise these policies on a regular basis.

262 Standard Operating Procedures

Standard operating procedures (SOPs) provide a written set of instructions for a particular task or process. Much like an instruction manual, SOPs establish safe, consistent, and effective ways to complete operational activities. They also:

- Maintain quality control
- Ensure employees perform tasks safely and effectively
- Function as an instructional training tool

SOPs should be clearly written for the individual who will be performing the task and should take into account his or her educational level, skills, knowledge, and experience.

In order to stay useful, SOPs should be updated regularly to reflect refinements and modifications made to the system that they describe. The updating process should rely on input from the worker performing the task. Updates are also necessary when there is an incident involving a machine or process, or when new information is available suggesting the potential for improved or safer performance.

SOPs are necessary for new procedures or machines, as well as for those tasks for which there may have been no previously written protocol. The length of SOPs varies with the process or task it describes with its intended use. For a new employee, a complete SOP is necessary. For review or reference, a shorter form of the SOP is adequate.

Remember that these SOPs will be used not only to train new workers, but also as a possible point of reference if accidents occur or the media questions any particular process.

Civil Rights Act— Title VII

Title VII of the Civil Rights Act of 1964 is one of the most important laws in business. This law was amended in 1972 by the Equal Employment Opportunity Act and applies to organizations with 15 or more employees. This act prohibits discrimination in hiring, firing, promoting, compensation, or conditions of employment, as well as any privileges of employment based on:

- Race
- Color
- Sex
- Religion
- National origin

Additional amendments to the Civil Rights Act include the Pregnancy Discrimination Act of 1987, and the Civil Rights Act of 1991. The Equal Employment Opportunity Commission vigorously enforces these laws.

The areas that you, as a manager, will be most concerned about are:

- Hiring
- Firing
- Job qualifications
- Discipline
- Interviewing
- Advertising

Exceptions to the Civil Rights Act are known as "bona fide occupational qualifications." The act also allows bona fide seniority merit systems, or incentive systems that have the effect of discriminating, provided such systems are not the result of an intention to discriminate. These exceptions are rarely used, since they are difficult to justify.

264

Americans with Disabilities Act

In 1990 the Americans with Disabilities Act (ADA) was passed, making it unlawful to discriminate in employment against a qualified individual with a disability. The ADA incorporates the remedies and procedures set out in Title VII of the Civil Rights Act (1964). Since the number of complaints filed with the Equal Employment Opportunity Commission is rising rapidly, it's important to be thoroughly familiar with this act. Unfortunately, the finer points of this law are extremely confusing and may require consultation with experts.

The ADA makes it illegal to discriminate in regard to:

• Job assignments
• Recruitment
• Promotions
• Hiring and firing
• Layoffs
• Pay
• Employee benefits
• Job training
• Leave
• Other benefits

The disability act does not restrict your right to employ the best qualified candidate for the job. The applicant with the disability must be able to carry out the duties of the job with or without reasonable accommodation. The ADA does not require employers to make accommodations that pose "undue hardship." This usually means significant expenses, disruptions, or major alterations to the operation of the business. The difficult parts may be defining what is *reasonable* accommodation and what is a *disability*. In any case, the employee must fulfill the requirements for the position, such as appropriate licensing, educational background, technical skills, or previous experience.

Family and Medical Leave Act

If your organization employs 50 or more employees, then the Family and Medical Leave Act (FMLA) requires that you allow employees to take the equivalent of 12 weeks of unpaid leave each year due to either:

- The birth or adoption of a child
- A serious health condition on the part of the employee or an immediate family member

Part-time employees who have worked more than 1,250 hours in the past year are entitled to a proportionate share of the standard leave.

Medical leave requires that either the employee, or the employee's child, spouse, or parent, be suffering from a serious health condition. Under the FMLA, a serious condition is:

- An illness requiring hospitalization
- An illness or incapacity of more than three consecutive days if treated at least twice by a health care professional during those three days
- Any incapacity due to pregnancy or childbirth
- A permanent or long-term problem being monitored by a physician but for which there is no effective treatment
- Any period of incapacity or treatment due to a chronic serious health condition
- Treatment for a problem that could result in a long-term illness if left untreated

After the 12 weeks, you must reinstate the employee in the same job or an equivalent one. The leave can be taken one day at a time. Additionally, if state law provides greater benefits to the employee, it supersedes the FMLA.

266

Understanding ERISA and COBRA

ERISA and COBRA are federal regulatory acts with which your organization must comply. You should have some knowledge of them to be sure your employees are receiving the benefits required by law.

ERISA

The Employee Retirement Income Security Act (ERISA) is a federal law that governs the operation of pensions and retirement benefits. The law does not require you to provide these benefits, but if you do they are subject to regulation by ERISA. This law prevents employees from being fired to keep them from being vested or from qualifying for benefits under qualified pension plans. ERISA also sets standards to make sure that everyone is treated equally in the plan and that employees receive promised benefits.

The Pension and Welfare Benefits Administration (PWBA) of the Department of Labor and the Internal Revenue Service (IRS) are responsible for enforcing ERISA. The PWBA has jurisdiction over Title I of ERISA, which governs the actions of the persons or entities managing and controlling plan funds. Title II of ERISA, which the IRS oversees, addresses vesting participation, discrimination, and funding standards. Willful violation of the law can bring not only civil but also criminal action.

COBRA

The Consolidated Omnibus Budget Reconciliation Act of 1985 (COBRA) mandates that employers offer the option of continuing group health care plan coverage to qualified beneficiaries who would otherwise lose benefits. The law applies to companies with 20 or more employees. Anyone covered under your group health plan on the day before an event that causes loss of coverage is considered a qualified beneficiary. This requirement applies to both full and part-time employees (if they are eligible to participate in the plan), their spouses, their dependents, retirees (unless they can receive Medicare), and partners in a partnership. The employee must receive COBRA information on the date of separation and is responsible for the cost of continued coverage.

Following OSHA Guidelines

Providing a safe environment for employees should be a major concern of every manager. The Occupational Safety and Health Act (OSHA), enacted in 1970, requires all employers to provide a working environment free from recognized hazards that cause, or are likely to cause, serious injury or death to employees. Every business is required to comply with some general rules under what is called a "general duty clause." The general duty clause makes it the employer's obligation to identify all potential safety hazards in the workplace.

Selected industries must also comply with industry-specific requirements and guidelines, known as OSHA standards. These standards fall into four classes, based on the type of work being performed:

1. General industry
2. Construction
3. Maritime
4. Agriculture

In addition, there is a general duty under OSHA to maintain a safe workplace even if there are no specific standards for your industry. This means that you have to evaluate the potential hazards of each new technology or situation.

The following are some of the areas that OSHA standards cover:

- Handling and disposal of hazardous materials
- Providing personal protective equipment
- Proper ventilation
- Maintaining medical and exposure records
- Employee rights

Employees may report any violations to OSHA and file complaints regarding safety and health conditions in their workplace. Workers are protected against employer reprisal and their identities remain confidential.

States have the right to enact their own standards, but these must be as effective as the federal OSHA regulations. Check with your state government to determine which regulations apply.

GOVERNMENT POLICIES

268 Employee Polygraph Protection Act

Federal law prohibits most private employers from administering lie detector tests for pre-employment screenings or to a current employee. Polygraphs, voice analyzers, or any mechanical device that attempts to analyze a person's honesty are all considered lie detectors. The employer may not discharge, discipline, or discriminate against an employee or job applicant who refuses to take a lie detector test.

Exemptions apply to security service companies, such as security guard, alarm, and armored car services, and to companies that manufacture, dispense, or distribute controlled substances, such as pharmaceutical companies. These organizations are allowed to administer polygraph tests. Additionally, employees at any company who are "reasonably suspected" of involvement in workplace theft can undergo polygraph testing, within strict standards concerning the conduct of the test and the person conducting the test.

Enforcing Child Support Withholding

Do you know what your responsibilities are as an employer if you receive a notice regarding child support from a state Child Support Enforcement (CSE) Office, other government agency, or attorney? In January 1994, wage withholding became a mandatory part of all child support orders, whether or not they were enforced by CSE programs. The federal Family Support Act of 1988 sets forth the rules and regulations covering wage withholding for child support.

Upon receipt of a court order, the employer must deduct a specified amount from the employee's pay check every pay period and send it to the appropriate enforcement agency. The notification sent to the employer will state when to begin the deduction, how much to deduct, and when and where to send the money. The most important point to know is a company will be liable for the entire amount if it fails to make required child support deductions.

The first deduction must take place no later than the first pay period that occurs within 14 days of the mailing date of the notice. The deduction is due within 10 days of that pay date. The deductions must continue until further notification or until the employee no longer works for the company. If the employee leaves, the company must notify the government agency and provide the employee's last known address and new employer if known.

The employee is protected in that there is a maximum dollar amount or percentage of salary that can be deducted. Child support deductions take priority over any other court-ordered withholding except for pre-existing federal tax levies.

Some states mandate that the employee's children be enrolled in a health plan if the support order specifies medical coverage and the employee is eligible to be included in the employer's plan.

Be sure that you keep a copy of the court order, as well as accurate records and proof of payment for each withholding. Again, noncompliance will leave you liable for the entire amount plus interest.

270

Personal Responsibility and Work Opportunity Reconciliation Act

The Personal Responsibility and Work Opportunity Reconciliation Act of 1996 (PRWORA) requires all employers to report information about new employees to the state within 20 days of the date of hire. Individual states are able to establish even stricter reporting requirements. The main goal of the act is to help enforce child support rulings. Filed reports will help the states locate parents, establish an order, or enforce existing orders for child support. Consider the following:

- One of two children in America will be raised in a single-parent household.
- More than $34 billion is owed in past due child support to America's children.
- The national recovery average of all child support owed is only 17 percent.
- In most states, case workers and attorneys are swamped with huge caseloads that take months to review.
- It may take months or even years before a state agency can help collect child support that is past due.

The reports your company files should include the employee's name, address, and social security number, along with the employer's name, address, and federal identification number. The reports will also help the states find and prevent fraudulent worker's compensation and unemployment claims. As with other federal requirements, there are financial penalties for noncompliance.

Age and Religious Discrimination Laws

271

The Age Discrimination Employment Act (ADEA) applies to companies with 20 or more employees. It specifically prohibits discrimination on the basis of age against employees who are more than 40 years old. The ADEA also specifically prohibits the following:

- Hiring younger employees because they are younger
- Paying older employees less because they are older
- Firing or laying off older employees before younger employees because of their age

The ADEA also eliminates mandatory retirement for most employees.

As an employer, you must also be aware that the Civil Rights Act (see tip #263) obligates you to reasonably accommodate the religious practices of employees and prospective employees. It is recommended that you allow religious observance and practices that do not harass coworkers, customers, or clients and that do not unreasonably interfere with your business. If your employee refuses your accommodation, record the refusal.

272

Sexual Harassment Update

So you thought you knew sexual harassment regulations? In June of 1998, the United States Supreme Court ruled in a seven-to-two majority that companies can be held legally responsible for a supervisor's sexual misconduct even if they knew nothing about it. They also ruled that employers are always liable when a supervisor's abuse results in a tangible job injury to the victim such as a firing, demotion, or a transfer to an undesirable job.

Under the ruling, a company can defend itself by showing that it exercised "reasonable care to prevent and correct promptly any sexually harassing behavior" or that the employee "unreasonably" failed to abide by anti-harassment policies. Unfortunately, the court did not offer employers any guidelines for developing acceptable anti-harassment policies or grievance procedures.

The following are some tips that employers can use as safeguards:

- Create a sexual harassment policy oriented to your business that includes examples of the range of unacceptable behaviors.
- Absolutely require that every employee from the CEO on down receives periodic training on sexual harassment awareness.
- Make sure every employee understands the internal recourse available for victims. Assure employees that outside investigators will be used if needed.
- Test your employees about their knowledge of the company's sexual harassment policies and grievance procedures.

After this decision, your company needs to reassess its sexual harassment policies and make sure that the procedures are more than written words. You will need to demonstrate that very serious efforts are in place to find and correct harassment.

GOVERNMENT POLICIES

Contracts

In order to be sure that both parties involved in an agreement understand and agree to all its terms, the agreement should be in writing. Creating a contract is a crucial step for self-protection. Everything must be spelled out or any future dispute will simply be a matter of one party's word against another's.

A contract is one of the basic tools of business. Contracts facilitate voluntary, mutually beneficial exchanges and serve to allocate risk among the parties involved. Sir William Blackstone, the famous English jurist, initially defined a contract as "an agreement, upon sufficient consideration, to do or not to do a particular thing." A more modern definition would describe a contract in terms of a promise or set of promises that if not performed will result in penalties. By either definition, a contract is a legal relationship consisting of rights and duties.

For a contract to be binding and legally enforceable, the following conditions must be met:

- The offeror, person making the offer, must have the intent to be bound to the contract, and that intent must be clearly manifested. In this context, preliminary negotiations are viewed as invitations to make an offer, not as an offer. An offer is a promise to do or refrain from doing something specific.
- There must be definite terms and conditions, so that sufficient detail is present to understand each party's promises.
- The offer must be communicated to the offeree, the party to whom the offer is made, prior to execution of the contract. If the contract was not communicated and accepted by the offeree, it is invalid.
- Termination of an offer can occur through action of the parties involved, withdrawal by the offeror (revocation), rejection by the offeree, or lapse of time (inaction of the offeree). Termination can also result by operation of the law through illegality, destruction of subject matter involved in contract, or death or insanity of either party.
- Acceptance must be unequivocal or definite (not "That's a good idea"), unconditional or without any conditions or alterations, and legally communicated to the offeror or offeror's agent.

Contracts are a necessity in both your business and private life. They serve to protect you as well as the parties you are dealing with. It is a good idea to have all contracts reviewed by an attorney before you sign. In particular, you must be sure to have legal advice before signing any contracts with foreign parties, because contract law differs from country to country.

Capacity to Contract

Any contract you create or sign might be void or illegal if you or the other party do not have the *capacity to contract*. Legally, *capacity* refers to the ability of a party to legally perform valid acts, incur legal liabilities, or acquire legal rights. If you claim incapacity to contract, the burden of proof is on your shoulders. The following are categories of individuals with *incapacity* or *reduced capacity* to contract.

Minors

A minor is a person under the legal age of majority, which is defined by common law as 21. Minors may enter into contracts; however, they have the right to disaffirm or void the contract at their option. Under a Mississippi Supreme Court case, Star Chevrolet Company v. Green [473 So.2d 157 (1985)], the law stated that "he who contracts with a minor does so at his own peril." This assumes that the minor did not falsely misrepresent himself or herself as being over the legal age of majority. The intent of the law is to discourage adults from contracting with minors. A minor therefore has only *partial capacity*.

Intoxicated Persons

If a person is intoxicated at the time a contract is signed, he or she may disaffirm the contract after becoming sober. Most courts agree that the test is whether the individual was too intoxicated to understand the contract. This is also defined as *partial capacity*.

Insane Persons

An individual who entirely lacks capacity to enter into a contract is insane. The term may sound a bit dramatic, but it is the legal classification often used. Any contract with such an individual would be void, since he or she has the right to disaffirm after restoration to competency. A guardian appointed by the court to act in the individual's behalf may also disaffirm the contract. The insane person has *no capacity* to contract. A few states will not, however, void a contract with an insane individual if the contract is just and reasonable.

It is extremely important to be sure that the individual you are contracting with has the capacity to contract. Otherwise the contract may not be worth the paper it's printed on.

275

Understanding Employment At-Will Policy

An employment at-will policy indicates that employment can be terminated at the will of either the employer or the employee for any or no reasons, and with or without advance notice. It is one of the most important policies listed in an employee handbook. Almost all states recognize at-will policies, and today it is rare to see contracts or commitments of guaranteed or continued employment. This policy generally applies to all staff, including managers and supervisors. It provides protection for the employer, but only if it is well advertised and is understood by the worker. As with other operational policies, it is the manager's responsibility to educate his or her staff on the importance of the at-will policy.

Your company's employment application form should contain mention of the at-will policy. Applicants are entitled to know that if they are hired their employment and compensation can be terminated with or without notice, with or without cause, and at any time by either party.

The company's written handbook should further strengthen the at-will policy. It should state that the company reserves the right to modify policies and procedures without advance notice, at its discretion, and without having to give cause or justification to the employee. By signing the handbook, the employee recognizes that accepting these policies is a condition for continued employment. The employee must also be informed that no written or oral statement to the contrary made by the employee's supervisor or any other manager should be relied upon as a contract for continued employment.

The handbook should contain a disclaimer giving the at-will policy additional teeth by stating that it is not feasible to list all rights and benefits and that policies are not limited to those stated in the handbook. This statement should advise the employee to discuss additional details concerning policies, rights, and benefits with his or her manager.

Managers must adhere to company policies when terminating employees. They are expected to use coaching and counseling for workers with performance deficiencies. They must strictly adhere to state and federal laws when firing staff. The at-will employment policy is a tool that should be used only when earnest attempts to rectify poor performance have not been successful.

Avoiding Litigation

Today, the federal and state laws that protect the rights of employees are more complex than ever. In addition to Title VII, the Age Discrimination in Employment Act (ADEA), the Americans with Disabilities Act (ADA), and the Equal Pay Act of 1963, there are state laws that favor the rights of the employees over those of the employer. The result of such laws restricts the employer's ability to terminate employees who are performing poorly.

The following are survival techniques to help prevent lawsuits:

- Be careful whom you hire. Before offering a position, be careful to check references and to be suspicious of gaps in work history. If the resume reads like a travel itinerary, be sure to examine the reasons for frequent job changes.
- Have a written personnel policy or manual. Make certain that all employees read and sign a document stating that they are "at will" employees.
- As a manager, clearly state that continued employment is dependent upon satisfactory performance.
- Define a progressive discipline process that can lead to termination. Document all instances of poor performance and discuss them with the employee. Have the employee sign all warnings.
- Conduct routine performance appraisals on at least an annual basis, and more frequently with employees who need coaching. Make sure that goals are reasonable, clearly defined, and agreed to in writing by the employee.

Having to terminate employees for "cause" is not only stressful but also a potential source of unfounded lawsuits. By hiring qualified employees and by having consistent, well-documented policies, a manager can hope to avoid, and at least successfully defend against, most litigation.

277

Working Through a Termination

To avoid litigation, it is not enough to hire the right people and to have the right policies. A manager must also be able to follow procedures that act as safeguards against lawsuits. It is expected that a manager will:

- Be consistent in his or her management style
- Consult the human resources department, his or her supervisor, and the company's attorney before terminating an employee with poor performance who has also filed a worker's compensation claim
- Have a witness present when terminating an employee
- Keep his or her supervisor and/or human resources representative informed of the discipline process and possible termination
- Openly explain the reasons for the termination to the employee
- Offer severance packages with clear explanations of health care benefits, as well as outplacement services and counseling
- Consult an attorney throughout the process if termination of a particular employee seems risky

Termination can be stressful for the employer as well as the employee. It is important to invest the same amount of time in handling the employee's departure as in his or her hiring. By upholding company policy and with displaying fair and consistent practices, a manager can do much to make the employee accept the termination without personal malice.

Providing References— Legal Risks

278

Companies know that providing information about previous employees can be risky business. There have been lawsuits for defamation brought by former employees who received references that were less than glowing. Managers have, therefore, often confined their remarks concerning former employees to their dates of employment and jobs held. However, the climate is changing as courts show impatience with a system that encourages the cover-up of poor performance or worrisome behavior.

A new tort called "negligent referral" refers to managers' attempts to disguise severe behavioral problems of past employees during reference checks. This is to say, the law does not accept taking a neutral stance when negative information should be divulged instead.

The trick is to develop policies that provide real information about former employees to prospective employers while minimizing exposure to potential lawsuits.

Some ways to achieve this are:

- *Get all requests in writing.* When you receive a telephone call, you can't be certain about the caller's identity. Ask the caller to write you a letter on company letterhead. You want to protect yourself against charges that you gave information to people who had no right to receive it.
- *Train one person to handle all requests.* You will limit exposure if one trained individual handles all references following a uniform procedure.
- *Train your staff not to respond to reference calls.* Funnel all such calls to the individual responsible for handling them, and put this policy in writing.

When responding to a reference check request, stick to job performance data. Discuss issues such as attendance records, job responsibilities, and attitude toward work that can be verified in written documents. If you have negative information to report about the employee, be accurate. Stick to objective documented data and leave subjective opinions out. In addition, try to have all departing employees sign a written consent form that allows the manager to give future references.

There are risks associated with both giving and withholding information to the prospective employers regarding your past employees. Your responsibility is to be prepared to offer fair, documented, objective information during a reference check.

OTHER LEGAL ISSUES

279

Protecting Intellectual Property

Intellectual property rights are an important way for both individuals and companies to protect inventions, products, or concepts. Innovation is a key component in establishing and maintaining a competitive advantage, and intellectual property rights are established to reward those who develop new ideas. There are four basic legal mechanisms used to protect intellectual property:

Trademarks. A trademark (™) is a symbol, slogan, logo, or word that identifies a particular company or entity. Others cannot associate their products or services with the identifying mark. The (®) symbol means that a trademark has been registered, which establishes indisputable rights regarding the mark's commercial use. Registration also enables the trademark to be filed in foreign countries. For these reasons, registration is a good idea, but a trademark does not have to be registered in order to provide legal rights to the owner.

Copyrights. Copyrights protect the author of a written work. This includes books, songs, software, articles, and even works of art. The point of a copyright is to protect the expression of an idea but not the idea itself. Other people are able to use the idea in a different manner or context. Use of the © symbol, along with the name of the creator and the year of the copyright, protects the work. In order to have a legal basis for claims of copyright infringement, you must register a copyright with the Library of Congress. The life of a copyright is the life of the author plus 50 years.

Patents. Getting a patent is considerably more complicated than getting a copyright, and it is often advisable to seek the help of a patent attorney. A patent protects an inventor by preventing anyone else from using or selling a particular invention; the inventor holds exclusive rights to the invention. There are three types of patents:

- Utility patents, which protect ideas for processes, machines, and chemical compounds
- Design patents, which protect the design and shape of useful objects
- Plant patents, which apply to living organisms

An invention must satisfy three requirements to be granted a patent:

- The invention must have a use.
- The invention must be new and different from what is currently available or known.
- The invention must not be obvious to a person of "ordinary skill" in the relevant field.

Trade Secrets. A trade secret is information about a product or service that is not disclosed when the product or service is sold. Keeping a trade secret avoids the risk associated with disclosing information that may encourage competitor imitation. Coca-Cola does not have a patent on its formula, but it is kept under tight wraps within the company. By keeping a trade secret, you also avoid the costs of searching, filing, and defending patents. There are risks associated with trade secrets, however, and the rights to a trade secret are only upheld as long as it is successfully kept a secret.

All of these methods are intended to provide legal protection for a unique idea, concept, or product. It is advisable to seek out legal counsel to ensure that intellectual property is sufficiently safeguarded. There are plenty of ideas out there, but an exceptional idea is hard to come by and is often extremely valuable.

280

Fixed and Variable Expenses

While it may be tempting to lump all the money that flows out of an organization into a single category, expenses, it is important to recognize that not all costs are created equal. They fall into two types: fixed and variable costs.

Fixed Costs

Fixed costs cannot be changed in the short term. The short term is usually defined as a period of less than one year, but the definition can vary from one business to another.

Here are some examples of fixed costs:

• Physical plant
• Property
• Equipment
• Rent

Fixed costs remain constant regardless of the volume of business. For example, a factory's rent will be the same whether or not it is operating at capacity. For this reason, fixed costs are often considered in the context of time, not volume.

Variable Costs

Variable costs can be changed in the short term and they vary as the quantity of output varies. If production is zero, so are the variable costs. A typical variable cost, such as direct labor or raw materials, is constant per unit of output, and it is assumed to be directly linked to production. In other words, if the cost of raw materials is variable, and one unit of final output requires $10 in raw materials, then 10 units of final output would require $100 in raw materials.

Recognizing a
Sunk Cost

In making strategic decisions, it's important to understand the nature and implications of different types of costs. One of the most important concepts is that of *sunk costs;* essentially, these are costs that cannot be recovered and should not be considered in the decision-making process. Here is an example: You buy a non-refundable airline ticket for the sole purpose of visiting an old friend in Seattle. Just before your trip, however, your friend is relocated to Miami. What do you do now? It's easy to say to yourself, "Well, I bought the ticket and it's non-refundable, so I might as well use it." In reality, however, the ticket purchase is a sunk cost, and taking the trip will incur further expenses that have nothing to do with the original purpose of your trip. It would be better to save these unrelated expenses even though it means accepting the loss of the plane fare. It's not easy to write off sunk costs, but it is often critical.

To think about sunk costs in a business context, consider the following scenario: You recently purchased a computer system. Within a few months, you realize that the system has become obsolete and that you made a poor purchase. But you consider upgrading your existing system at significant expense rather than purchasing a new system. You know that this improved system will still not be as good as a new system, but you are reluctant to admit that your original purchase is no longer useful.

It's important to prevent emotions from factoring into business decisions. The money you spent on the original computer system is a sunk cost or, to use a more common expression, "water under the bridge." The existing computer system is obsolete, and the money spent to purchase it should not be considered in the decision to buy a new system.

282

Understanding an Opportunity Cost

FINANCIAL CONCEPTS

One type of cost that is frequently overlooked is *opportunity cost*. This is the cost associated with picking one alternative over another.

Consider the following situation: You have been considering going back to school to obtain a particular degree. You have been working for several years and you are making a comfortable salary. Option A is to go back to school and Option B is to keep working. If you pick Option A, you will give up your salary and benefits. This is considered the opportunity cost of Option A. If you pick Option B and choose to keep working, you give up the potential that the degree would provide, for example, an eventual increase in salary or a promotion.

As another example, consider an investment opportunity for your business. Option A is to pursue a project in an attempt to expand your business. Option B is to leave that money in secured government bonds. If you choose Option A, the opportunity cost is the interest that you would have received if you had left your money in government bonds. The opportunity cost of Option B is the loss of the potential benefits of expanding your business.

It's not always easy to quantify opportunity costs; there may be hidden costs involved. Opportunity costs should always be considered in terms of the potential benefits versus the risks associated with a given strategy.

Understanding the Time Value of Money

Is one dollar today the same as one dollar 10 years from now? This simple question raises one of the most important concepts in finance—the time value concept of money. In essence, the certainty of having a given sum of money today is worth more than the certainty of having an equivalent sum at a later date.

If you were given $1,000 today, you could put that money into a risk-free investment, such as a government bond. If this money was earning a modest interest of 6 percent each year, at the end of ten years you would have $1,791. The general rule is that you will approximately double your money at 7 percent interest per year over 10 years.

If you are considering investing in a project that will cost $100,000 and will provide an estimated revenue return of $15,000 per year for 10 years, here are some things to think about:

- How certain are you that the project will be successful and will generate the expected returns?
- If you don't put money into the project, the $100,000 could be put into a low-risk investment that will earn interest.
- If the project performs as expected, it should generate, at the very least, the same revenue as a moderate-risk investment. Is the risk worth the trouble?

The time value concept of money is an important consideration in a variety of circumstances. For example, the sooner you collect your accounts receivable, the sooner you will be able to deposit the money and earn interest on those funds. Likewise, the longer you delay your accounts payable, the more interest you will earn on those funds as they sit in the bank. There are limitations to this strategy, of course, since your suppliers will want to collect as soon as possible, and your customers will want to delay payment as long as possible.

The time value of money is also an important concept when you are spending money. Money spent today is worth more than the same amount of money spent some time in the future because of the interest that could be earned in the interim. Therefore, delaying spending or payments can increase your buying power.

284

Understanding
How to Float

Float is the difference between book cash and bank cash; it represents the delay involved in using checks. The concept of float is easiest to understand with a simple example:

Say you write a check for $100 to your credit card company. You write the check on a Monday, and you immediately make an entry in your checkbook. According to your checkbook, you have $100 less in that account, even though the check is still sitting in the mailbox. That money will not be deducted from your account until your credit company deposits it. The balance reflected in your checkbook will not be the same as the balance that is actually in your bank account. Checks you write create a *disbursement float,* causing an immediate decrease in book cash but no immediate change in bank cash.

When you receive checks and enter them into the books, you increase book cash, but bank cash does not change until the check clears. This is known as *collection float.*

It is critical to keep track of float and to know how much cash you actually have in the bank. Speeding up collections and delaying payments lets your money sit in the bank and earn interest just a little bit longer. This can have a significant effect for companies with millions of dollars in daily transactions. For example, Exxon's average daily sales are about $248 million. If Exxon speeds up the collection process or slows down the disbursement process by one day, it frees up $248 million, which can be invested in marketable securities. With an interest rate of 10 percent, this represents overnight interest of approximately $68,000 [($248 million/365) × 0.10].[9]

Your company may like to collect early and pay late, but customers and suppliers would like to do the same. Trade-offs are inevitable to preserve good working relationships.

---

[9]Stephen Ross, Randolph Westerfield, and Jeffrey Jaffe, *Corporate Finance,* 4th ed. (Chicago: Irwin, 1996).

Simple Versus Compound Interest

When you take out a loan or invest your money, it is important to know whether you are collecting or paying simple or compound interest. This difference can amount to a large sum of money over time. Compound interest is interest earned both on the initial principal and on the interest that has accumulated on that principal. The interest earned previously becomes part of the principal.

When you take out a U.S. Treasury bill or note, you will receive simple interest, paid directly to you or to your bank account. It will not accumulate and increase the value of your investment. When you invest your money in a money market account or reinvest your dividends and interest in an investment such as a stock, you are compounding your return. The initial investment will grow and the resulting interest on the new, higher principal will also grow with each payment. This is compound interest, which will make an investment grow faster than it would earning simple interest.

Table 10 shows the difference between simple and compound interest across 10 years for an investment of $1,000 at 10 percent.

Table 10
Simple and Compound Interest Compared

Year	Simple Interest	Compound Interest
1	$1,100.00	$1,100.00
2	$1,200.00	$1,210.00
3	$1,300.00	$1,331.00
4	$1,400.00	$1,464.10
5	$1,500.00	$1,610.51
6	$1,600.00	$1,771.56
7	$1,700.00	$1,948.72
8	$1,800.00	$2,143.59
9	$1,900.00	$2,357.95
10	$2,000.00	$2,593.74

The investment yielding compound interest would have earned $593.74 more. If the amount invested was $100,000, the difference would be $59,374.

286

Investment Risk

When you invest in a riskier security, you should expect a higher potential rate of return. When you invest for safety, you must be willing to earn a lower rate of return. The rate of return and the risk are inversely related. You cannot expect both a high rate of return and a very safe investment.

The *beta coefficient* shows the risk of an individual security in statistical terms. The beta usually represents the relationship of a security to the entire market (for example, the Standard and Poor's composite index). The value of a stock with a beta of one tends to move up or down at the same rate as the market. A beta coefficient lower than one means the value of the security will move less than the market; a beta higher than one means the value of the security will move more than the market.

A formula for determining the expected return on an individual security, using the security's beta coefficient is:

Expected return = Current risk-free return + (Beta of security × Historical market risk premium)

The current risk-free return on a security is the current interest rate of a short-term U.S. government bond, the least risky security. The market risk premium has, over the long term, historically been much higher than returns on short-term government securities, which have averaged approximately 8.5 percent.

Diversification reduces the risk of your investment portfolio. Combining risky stocks with low-risk investments reduces your overall portfolio beta; however, risk cannot be entirely diversified away. Another way of reducing your risk is to diversify into markets in other parts of the world. These markets do not react in exactly the same way as the U.S. market to economic changes. A drop in the European market would not necessarily accompany a drop in the U.S. stock market.

The risk of your portfolio also depends on the percentage of your total assets that are invested in each category. For example, placing 70 percent of your portfolio in risky securities will result in a high-risk portfolio, even with the remaining 30 percent invested in low-risk securities.

Generally Accepted Accounting Principles (GAAP)

287

GAAP stands for "generally accepted accounting principles" and refers to the framework on which modern accounting is built. It is a good idea to be familiar with these ground rules of accounting.

Accounting principles usually depend on three criteria—relevance, objectivity, and feasibility—and must establish a balance among them.

Relevance: The principle contains information that is meaningful or helpful.

Objectivity: The principle contains unbiased information that can be verified.

Feasibility: The principle can be implemented without undue expense.

The Financial Accounting Standards Board (FASB) is the ruling body that sets these principles. There are seven members on the FASB, and five of the seven must agree on any new principle or statement. Companies are not obligated to use GAAP, but if they do not, they must call the public's attention to that fact. In addition, the Securities and Exchange Commission requires companies with more than 500 shareholders or $5 million in assets, to file their accounting reports in accordance to GAAP.

The FASB also determines *interpretations,* which are modifications or extensions of existing standards; *financial accounting concepts,* the concepts and objectives that will underlie future standards; *technical bulletins,* providing guidelines for implementing or using FASB standards; and *emerging issue task force statements,* which describe how to handle new and unusual financial transactions that have the potential for creating controversial accounting situations.

Contact the FASB at (203) 847-0700 or at www.fasb.org.

288

Activity-Based Costing

Previously, conventional cost accounting systems focused on assigning costs to production cost centers (such as service center costs) and to unit-lever drivers (such as direct labor hours or direct labor dollars). This method of accounting has several deficiencies. First, it cannot correctly determine the actual total product and service cost. Second, it cannot generate enough useful information to allow management to make good operating decisions. As a manager, you should be familiar with another accounting system, called activity-based costing (ABC). This method will allow you to make better decisions about pricing, product mix, and technology.

ABC identifies the areas or activities that are responsible for the costs. This approach allows you to accurately identify the activities that contribute to the costs of a product or service. If the number of activities increases, ABC can help you analyze the underlying economics of the company's operations. It also helps bring to light all aspects of bringing the product or service to market. After identifying product costs by using the activity-based costing system, you are better able to make management decisions about streamlining operating costs.

The basic premise behind ABC is that cost objects, such as products and services, consume activities and materials, that in turn consume resources, and the consumption of these resources is what drives costs. The most appropriate time to use ABC is when overhead is high, your products are diverse, the cost of errors is high, and competition is stiff.

In using ABC:

- Identify the activities
- Find the cost of each activity
- Determine the cost drivers
- Find activity data
- Determine product cost

If you follow ABC, you will have better information regarding the driving costs of your products, services, and customers, and you will be better able to identify if a particular area is consuming a disproportionate amount of resources.

Understanding Depreciation

Understanding the accounting principles governing financial statements will help you assess your company's performance and plan for the future. There are certain major business assets, such as vehicles, office equipment, machinery, and buildings, that businesses must own or lease in order to operate. These are all tangible assets with a long life. On the balance sheet, long-lived assets usually appear under the heading "property, plant, and equipment" (PP&E) and are sometimes called fixed assets. Assets that will give service for no more than several years are considered capital assets.

Depreciation is the annual write-off of a portion of the cost of a fixed asset, such as a vehicle or piece of equipment. This accounting process converts the original cost of the fixed asset to an expense. An item is depreciated to make sure that there is an accurate measurement of a business's gross and net income in a given year. Allowing the full cost of a fixed asset to be charged to one year would clearly distort reported income. There would be an understatement of net income in the year the asset was bought and an overstatement of net income in future reporting years. Depreciation allows the cost to be spread out over the expected lifetime of the asset.

In order to determine how much depreciation can be taken on an asset, the following estimates must be known: the asset's useful life, its salvage value (what it can be sold for when its useful life is over), and the method of allocation to be used in writing it off. This will usually be either the *straight-line method* or the *accelerated depreciation method*.

In the straight-line method, the asset is depreciated a set amount each year. An example is a $10 million asset with a useful life of 10 years. It has a salvage value of $1 million dollars. After selling the asset, the net amount spent on the purchase will therefore be $9 million. Straight-line depreciation determines how to spread out this $9 million equally over the 10 years. The straight-line depreciation would be:

$$\frac{\$10 \text{ million} - \$1 \text{ million}}{10 \text{ years}} = \$900,000/\text{year}$$

The accelerated method allows more depreciation to be taken in the early years and less in the later years. Two methods commonly used are the *dou-*

FINANCIAL CONCEPTS

ble-declining-balance method and the *sum of the years' digits method*. Both of these methods write off two thirds of the asset's cost in the first half of the asset's estimated life.

If a company chooses to use the straight-line method, it will overstate current earnings. It will understate them if it chooses to use the accelerated method. In the United States, it is acceptable to keep two sets of books. One is for reporting to shareholders and for managing the company, and gives a more accurate accounting of the financial picture. The other set of books is for tax purposes. Using the most rapid method of depreciation over the shortest useful life allowed by law will minimize taxes. Other countries do not allow different books to be kept in this manner.

Knowing the type of depreciation used for your company's assets as well as reviewing both sets of accounting books will help you understand the finances of the business.

Understanding
Inventories

A company's inventory is the collection of items that are being held for sale, are in the process of being made, or are being used to create products or services that are to be sold. It is important to carefully maintain an inventory record system. There are two methods of accomplishing this task:

The Perpetual System

The perpetual system requires continuous recording of changes in inventory levels. The availability of computers and scanners has popularized this system, which gives the accounting, sales, and purchasing departments instant access to much-needed information.

The Periodic System

This system records the amount of inventory periodically. It was more common before the computer era but is still used in some small businesses. With this system, up-to-date information is not available at all times.

After you choose an inventory system, the next item is to pick a costing or valuation method (see tip #291). Remember that inventory control and planning are vital to any business. Having too much or too little inventory can mean lost sales, lost customers, or additional costs.

291

Putting Value on Inventory

There are several ways to characterize the cost of carrying inventory. The choice of method can significantly affect a company's reported earnings and tax consequences. There are four main systems in use:

Specific Identification

The specific identification method keeps track of the purchase cost of each item sold. This method works well with big-ticket items, and the advent of computers and bar code scanners allows tracking of smaller items as well. This method does make manipulation of net income possible by selecting the cost of goods sold, or COGS (see tip #52). For example, if three shipments of an identical material that have different purchase costs are received during the year, the merchant can change the net income by shipping the lower- or higher-priced material depending on whether higher or lower reported earnings are desired for that reporting period.

Average Cost

The average cost method figures the average price of the items in the inventory on the basis of the average cost of all like goods available during the period. In the periodic inventory system this is a weighted average, while in the perpetual inventory system a new average unit cost is sometimes calculated after each purchase.

First-In, First-Out (FIFO)

The FIFO method assumes that the product purchased first is sold first and that the most recently purchased or produced merchandise is in the ending inventory. The basic disadvantage of this method is that the income statement does not compare current costs to current revenues.

Last-In, First-Out (LIFO)

The LIFO method assumes that the most recent inventory goes out first. It values ending inventory at the cost of the oldest items available. Assuming that inventory is more expensive as time goes on, LIFO deflates the gross margin and, therefore, the net. Inventory as an asset also has a lower stated value. If investors misunderstand this, stock prices may fall.

Inventory errors can affect both balance sheets and income statements. If ending inventory is not correct, working capital, retained earnings, cost of goods sold, accounts payable, and net income will all be incorrect as well.

292

Profit Margin

Profitability ratios provide a way of looking at a company's performance on a yearly basis. Two ratios commonly used to evaluate the profitability of a company are the *gross profit margin* and the *net profit margin*. These ratios show performance and growth potential. Evaluating trends over several years can help management with long-term planning and provide projections of future profits.

The gross profit margin equals gross profits divided by sales. These numbers come from the company's income statement (see tip #305). This ratio is important because it shows the business's pricing strategy and its ability to control operating costs. If your profit margin is falling over time, you should look at your inventory management or check your selling prices. Usually companies that add significant value to an item can obtain high profit margins, but they also usually have lower asset turns. An example is an airplane manufacturer compared to a supermarket.

The net profit margin equals net income divided by sales. This ratio reveals how much of each dollar is available as profit or dividend.

Remember that profits available each year are only a short-term indication of the financial health of a company. Various accounting practices may inflate or decrease profits. Companies frequently perform large write-offs of assets after mergers or acquisitions, and this might temporarily decrease profits. Sales of divisions or assets might temporarily increase profits. Trends in profits over several years are much more important to investors who are following the overall performance of a company.

Rate of Return

How well is a company using its assets to produce profits? How well are investors doing on their investment in a business? The rate of return demonstrates how well management is using its assets and the investors' money to produce results. Looking at the rate of return of other companies in your industry is one way to benchmark your company against others.

Return on Assets (ROA) equals net income divided by average total assets. This ratio calculates how well the company is using its assets to provide more income. Another way to write this equation is

$$ROA = \frac{\text{Net income}}{\text{Sales}} \times \frac{\text{Sales}}{\text{Total assets}}$$

or

$$ROA = \text{Profit margin} \times \text{Asset turnover}$$

As you can see from the formulas, a large return on assets may reflect a high profit margin, a rapid turnover of assets, or a combination of both.

Return on Equity (ROE) may be the most popular ratio for measuring financial performance. It calculates the percentage return to owners of the company on their investment. ROE equals net income divided by owner's equity. The figure for net income comes from the income statement and owner's equity comes from the balance sheet.

In *Analysis for Financial Management,* Robert C. Higgins breaks ROE down to three principal components[10]:

$$\text{Profit Margin} = \frac{\text{Net Income}}{\text{Sales}}$$

$$\text{Asset Turnover} = \frac{\text{Sales}}{\text{Assets}}$$

$$\text{Financial Leverage} = \frac{\text{Assets}}{\text{Owner's equity}}$$

FINANCIAL CONCEPTS

---

[10]Higgins, R. C., *Analysis for Financial Management,* 4th ed., The University of Washington: Irwin, 1995.

Another way to look at ROE is through the following formula:

$$\text{ROE} = \frac{\text{Net income}}{\text{Sales}} \times \frac{\text{Sales}}{\text{Assets}} \times \frac{\text{Assets}}{\text{Owner's equity}}$$

or

$$\text{ROE} = \text{Profit margin} \times \text{Asset turnover} \times \text{Financial leverage}$$

When ROE is viewed this way, the company can control the earnings from each dollar (profit margin), the efficiency of utilizing assets to generate sales (asset turnover), and the amount of equity used to finance the assets (financial leverage). This ratio also allows an investor to see if the return on equity compares to an investment in the stock market or a certificate of deposit.

Understanding Your Assets and Liabilities

The term *asset,* commonly used in financial statements, means things of value possessed by a company. *Liabilities* represent the financial claims on those assets. For example, if a company wants to purchase a new building, it must first figure out how it is going to pay for such an asset. This usually comes from some sort of debt financing, or through the sale of stock to shareholders. The asset (what the company owns) is directly linked to the company's liabilities (where the money for the asset came from). This relationship is the main focus of the balance sheet (see tip #304).

Assets fall into two main categories, *fixed* and *current.* Fixed assets are those that have a long life, such as equipment, buildings, property, and machinery. The items cited are *tangible* fixed assets, since they are material items that can be appraised with relative ease. Other fixed assets may be a bit more abstract. How do you place a monetary value on the skill of a management team, or on a patent owned by a particular company? These are *intangible* assets.

The other broad category of assets is *current* assets, which consists of assets with short lives, such as inventory and accounts receivable. There is no universal time frame for categorizing assets as either current or fixed, although many people use one year as the dividing line.

Liabilities are also categorized according to a time scale. *Short-term* debt, also called *current* liability, is a debt that must be paid within one year. If it does not need to be paid within one year, it is *long-term* debt. A firm's total debt is simply the combination of short and long-term debt obligations.

There is only one more piece missing. Let's say a company has total assets worth $1 million dollars. On the balance sheet, the total debt for the company is $750,000. The $250,000 in assets must also be associated with a liability, since liabilities tell you where the money for assets comes from. The answer is *shareholder's equity.* Financing for this portion of the assets came from the sale of company stock.

FINANCIAL CONCEPTS

295 Dealing with Debt

Many people shudder at the mention of debt, but it is a fact of doing business. Debt is something owed, such as money, goods, or services, or is an obligation or liability to pay or render something to someone else. While there is a cost associated with debt, it can often provide financing for projects or for acquisition of materials that would otherwise be impossible. You should scrutinize very carefully the following points concerning debt:

- How much are you borrowing and how much will you have paid after the loan is paid off? Can you afford these payments?
- The length of time you have to pay off the debt will determine the interest rate on your loan (usually, the longer the time, the higher the interest rate) and will also determine how much you will end up spending by the time the loan is paid off. A longer time period will, however, mean lower individual payments.
- How often must you make payments (monthly payments will cost you less than quarterly or yearly payments), and do you pay interest and principal with each payment thereby reducing the remaining loan, or do your payments at first only pay off interest, keeping the principal to be paid off later? How much principal will you pay up front? Reducing the amount of principal to be paid off will also reduce the amount of interest you will pay.
- The interest rate is your cost of the loan. Always compare APRs (annual percentage rates) since quoted monthly interest rates are often misleading. A higher interest rate means your loan will cost more.

How do you settle debts that you cannot pay when they become due? Usually it is best to enter into a settlement agreement with the creditor. This means that the creditor releases the debtor from the full obligation of the debt in return for some mutual arrangement. Frequently, the creditor will accept partial payments if they are the only alternative to no return of the debt.

A *liquidated* debt is one in which the debtor and creditor have no disagreement regarding the amount owed. If a settlement agreement involves payment of an amount less than the original debt, the creditor may still make a later claim on the remainder owed. An unliquidated debt means that there is no agreement regarding the amount owed between the parties involved. Generally, a settlement agreement for an unliquidated debt is usually binding. Both creditor and debtor have agreed that they will settle the debt for a stated amount, even though there is no agreement on the amount of the original debt.

FINANCIAL CONCEPTS

Factoring

Cash is the lifeblood of every business, and sometimes a company must make obtaining cash its highest priority. Frustrated banks may call in a loan, and if the company is unable to pay it, even more difficult times are ahead. Creditors may also impose penalties on late or insufficient payments.

One method of generating cash quickly is the factoring of accounts receivable. A firm may have $100,000 in accounts receivable that it expects to have within 30 days, but these will not provide cash for immediate financial obligations. The firm will therefore find a financial institution willing to purchase the accounts receivable. The financial institution is known as the factor. The factor obtains the accounts receivable at a discount, and the customer then sends payment directly to the factor. This provides a quick source of cash for the troubled firm, and it transfers the risk of nonpaying customers to the factor.

Because of the cost of factoring, an organization should first consider these alternatives:

- Communicate with creditors and debtors and get their input. Debtors may be induced to pay earlier, or creditors may permit a delay in required payments for a reasonable interest charge.
- Are there unnecessary assets that can be liquidated?
- Would refinancing help?

But in some instances, a company that is desperate for cash may have no other choice but to accept factoring of its accounts receivable.

297

Understanding Cost of Capital

Cost of capital is the company's cost of long-term financing—in other words, the expected return required by creditors and shareholders.

To calculate its cost of capital, a company should figure out the proportions of each component of capital. This includes the cost of debt, the cost of preferred stock, and the cost of common stock. After this has been determined, the company then determines the cost of each source of capital. The cost of capital is the weighted average costs of the various costs of capital.

The best way to explain the weighted average cost of capital (WACC) is with an example. Lender A invests $10,000 and expects a 7 percent return. Investor B invests $20,000 and expects a 10 percent return, while Bank C invests $20,000 and expects a 15 percent return. The total capital received is $50,000, and Table 11 shows the resulting cost of capital.

Table 11
Calculating the Cost of Capital

Investor	Rate	Weight	Weighted Cost	$
A	7%	$10,000 / $50,000 = 20%	7% × 20% = 1.4%	$700
B	10%	$20,000 / $50,000 = 40%	10% × 40% = 4.0%	$2,000
C	15%	$20,000 / $50,000 = 40%	15% × 40% = 6.0%	$3,000
		WACC	**11.4%**	**$5,700**

The total cost of capital is 11.4 percent. This means that the company must earn $5,700 after subtracting all other costs. The WACC may also be called the "hurdle rate." In the example given, if the company cannot earn more than 11.4 percent on the $50,000 given to it by investors, it should abandon the investment opportunity.

Overview of
Bankruptcy

Under the U.S. Constitution, bankruptcy is a matter of federal law, and the Bankruptcy Reform Acts of 1978 and 1984 presently govern it. Generally, individuals, corporations, and associations whose assets are less than their liabilities can file for bankruptcy. The Bankruptcy Code provides for the following major types of bankruptcy proceedings:

Chapter 7, or liquidation, requires that a trustee sell off the debtor's property to pay the debts owed to creditors. Under federal and state exemptions, an individual debtor is allowed to keep a modest amount of household property. Declaration of Chapter 7 bankruptcy may be a voluntary act on the part of the debtor or may be the result of a lawsuit filed by the creditors. The trustee is elected by the creditors or appointed by a court. The debtor must also pay legal and accounting fees. This is the most common form of bankruptcy.

Chapter 13, the second most common form of bankruptcy, allows individuals or proprietorships with a regular income to pay off their creditors with the assistance of a trustee. A debtor enters this form of bankruptcy voluntarily. The creditor's claims are frozen until a plan is presented to pay off the creditors from income. If the court and creditors agree, debts may be stretched out or compromised. This might prevent the seizure of the debtor's property and allow the business to keep operating.

Chapter 11 applies to corporations and allows management or a trustee to continue a company's operations while creditors' claims are frozen pending approval of a plan. With court approval, the plan can modify or forgive debts, recapitalize a corporation, provide for mergers or takeovers, or dispose of assets. Many firms wait too long to file for Chapter 11 bankruptcy and few, approximately 25 percent, manage to survive.

FINANCIAL CONCEPTS

299

Bankruptcy from the Creditor's Viewpoint

Have you or your organization ever received a notice from the federal district court stating that there will be a creditor's meeting concerning Company XYZ's bankruptcy? While bankruptcy can be voluntary, creditors can also press a company into involuntary bankruptcy. If there are more than twelve creditors, three or more must file the petition. Otherwise, a single creditor can file. The outstanding debt must be at least $5,000.

After learning that a customer is in bankruptcy proceedings, there are several things you should do. The first step is to cease all attempts to collect the outstanding debt. The next is to have your lawyer or the proper department in your company file a proof of claim. Finally, if you received any payments within 90 days of the filing, you may be required to return the payment to the bankruptcy estate.

The federal bankruptcy system ensures that creditors get fair treatment. As soon as someone has filed for bankruptcy, no creditor can better its position by getting to the debtor's property first. This is in contrast to some state laws under which those creditors who act most quickly gain an advantage.

Bankruptcy laws give debtors a way of recovering from an oppressive financial burden that would keep them from being productive members of society. The law tries to distribute debtors' property equally to creditors of the same ranking. If you are contemplating bankruptcy or have had customers declare bankruptcy, the assistance of a bankruptcy attorney is recommended.

Understanding
Chapter 7 Bankruptcy

A debtor who chooses voluntary bankruptcy files a federal district court petition. As soon as the petition is filed, the court automatically declares the debtor bankrupt.

Your company may receive notice from the bankruptcy court that customer XYZ has filed Chapter 7 bankruptcy, usually accompanied by notice of a first creditors' meeting. At this meeting, the trustee (the creditors' representative) will be selected. The role of the trustee is to maximize the debtor assets that can be used to pay the creditors. In Chapter 7, debtors give up the right to nonexempt property at the time of the filing and any property that they may receive a right to own after the bankruptcy filing. Federal law allows states to make some of the debtor's property exempt, usually items such as the debtor's house, car, household furnishings, or necessary business equipment. In other words, debtors can keep property that is necessary to support them and their dependents.

After petitioning the court for Chapter 7 protection, the debtor must provide a list of the following:

- All creditors and the amount owed to each
- All the debtor's financial affairs
- All property owned by the debtor
- All current income and expenses

After obtaining this information, the trustee liquidates all the debtor's nonexempt property at a public auction, unless the court rules otherwise. Following the sale of property, the trustee distributes the sums among the creditors. All creditors with a claim against the debtor are entitled to share in the distribution.

According to the law, certain creditors or obligations have priority over others in receiving the proceeds of the debtor's assets. The following is the usual order of priority:

- Secured creditors
- Costs associated with preserving and administering the debtor's estate
- Taxes
- Rent
- General creditors

A secured creditor usually has collateral for the debt, such as a car loan. Such creditors can take possession of the property and either sell it or keep it. Statistics show that the average recovery for a secured creditor is 75 to 80 cents on the dollar and only several cents for an unsecured creditor.

Understanding Chapter 11 and 13 Bankruptcy

301

This type of bankruptcy is known as reorganization. Chapter 11 applies to businesses and Chapter 13 to individuals. Under Chapter 11, a company is allowed to reorganize and to continue operations under the court's jurisdiction while paying off a portion of its debt. The courts can discharge the debt that cannot be paid off. This type of bankruptcy significantly increases creditors' chances of receiving some payment. The standards for paying the creditors are identical to those in Chapter 7. If the company were liquidated, there is a good chance the amount of money received would not be sufficient to pay off the creditors. But Chapter 11 enables a company to continue operations and continue making debt payments.

After filing a petition for Chapter 11, the debtor is now known as the debtor-in-possession. The debtor-in-possession's responsibilities now consist of filing monthly operating reports, and any other reports required by the court and the U.S. trustee, examining and objecting to claims, and accounting for property. Other duties are employing attorneys, accountants, appraisers, auctioneers, or other professionals, if needed. There is no case trustee for Chapter 11, but the U.S. trustee monitors the progress of the bankruptcy, making sure that the debtor-in-possession is operating the business correctly and is filing the proper reports. The U.S. trustee also runs the meetings of creditors.

Normally a debtor has 120 days to file a plan and 180 days to gain acceptance of the plan. After this time period, a creditor or other interested party can file a competing plan. Once the plan is confirmed, the debtor must make plan payments and is bound by the provisions of the plan of reorganization. Periodically the debtor must make progress reports to the courts and, when the plan is completed, will apply for a final decree and have the case closed.

In Chapter 13, the individual must have a plan that will pay off the debts within three years. Again, a court-ordered trustee supervises the proceedings, and may put the debtor into Chapter 7 bankruptcy if he or she cannot meet the obligations. Remember, the debtor cannot be hassled by collection efforts while under the protection of Chapter 13. Chapter 13 bankruptcy is open to anyone with unsecured debts of less than $250,000 and secured debts of less than $750,000.

FINANCIAL CONCEPTS

302

Advantages and Disadvantages of Declaring Bankruptcy

Chapter 7 and Chapter 13 bankruptcy provide certain advantages to the debtor:

- A debtor can get a fresh start. After the discharge order is obtained, there is no further obligation to pay the debt.
- Creditors cannot foreclose on homes or repossess automobiles.
- The debtor can recover property taken in the last 90 days.
- Collection agency harassment will stop.
- Lower payments on existing debt can be arranged.
- Utilities can be restored.
- Creditors who may be gouging the debtor will be blocked.

The major advantage of Chapter 11 bankruptcy is that it allows a company to continue business while trying to find a way to repay its debt.

There is, of course, a downside to declaring bankruptcy. Financial obligations that will not be excluded include alimony and child support payments, certain types of student loans, certain debts incurred just prior to filing for bankruptcy, fraudulent debts against creditors, certain governmental fines and taxes, and debts incurred after the bankruptcy filing. Also, a cosigner's obligation may not be eliminated.

In addition, the bankruptcy will remain part of the debtor's credit history for 10 years. This may make it much more difficult to secure future credit. Once you file bankruptcy, you cannot do so again for six years. Bankruptcy can help you to make a fresh start, but the laws are designed so that you cannot use bankruptcy to avoid certain responsibilities.

Foreign Exchange Risk

In today's global marketplace, companies are doing more and more business with foreign corporations. These transactions present a factor known as foreign exchange risk. Imagine that your company sells a large piece of manufacturing equipment to a Japanese firm and the foreign firm will pay for the equipment in thirty days. The deal was closed on March 1, and payment will be received April 1. The Japanese company has agreed to pay $100,000 for the equipment in Japanese yen (JY). The exchange rate on March 1st is 132JY to the dollar. According to the terms of the agreement, your company will receive 13,200,000JY (132 × $100,000) and will then exchange the yen for dollars in the foreign exchange market.

Foreign exchange values change on a daily basis as currencies strengthen or weaken against each other. What happens if the yen weakens against the dollar so that there are 136JY to the dollar 30 days later? On April 1, you receive 13,200,000JY, as agreed in the sales contract. Now you need to exchange the yen for dollars and, at an exchange rate of 136JY per dollar, receive $97,058. The change in the foreign currency market caused your company to lose $2,942.

One way to avoid the risk of exposure to foreign currency exchange is the process of *hedging*. A hedge is a safeguard to protect against loss. Hedging usually involves a contract that guarantees a specified exchange rate at a future date. That way, changes in the exchange rate will not cause your company to lose money.

Understanding the Balance Sheet

A balance sheet is important because it reflects the company's present financial state. It is a snapshot showing the company's assets (everything the company owns), liabilities (debts), and stockholder's equity (value remaining after liabilities are subtracted from the assets). This can be expressed as the equation:

$$\text{Assets} = \text{Liabilities} + \text{Stockholder's equity}$$

Comparing balance sheets from several different years allows you to see changes in profits and losses, sales, short-term and long-term debts, collectable accounts, and accounts payable. You can thereby understand whether the company is reducing its debts, increasing sales, decreasing costs, purchasing new equipment, or investing in research and development. You can also track changes in stockholder's equity.

Assets

The ease and speed with which assets can be turned into cash is known as *liquidity*. *Current assets* are the most liquid and include cash and other assets that can be converted into cash within one year. The more liquid assets (cash, for example) usually earn lower rates of return than fixed assets (such as long-term bonds). *Accounts receivable* are assets that are owed by customers for goods or services. *Inventory* includes raw materials, work in progress, and finished goods. *Fixed assets* are the least liquid of the assets. The tangible fixed assets include property, plant, and equipment owned by the business. Non-tangible assets include trademarks, patents, and licenses. The more liquid assets the firm has available, the less likely it is to have difficulties meeting expenses such as payroll, rents, and accounts payable.

Liabilities and Stockholder's Equity

Just as money does not grow on trees, the assets of a company must come from somewhere. Liabilities and stockholder's equity represent the resources the company uses to obtain assets. Looking at the proportion of liabilities to stockholder's equity indicates how the company is financed in regard to debt and equity.

Book Value

The *book value* or carrying value of a business is the accounting value of its assets. These are determined using generally accepted accounting principles, or GAAP (see tip #287). In contrast, *market value* is the price that investors will pay for the company. If the company has gone public and stock has been issued, the value is whatever buyers and sellers of the stock are willing to pay. The job of management is to make the market value greater than the book value.

305

Understanding the Income Statement

An income statement measures performance over a period of time. The statements present the financial transactions that took place over each quarter and the year as a whole. Generally Accepted Accounting Principles, or GAAP (see tip #287), provide guidelines for the determination of income, revenue, and expenses. The relationship among the three is:

$$\text{Net income} = \text{Revenues} - \text{Expenses}$$

Revenue, or gross income, includes:

- *Total revenue,* which is the total amount of funds received by the business during the time period
- *Operating income,* which is comprised of the funds the company receives from sales
- *Non-operating income,* the funds received from interest on investments and from other sources such as rent of space

Expenses include:

- *Cost of goods sold,* the total of the funds spent to prepare products for sale
- *Fixed costs,* which are costs that cannot be changed in the short run because of fixed commitments, including rent, property taxes, and interest on bonds
- *Variable costs,* such as production labor costs and raw material costs, which change according to the amount of sales
- *Selling, general, and administrative expenses,* including all expenses related to the management and marketing of the business
- *Depreciation,* the decrease in value of fixed assets over their useful life, which is considered an expense
- *Taxes*
- *Interest*

Net Income is the income after all expenses, including taxes and interest payments, are subtracted. It is also known as net profit and may be expressed as earnings per share of common stock.

Understanding Financial Cash Flows

Does the company have enough cash on hand to pay the bills? This is one of the most critical bits of financial information for a company, and it is depicted in the *cash flow* financial statement. Cash is the lifeblood for any company, and knowing where and when the money is coming in and going out is necessary for survival. This information comes from two other financial statements, the *balance sheet* (see tip #304) and the *income statement* (see tip #305). Cash flow from the company's assets must equal the cash flow to the creditors and investors.

Cash flow can be divided into:

- *Operating cash flow.* This is the cash resulting from business activities (sales and services). Depreciation and tax payments also fall into this category.
- *Investing cash flow.* This includes any changes in fixed assets such as property, plant, or equipment, as well as additions or subtractions to net working capital.
- *Financing cash flow.* This category covers cash flow to investors (interest on loans, payment of debt, dividends, and repurchase of equity) and cash flow from investors (long-term debt financing and new equity or shares of stock sold).

The general purpose of the cash flow statement is to take into account that not all business transactions actually involve cash. It therefore more accurately depicts the amount of cash that is immediately available to the company and therefore gives a better picture of the company's solvency. For example, depreciation for a piece of equipment is considered an expense, but there is no actual cash involved, and the amount should therefore not be deducted from available cash funds. Conversely, if you have $10,000 in accounts receivable, you should not consider that as a cash asset since you don't yet have the money, only an invoice saying that you are owed it. Many companies run into trouble when they miscalculate the amount of cash on hand and find themselves without enough to pay bills.

307

Using Efficiency Ratios

Efficiency ratios help a business determine how well its assets are being used and how well it is being managed. The following ratios provide this assessment:

Asset Turnover Ratio

$$\text{Asset turnover} = \frac{\text{Net sales}}{\text{Average total assets}}$$

This ratio measures the sales generated per dollar of assets. The net sales amount comes from the income statement and the total assets from the balance sheet. A high turnover ratio indicates a higher return on assets, which can compensate for a low profit margin. You can also find turnover ratios for other assets, such as fixed assets, by substituting fixed assets for total assets in this equation. If you have a falling ratio, it may indicate that too much capital is invested in plant, property, or equipment.

Inventory Turnover Ratio

$$\text{Inventory turnover} = \frac{\text{Cost of goods sold}}{\text{Average inventory}}$$

Inventory management can have a significant effect on your cash flow. The inventory turnover ratio tells you approximately how many times an item turns over in a year, or how long an item sits on the shelf. If a company does this for individual products, it can see which items are moving and which ones are accumulating. With computers and bar coding, this kind of control over inventory has become much easier.

Account Receivable Turnover Ratio

$$\text{Accounts receivables turnover} = \frac{\text{Net sales}}{\text{Average receivables}}$$

$$= \frac{\text{Net sales}}{(\text{Beginning} + \text{ending receivables} / 2)}$$

Receivables turnover measures the liquidity of your company's accounts receivable. This ratio measures the number of times receivables are collected during the time period. You can calculate the number by dividing net sales by the average receivables outstanding during the year. Usually average receivables outstanding can be derived from the beginning and ending balances of net trade receivables.

Divide 365 days by the accounts receivable turnover number to determine how often to collect accounts receivable. This information can tell you if your credit and collection policies need to be tightened or changed.

308

Using Financial Ratios

Managers need to know how well their business is doing from quarter to quarter and to compare it to others within the same industry. One way to analyze business performance is the use of financial ratios. These ratios fall into four categories:

- *Liquidity ratios.* These ratios compute the business's short-run ability to pay its current obligations. Is there enough cash on hand to pay the bills?
- *Efficiency ratios or activity ratios.* These ratios measure how well the company is using its assets. Is management doing its job?
- *Profitability ratios.* These ratios compute profit or loss over a given period of time.
- *Solvency ratios or coverage ratios.* These ratios compute the company's debt obligations.

Using these ratios will enable you to evaluate the size of a company's debt, the company's ability to pay its bills, how efficiently its assets are being used, and its profitability. Tracking these ratios over time will give you a good picture of the strength of the business and its ability to survive.

Using Liquidity Ratios

Liquidity ratios are the most widely used ratios. They show the company's ability to paying short-term debt to its suppliers and lenders. Does the company have enough cash on hand to meet its expenses and stay solvent? The liquidity ratio will quickly tell you if your company is in financial trouble and may be unable to pay its bills.

The two commonly used ratios are the *current ratio* and the *quick ratio*.

The current ratio is the sum of a company's current assets divided by its current liabilities:

$$\text{Current ratio} = \frac{\text{Current assets}}{\text{Current liabilities}}$$

A current ratio of 2:1 is considered good. This means that there is $2 in current assets (cash, accounts receivable, and inventory) to meet each $1 in current liability. A current ratio of 1:1 or less is not sufficient to meet financial demands, and a ratio that is constantly declining indicates that the company is experiencing problems. To improve this ratio the company can take steps to increase the current assets, decrease the current liabilities, or both.

A more conservative measure of liquidity is called the quick ratio or acid test. In this test the numerator is reduced by the value of the inventory. This ratio allows you to see whether you have the ability to meet your short-term obligations regardless of the company's sales.

$$\text{Quick ratio} = \frac{\text{Current assets} - \text{Inventory}}{\text{Current liabilities}}$$

If the ratio is 1.5:1 or greater, the company is in good shape to pay its current bills. This ratio improves with the use of the same methods that improve the current ratio, and also when inventory changes to cash or accounts receivable.

Management plays a key role in determining these measures of liquidity. Check periodically to see how your company, or a company you have invested in, is doing.

310

Understanding Solvency or Coverage Ratios

The following set of ratios will help you determine the ability your firm has to pay its debts as they mature. A certain amount of debt is acceptable, but if debt starts to increase there will be concern that the company cannot meet its financial obligations. Analyzing solvency ratios helps the company to determine whether it will be able to meet the interest costs and repayment schedules that accompany long-term debt.

Four often-used coverage ratios are:

Debt to Equity Ratio

$$\text{Debt to equity} = \frac{\text{Total debt}}{\text{Owner's equity expressed as a percentage}}$$

This ratio tells the company the amount of financial leverage it is using (for example, whether it is using too much debt for financing purposes). An increasing ratio may indicate that the company should look at its fixed assets or purchases of inventory. Companies that are highly leveraged usually have less financial flexibility and more risk. The information for making this calculation can be obtained from the company's balance sheet.

Debt to Assets Ratio

$$\text{Debt to asset ratio} = \frac{\text{Total liabilities}}{\text{Total assets expressed as a percentage}}$$

This ratio determines the percent of a company's assets that are financed with debt. Another ratio that shows this is the percentage of assets financed by creditors versus the percentage financed by the company. The higher the percent of debt to total assets, the larger the risk that the business will not be able to pay its financial debts. Usually, a 50 percent ratio is desired. In order to accomplish this goal, the company may have to pay off some of its debt or increase the value of its assets.

Times Interest Earned Ratio

$$\text{Times interest earned} = \frac{\text{Earnings before interest and taxes}}{\text{Interest expense}}$$

This ratio measures the company's ability to meet interest payments as they become due. The larger the ratio, the better able the company is to meet its obligation. Falling ratios can indicate possible cash flow problems.

Times Fixed Charges Earned Ratio

$$\text{Times fixed charges earned} = \frac{\text{Net income before taxes and fixed charges}}{\text{Fixed charges}}$$

Again, the larger the number, the better able the company is to meet its fixed obligations. Many lenders specify the ratio that must be maintained. Once again, falling ratios can indicate possible cash flow problems. Examining this and other important financial ratios, and checking on trends regularly, can help management make better monetary decisions.

311

Understanding Breakeven Analysis

Most employees never have to analyze the effect that increases or decreases in goods or services sold or produced have on the bottom line. As a manager, however, you will likely be involved in a breakeven analysis of current or proposed business. The purpose of the analysis is to be able to price goods or services at a level that will include all the fixed and variable costs. The point at which enough goods or services have been sold to cover this cost is the breakeven point. From this point on, a profit is achieved for each unit sold minus its variable cost. A breakeven analysis looks at the interaction between fixed costs, variable costs, prices, and unit volume.

A fixed cost is money that is paid out by your business no matter what revenue is generated. Some examples are rent, salaries for full-time employees, repayment of loans, and utilities. Variable costs are those costs that change depending on volume and are directly proportional to output. Some examples are sales commissions, materials, and delivery charges.

Use the following formula to calculate the breakeven point:

$$\text{Breakeven Costs} = \frac{\text{Fixed costs}}{(\text{Selling price per unit} - \text{Variable cost per unit})}$$

Assume a company's fixed costs are $50,000. Its variable costs per unit are $1, and its sales revenue per unit is $3. Therefore, each unit sold will contribute $2 toward covering fixed costs.

Now divide fixed costs by cost per unit of sales. This tells you how many units have to be sold to break even. $50,000 divided by $2.00 equals 25,000. If sales exceed 25,000 units the company will make a profit. If sales are lower it will lose money.

See Figure 25, on the following page, for a graph of the breakeven point. It illustrates what will happen if fewer items are sold. If variable cost is frozen, can fixed costs be lowered or could more be charged for the item? The results may indicate that you can still make a profit with fewer units sold. If your business has only a single product, there are only four ways that you can increase your profitability: increase the number of units sold, decrease fixed costs, decrease variable costs, or increase the price.

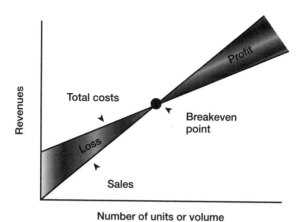

Figure 25. The breakeven point.

312

Understanding Contribution Margins

Contribution margin analysis allows you to understand whether a given product is producing a profit or loss, whether to reprice a product or service, or whether it's appropriate to offer sales bonuses. The contribution margin is the percentage of each sales dollar that remains after subtracting the variable costs. To use contribution margins, you must break down the variable costs on the income statement.

Items that might be included in the variable costs are costs of goods sold, sales commissions, freight charges, and maintenance on machinery used in production. The higher the contribution margin is, the more profitable the product line is. Table 12 gives an example.

Table 12
A Contribution Margin Calculation

Company XYZ	Product A	Product B	Product C
Sales	$500,000	$600,000	$450,000
Less Variable Costs			
Cost of Goods Sold	$200,000	$325,000	$175,000
Commissions	$100,000	$75,000	$20,000
Freight	$50,000	$15,000	$20,000
Maintenance	$25,000	$10,000	$10,000
Total Variable Costs	$375,000	$425,000	$225,000
Contribution Margin	$125,000	$175,000	$225,000
	(25%)	(29%)	(50%)

In the example given in Table 12, Product C has the largest contribution margin. You now can try to determine why Product C has such a high contribution margin and see if you can alter anything in the other product lines to help increase their profitability. In this example, changing the freight company for Product A and the sales commission structure might allow for more profit.

Understanding Operating Leverage

Having determined your breakeven point (see tip #311), you can see that a small increase or decrease in the number of units sold can have a significant effect on profit or loss. The concept of operating leverage offers an explanation of how fixed and variable costs can have this effect on your profit or loss.

You will find that these phenomena are often related to the amount that fixed costs contribute to the revenues generated. What you are examining is the average profit per unit volume and the way it changes with volume. In other words, as volume increases, the average per unit cost decreases because the average fixed cost is decreasing. If the opposite occurs, the average unit cost increases because the average fixed cost is increasing. The object of operating leverage is to distribute the fixed costs over a larger volume.

Here is one example. Company XYZ has the following cost and pricing structure: Total fixed costs are $500, variable costs are $5 per unit, and the selling price is $7.50 per unit. To calculate the breakeven point, the sales volume at which revenues are equal to costs, take the total fixed costs and divide this figure by the selling price minus variable costs. The breakeven point is 200 units. This means that if 200 units are sold, revenue would be $7.50 multiplied by 200, or $1,500. This revenue provides no profit since the total cost is also $1,500. This cost is the variable cost ($5) times the number of units (200), plus the total fixed costs ($500).

If 250 units are sold, revenue would be $1,875, costs would be $1,750, and profit would be $125, with an average profit of $0.50 per unit. If 300 units are sold, revenue would be $2,250, costs would be $2,000, and profit would be $250, with an average profit of $0.83 per unit.

When volume is 250 units, the profit is $125. When the volume goes up to 300 units, a 20 percent increase, the profit goes up by $125, a 100 percent increase. If sales slip, there is a similar effect in the opposite direction. It's clear to see how a slight change in sales can have a much more dramatic effect on profits.

314 Capital Budgeting

If you are involved in the budgeting decisions for your company, sooner or later you will be involved with the financial process that helps determine whether or not to undertake a major project or purchase. Some managers fly by the seat of their pants and go on instinct, but there are methods to help you take calculated risks.

A major project or purchase is usually anything that will last for more than a year and cost more than a set amount. This amount will vary anywhere from $5,000 on up, depending upon the industry. The larger the project, the more carefully it should be analyzed. Your company may have several projects that it is interested in simultaneously but it may also have only a given amount of capital to spend. Your analysis may mean the difference in whether your department is awarded the project or not. Analysis of the project or purchase can involve many uncertain factors, including consumer trends, future interest rates, technological advances, and future business conditions.

You must first ask yourself what the project is trying to accomplish. What benefits will be forthcoming from this new undertaking? In making your assessment, be sure to include intangible benefits, like changing the company's image, and very tangible benefits, like increasing profit and decreasing costs. Sometimes companies have little choice in the projects they undertake just to stay in business. Some major projects may be mandated by law, like removing gasoline from the soil underneath a gasoline station. Others may be substantial repairs required for existing equipment or property, or safety or accessibility improvements.

After you select the goals that the project should accomplish, details will start to fall in place. Since most major projects will require an influx of capital, the next step is to start evaluating the costs of the project. Develop a projected cash flow budget and determine the effect the project will have on your company. Finally, a financial analysis needs to be performed to determine whether to undertake the project, abandon it, or choose another project. This decision will most likely be made by your superiors, so give them complete and accurate data.

Costs of the Proposed Capital Budget 315

When a company decides to move forward with a major undertaking or purchase, it must evaluate the costs involved. This evaluation may require knowledge about construction costs, real estate values, or financing alternatives, or may require information from knowledgeable suppliers, production line consultants, or engineers.

In figuring out costs of the project, be sure to include items that are often left out of original estimates but that can add a substantial amount of capital to the completed project. Examples of these are:

- New employees
- Additional insurance
- Training costs
- Extra supplies
- Janitorial services
- Extra maintenance
- Increased use of utilities
- Number of hours taken away from current employees' regular jobs and expenses resulting from neglect of these jobs or of additional staff to handle these tasks
- Increased delegation to lower-level staff
- Consultants' fees
- Upgrades of existing equipment so that it will perform with the new equipment

Depending on the size or scope of the project and the additional dollars needed to finance the new project, you must balance the analytical and the practical, the pros and cons, and all the alternatives before making a commitment.

316

Developing a Cash Flow Statement for Capital Budgeting

Once you have assessed the costs associated with a new project or purchase, the next step is to analyze the effect it might have on revenues. The first step in this procedure should be developing a projected cash flow statement.

The cash flow statement shows a company's investing and financing activities and its revenue over a certain time period in the past. Projected cash flow statements, on the other hand, can help in assessing the costs and financial benefits of a potential project. This analysis should demonstrate if, from a financial perspective, the project should be pursued or not. If your company anticipates having to borrow money for the new project, the lending institutions that review your application will most certainly request a projected cash flow statement.

In preparing a cash flow statement, try to show cash inflows and outflows on a monthly basis for the first year or two. Remember that the farther out you extend your projection, the less sure you can be of your assumptions. Depending on the project or purchase, include the items shown in Table 13 in your statement.

Table 13
Projected Cash Flow Statement

| | | YEARS PROJECTED OUT | | |
	Current year	Year 1	Year 2	Year 3
Net sales	A			
Variable costs	B			
Fixed costs	C			
Depreciation	D			
Pretax income	E			
Tax expense	F			
Net Income (NI) = A − (B + C + D + E + F)				

Include additional numbers for each year depending on how detailed the analysis must be, but always try to make sure that the numbers used are realistic. Some items, such as depreciation expenses and asset purchases, will affect actual future cash on hand and need to be factored into the cash flow projections.

Analysis of Capital Budgeting Project— Payback Period

317

The final step in the decision-making process for a major purchase or project is a financial analysis using one of the following methods: the payback period method, the accounting rate of return method, the net present value method, or the internal rate of return method. The first two methods are the easiest to calculate, while the last two take into consideration the time value of money.

The payback method is probably the easiest of the four. It shows the company how long it will take to recapture the money that is spent on the new project or purchase. It ignores the timing of cash flows, the time value of money, and the length of the project.

$$\text{Payback period} = \frac{\text{Cost of project or purchase}}{\text{Annual cash inflow}}$$

If the project cost $100,000 and returned $27,500 annually, the payback period would be 3.64 years. If the returns vary over time, just add them together and divide by the number of years.

This method gives projects with the shortest payback period higher priority. The rationale for this is that capital is returned quickly and can be reinvested. There is also less chance that other market conditions such as technology and interest rates will change. The major objections to this analysis are that it does not look at returns after the payback period and that it does not take into consideration the time value of money (see tip #283).

318

Analysis of Capital Budgeting— Accounting Rate of Return

The accounting rate of return (ARR) is one of the traditional methods of calculating the return on your company's proposed investment. The accounting rate of return looks at the project's annual income, not its cash flow. The ARR is:

$$\text{Accounting rate of return} = \frac{\text{Annual cash inflows} - \text{Depreciation}}{\text{Initial investment}}$$

This equation uses the straight-line method of depreciation:

$$\text{Depreciation} = \frac{\text{Cost} - \text{Salvage value}}{\text{Useful life}}$$

Let's look at an example using ARR:

Cost of equipment = $20,000

Returns = $5,000 per year × 5 years

Salvage value of equipment = $1,000

$$\text{Depreciation} = \frac{\$20,000 - \$1,000}{5} = \$3,800$$

$$\text{ARR} = \frac{\$5,000 - \$3,800}{\$20,000} = 6\%$$

A positive ARR indicates that the project should be considered.

The advantage of using ARR is that it gives the company a rapid way to compare several different projects. It evaluates the return on the investment for the entire useful life of the project. Remember, though, that the ARR uses income rather than cash flow and never considers the time value of money (see tip #283).

Analysis of Capital Budgeting—Net Present Value

319

The usual method for calculating acceptance or rejection of new projects is the net present value analysis (NPV). NPV is a discounted method of capital investment analysis; that is, it incorporates the time value of money by using a discount rate on future cash flows. This means you can calculate the value in today's dollars of the future net cash flow of a project, and you can compare this value to the amount of capital needed to start the project.

Today, computer spreadsheet programs and financial calculators will automatically calculate NPV, but it is still helpful to understand the components of the formula. The first step is to calculate the present value (PV).

$$PV = \frac{CF_1}{(1 + r)^1} + \frac{CF_2}{(1 + r)^2} + \frac{CF_3}{(1 + r)^3} + \frac{CF_n}{(1 + r)^n}$$

where CF is cash flow during a single period of time x, n is the number of such periods, and r is the discount rate.

If the project is to be financed, this is usually the interest rate on the loan. Otherwise this should be the average cost of capital.

The following equation is then used to calculate NPV.

$$NPV = PV - \text{Cost of project}$$

If the NPV is positive, that means the present value of the future cash flows is greater than the cost of the project, which is like saying that the project will be profitable. Alternatively, if the NPV is negative, the cost of the project is greater than the present value of future cash flows, which is like saying the project will cost more money than it will generate.

Essentially, NPV indicates how much a given amount of money would be worth in today's dollars if invested in a given project for a given amount of time. NPV can also be used to compare and rank competing proposals, and the higher the positive NPV, the more lucrative the project. The discount rate used in assessing a project can make the difference between acceptance and rejection, so care should be taken in selecting an appropriate rate.

More information on utilizing this manual method of NPV calculation can be found in most basic finance textbooks.

FINANCIAL ANALYSIS

320

Analysis of Capital Budgeting—Internal Rate of Return

Internal rate of return (IRR) is another popular method of determining whether a project should be undertaken. IRR is similar to the NPV (see tip #319), but while NPV uses a selected discount rate to calculate the present value of future cash flows, IRR considers the discount rate to be unknown. In fact, the same equation is used for both approaches, but, in general terms, the IRR is the discount rate that causes the NPV to equal zero. In other words, the NPV equation is set equal to zero and solved for r.

Recall this equation from the tip on NPV:

$$NPV = PV - \text{Cost of project}$$

Set NPV equal to zero to give:

$$0 = PV - \text{Cost of project}$$

Now plug in the formula for PV:

$$0 = \frac{CF_1}{(1+r)^1} + \frac{CF_2}{(1+r)^2} + \frac{CF_3}{(1+r)^3} + \frac{CF_n}{(1+r)^n} - \text{Cost of project}$$

Now, using trial-and-error, plug in values of r to find the one that makes the equation true; that is, make the right side of the equation equal to zero. This value of r is the IRR.

This rate was calculated using internal information and did not rely on any external information. It is therefore not affected by market conditions and other factors. The IRR provides the interest rate equivalent to the dollar returns you expect from the project. If this rate is less than the cost of financing the project, the project will definitely lose money. If the IRR is greater than the cost of financing the project, then the project should be considered.

The IRR can be easily calculated using spreadsheet programs and financial calculators, and it usually gives the same answer as the net present value method. But if the cash flows have large variances from year to year, IRR calculations become time consuming. The IRR method cannot be used to evaluate mutually exclusive projects or cases where there is a limit on capital spending.

Economic Value Added (EVA®)

Capital budgeting is the process a company uses to make long-term investment decisions that eventually will add wealth to a company. A new method, economic value added (EVA®, which is a registered trademark of Stern Stewart & Co.), recently gained popularity with many corporations in the United States.

EVA is the net operating profit after tax (NOPAT)—that is, the profit after removing the costs of sales, operating expenses, taxes, and other adjustments from revenue—minus all the capital employed to produce those earnings:

$$EVA = NOPAT - Capital\ change.$$

Capital change is the cost of all capital employed in the business. Included in this cost, besides the time value of money and compensation for risk, are net assets which include accounts receivable, inventory, property, plant, equipment, long-term debt, and capitalized lease obligations, among other items. The cost of capital charge probably plays the most important part in this formula. Using EVA, a company can see if it is truly earning a profit and can show every division and every manager that they must account and pay for the capital they use.

To increase EVA, you can take any or all of the following steps:

- Increase operating profits without investing more money, or decrease capital expenditure while maintaining or improving profits
- Invest new capital in projects that earn more then the cost of capital
- Eliminate business activities that do not provide adequate returns

EVA shows managers and divisions of the company that assets as well as income have to be managed. With continuous growth in EVA, there will be continuous growth in shareholder wealth. Companies that have adopted EVA feel that it allows all employees, owners, and shareholders to communicate in a common language about performance, decision making, and compensation.

A disadvantage of EVA, according to Gary Hamel (*Fortune,* August 4, 1997), is that it is not an adequate way to measure corporate wealth. He argues that "a better way of determining whether a company is winning is to look at what happens to its percentage share in the total market value in its industry. If the market value of an industry increases and a company's share grows larger, it is a superior wealth creator."

322 Family Business Basics

There are over 12 million family businesses in the United States. It is estimated that these businesses generate more than half the country's gross domestic product and generate most of the new jobs as well. The Arthur Andersen/Mass-Mutual American Family Business Survey of 1997 received more than 3,000 responses to questionnaires sent to approximately 37,000 family businesses. The companies that responded accounted for approximately $67 billion in revenues. The mean sales volume was $9 million, the mean number of employees was 50, and the businesses had been in existence an average of 46 years.

According to the survey, possibly turbulent times lie ahead for family businesses. The reason for this is that 53 percent of the current CEOs are expected to retire in the next 5 to 10 years, with about 74 percent going into semiretirement. This situation places a tremendous burden on existing leaders. Succession planning is an absolute must. Failure to do so is probably the main reason that only one in three family-owned businesses make it to a second generation and only one in nine makes it to a third generation.

Succession planning should include consideration and discussion of the following:

- The goals of the business and the family
- Expectations of the founder
- Possible differences in generational agendas
- Adequate tax planning
- A transition timetable
- The business' capacity to support the people dependent on it after the change
- The degree and kind of training the intended successor will need
- The role the founder's spouse will play, especially if the founder dies unexpectedly

In order for these family businesses to survive in the 21st century, they will have to learn to use both family and non-family personnel, choose new CEOs, and plan for estate taxes—all while continuing to grow the business. The transfer of power can take place with minimal disruption if there is good communication and planning that involves all parties.

Funding Family Succession

A good succession plan should address the transfer of power and the transfer of assets. Of these two, it is the assets that are most often neglected or overlooked. Without the correct asset planning, the company may be forced into divesting itself in order to pay estate taxes or satisfy other financial demands.

About 75 percent of the current heads of family businesses report a "good" understanding of the estate taxes due upon their death. Even so, 25 percent have not completed any estate planning. This lack of preparation leaves a tremendous potential void in money to meet the estate tax liabilities and possible stock pay-out plans.

To avoid putting the succeeding generation at risk, using experts to help with estate planning is absolutely essential if sufficient assets have been accumulated. This is not the place to skimp on the quality of the professionals hired.

The following are some of the strategies commonly used to minimize taxes and to ensure that there is enough capital to keep the company liquid:

- Have the business valued.
- Consider life insurance to cover estate tax liability.
- Consider paying estate taxes across 14 years if the business interest is more than 35 percent of your adjusted gross estate. The IRS charges interest at a rate set by law.
- Consider buy/sell agreements backed by life insurance on the principals.
- Consider the yearly $10,000 gift exclusion.
- Using a private annuity. The owner sells his or her interest in the business for a guaranteed lifetime income.
- Use grantor retained annuity trusts, fixed annuities for a fixed number of years. This strategy will definitely require legal input.
- Issue two types of stock, voting and nonvoting. This process is usually called recapitalization and should be undertaken with legal counsel.
- Keep the planning updated.

If you feel that the estate must be shared equally, contemplate providing equal financial packages while avoiding equality of roles in the business. No matter how you plan, family members will have their own successes and failures according to their own skills, opportunities, and luck.

324 Planning Family Succession

One of the most difficult tasks a family business or any business can undertake is to choose the next chief executive officer. Unfortunately, too many family-owned businesses wait until the last minute to make this decision. Maybe the founder is not ready, willing, or able to give up control of the company. Or perhaps it is not certain which family member or non-family member should be chosen to be the new leader. These family businesses are challenged with trying to make everything "fair" and must effectively handle generational differences. Unfortunately, if there has not been proper succession planning done, there is an excellent chance that the business might have to be sold to pay estate taxes or satisfy the demands of various heirs.

Planning for succession in a family business is a complicated process but one that should be started early on. The current CEO must:

- Decide who will be the next CEO. This may be a sibling, non-family manager, or an outside candidate.
- Decide how to deal with spouses.
- Make sure there is enough money to pay estate taxes.
- Make sure there is enough money to buy out a family member or other party who no longer wants to be a part of the business.
- Formulate a business plan to ensure the business will continue to operate without any interruption.
- Determine the role that important nonfamily managers will play.
- Be sure your estate plans are in order.
- Decide to deal with the remaining family members.
- Assess how the choice of successor will affect current family dynamics.
- Devise a way to handle divorces or demands of in-laws.

Think of preparing for family succession as a process rather than an event. It requires planning, teamwork, communication, and constant re-evaluation. Bringing together family members, nonfamily members, accountants, lawyers, advisors, and members of the board of directors can be helpful in finding and solving issues that are critical to the success of the company.

If no one takes the time and trouble to plan for succession, the day will come when everything will have to be decided on the spur of the moment, and this may have catastrophic consequences. Remember that a good succession plan usually has two parts. The first is the transfer of authority and the second is the transfer of assets.

325 Choosing a Successor for a Family Business

Changing leadership in any company is a difficult time, but in a family-owned business it can be the most challenging of all the decisions the founder will have to make. He or she has to decide if there is a family member capable of taking the reins of the company. If not, then the management has to be turned over to someone outside the family.

There are several scenarios that can occur in choosing the next leader. The first is that there is one excellent family candidate for the position. This candidate already possesses the knowledge, training, ability, and desire to be the next leader. Even if this situation occurs, it is important that other problems be avoided. Long-time key employees should be kept informed about the time frame for the transition. The new successor should be given the necessary control over the business so that other family members cannot hinder its operation. Remember that voting rights can be separated from financial rights, and that there are assets unrelated to the company that can be left to family members who will not share in control of the business.

If two or more family members are qualified to replace the founder, then use other means to determine the successor. Again, seek advice from long-time, key executive employees who are outside the family. Using outside advisors or directors to help determine the next leader is another excellent approach. You may decide to name co-presidents. This strategy may or may not work well, but it is gaining in acceptance. In the Arthur Andersen/Mass Mutual Survey of 1997, about 42 percent of businesses are considering co-leaders. The danger of giving two people equal power is that a stalemate may develop that would threaten or destroy the company. Another change is that more businesses are choosing a woman in the family as the new leader. If there is rivalry for the top position, the founder or new successor must recognize that the unsuccessful candidate may decide to seek employment elsewhere.

It may be that there is no family member who can or wants to continue the business. If this is the case, then consider selling the business to an employee or employees, selling it outright, or liquidating it.

No matter what the decision is, early planning with proper preparation and regular updates will lead to an orderly transition for all involved.

References

Adams, Bob, et al. *Streetwise Managing People: Lead Your Staff to Peak Performance.* Holbrook, Massachusetts: Adams Media Corporation, 1998.

Anthony, Robert N., Reece, James S., and Hertenstein, Julie H. *Accounting: Text and Cases,* 9th Ed. Chicago: Irwin, 1995.

Bittel, L. R. and Newstrom, J. W. *What Every Supervisor Should Know,* 6th Ed. New York: McGraw-Hill, Inc., 1992.

Blake, Robert R. and Mouton, Jane S. *The Managerial Grid.* Houston: Gulf Publishing Company, 1964.

Blake, Robert R. and McCanse, Anne Adams. *Leadership Grid Dilemmas— Grid Solutions.* Houston: Gulf Publishing Company, 1991.

Gordon, Gus. *Understanding Financial Statements.* Cincinnati: South-Western Publishing Co., 1992.

Greer, C., Jackson, D., and Fiorito, J. "Adapting Human Resource Planning In a Changing Business Environment," *Human Resource Management,* Vol. 28, 1:110, 1989.

Hamel, Gary, and Ehrbar, Al. "Debate: Duking It Out Over EVA." *Fortune,* Vol. 136, 3:232(1), August 4, 1997.

Harvey, Jerry B. *The Abilene Paradox and Other Meditations on Management.* San Francisco: Jossey-Bass Publishers, 1996.

Hesselbein, Frances, Goldsmith, Marshall, and Beckhard, Richard (Editors). *The Leader of the Future: New Visions, Strategies, and Practices for the Next Era.* San Francisco: Jossey-Bass Publishers, 1996.

Higgins, Robert C. *Analysis for Financial Management,* 4th Ed. Chicago: Irwin, 1995.

Hilton, Margaret. "Shared Training: Learning from Germany." *Monthly Labor Review,* Vol. 114, No. 3, 1991, pp. 33–37.

Hunsaker, P. L., and Alessandre, A. J. *The Art of Managing People.* New York: Simon & Schuster, Inc., 1986.

Janis, Irving L. *Groupthink: Psychological Studies of Policy Decisions and Fiascoes,* 2nd Ed. Boston: Houghton Mifflin Company, 1982.

Kotler, Philip. *Marketing Management: Analysis, Planning, Implementation, and Control,* 8th Ed. Englewood Cliffs, New Jersey: Prentice-Hall, 1994.

Kubler-Ross, Elisabeth. *On Death and Dying.* New York: Macmillan, 1969.

MacKenzie, R. Alec. *The Time Trap,* 3rd Ed. New York: American Management Association, 1997.

Meiners, Roger E., Ringleb, Al H., and Edwards, Frances L. *The Legal Environment of Business,* 5th Ed. St. Paul: West Publishing Company, 1994.

Mintzberg, Henry. *The Rise and Fall of Strategic Planning.* New York: Free Press, 1994.

Penrose, J., Rasberry, R., and Myers, R. *Advanced Business Communication,* 2nd Ed. Belmont, California: Wadsworth, 1993.

Peter, Laurence J., and Hull, Raymond. *The Peter Principle: Why Things Go Wrong.* New York: Morrow, 1969.

Ross, Stephen, Westerfield, Randolph, and Jaffe, Jeffrey. *Corporate Finance,* 4th Ed. Chicago: Irwin, 1996.

Russell, Roberta S. and Taylor, Bernard III. *Operations Management: Focusing on Quality and Competitiveness.* Englewood Cliffs, New Jersey: Prentice-Hall, 1998.

3M Meeting Management Team. *How to Run Better Business Meetings: A Reference Guide for Managers.* New York: McGraw-Hill, 1987.

Trevino, Linda K. and Nelson, Kathy. *Managing Business Ethics: Straight Talk On How To Do It Right.* New York: John Wiley & Sons, 1995.

Tuckman, Bruce W. "Developmental Sequence in Small Groups." *Psychological Bulletin,* Vol. 63, 6:334–99, 1965.

Zenger, John H., et al. *Leading Teams: Mastering the New Role.* San Francisco: McGraw-Hill, Inc., 1994.

Index